PREDATOR NATION

PREDATOR NATION

Corporate Criminals,
Political Corruption, and the
Hijacking of America

CHARLES FERGUSON

CROWN
BUSINESS

New York

Published in the United States by Crown Business, an imprint of the Crown
Publishing Group, a division of Random House, Inc., New York.
www.crownpublishing.com

CROWN BUSINESS is a trademark and CROWN and the Rising Sun colophon
are registered trademarks of Random House, Inc.
Originally published in hardcover in the United States by Crown Business,
an imprint of the Crown Publishing Group, a division of Random House, Inc.,
New York, in 2012.

Library of Congress Cataloging-in-Publication Data
Ferguson, Charles H.
Predator nation : corporate criminals, political corruption, and the hijacking of
America / Charles Ferguson. — 1st Ed.
p. cm.
Includes bibliographical references and index.
1. Financial crises—United States. 2. Banks and banking—United States.
3. Global Financial Crisis, 2008–2009. 4. Equality—United States. 5. United
States—Economic conditions—2009– 6. United States—Economic policy.
7. United States—Politics and government. I. Title.
HB3722.F458 2012
330.973'0932—dc23   2011052366

ISBN 978-0-307-95256-1
eISBN 978-0-307-95257-8

Printed in the United States of America

Book design by Nicola Ferguson
Jacket illustration and design by Jamie Keenan

10 9 8 7 6 5 4 3 2 1
First Paperback Edition

To Athena Sofia and Audrey Elizabeth,
two women who changed my life

CONTENTS

PREDATOR NATION

CHAPTER 1

WHERE WE ARE NOW

MANY BOOKS HAVE ALREADY been written about the financial crisis, but there are two reasons why I decided that it was still important to write this one.

The first reason is that the bad guys got away with it, and there has been stunningly little public debate about this fact. When I received the Oscar for best documentary in 2011, I said: "Three years after a horrific financial crisis caused by massive fraud, not a single financial executive has gone to jail. And that's wrong." When asked afterward about the absence of prosecutions, senior Obama administration officials gave evasive nonanswers, suggesting that nothing illegal occurred, or that investigations were continuing. None of the major Republican presidential candidates have raised the issue at all.

As of early 2012 there has *still* not been a single criminal prosecution of a senior financial executive related to the financial crisis. Nor has there been any serious attempt by the federal government to use civil suits, asset seizures, or restraining orders to extract fines or restitution from the people responsible for plunging the world economy into recession. This is not because we have no evidence of criminal behavior. Since the release of my film, a large amount of new material has emerged, especially from private lawsuits, that reveals, through e-mail trails and other evidence, that many bankers, including senior management, knew *exactly* what was going on, and that it was highly fraudulent.

But even leaving this crisis aside, there is now abundant evidence of widespread, unpunished criminal behavior in the financial sector. Later in this book, I go through the list of what we already know, which is *a lot*. In addition to the behavior that caused the crisis, major U.S. and European banks have been caught assisting corporate fraud by Enron and others, laundering money for drug cartels and the Iranian military, aiding tax evasion, hiding the assets of corrupt dictators, colluding in order to fix prices, and committing many forms of financial fraud. The evidence is now overwhelming that over the last thirty years, the U.S. financial sector has become a rogue industry. As its wealth and power grew, it subverted America's political system (including *both* political parties), government, and academic institutions in order to free itself from regulation. As deregulation progressed, the industry became ever more unethical and dangerous, producing ever larger financial crises and ever more blatant criminality. Since the 1990s, its power has been sufficient to insulate bankers not only from effective regulation but even from criminal law enforcement. The financial sector is now a parasitic and destabilizing industry that constitutes a major drag on American economic growth.

This means that criminal prosecution is not just a matter of vengeance or even justice. Real punishment for large-scale financial criminality is a vital element of the financial re-regulation that is, in turn, essential to America's (and the world's) economic health and stability. Regulation is nice, but the threat of prison focuses the mind. A noted expert, the gangster Al Capone, once said, "You can get much further in life with a kind word and a gun than with a kind word alone." If financial executives know that they will go to jail if they commit major frauds that endanger the world economy, and that their illegal wealth will be confiscated, then they will be considerably less likely to commit such frauds and cause global financial crises. So one reason for writing this book is to lay out in painfully clear detail the case for criminal prosecutions. In this book, I demonstrate that much of the behavior underlying the bubble and crisis was quite literally criminal, and that the lack of prosecution is nearly as outrageous as the financial sector's original conduct.

The second reason that I decided to write this book is that the rise of predatory finance is both a cause and a symptom of an even broader, and even more disturbing, change in America's economy and political system. The financial sector is the core of a new oligarchy that has risen to power over the past thirty years, and that has profoundly changed American life. The later chapters of this book are devoted to analyzing how this happened and what it means.

Starting around 1980, American society began to undergo a series of deep shifts. Deregulation, weakened antitrust enforcement, and technological changes led to increasing concentration of industry and finance. Money began to play a larger and more corrupting role in politics. America fell behind other nations in education, in infrastructure, and in the performance of many of its major industries. Inequality increased. As a result of these and other changes, America was turning into a rigged game—a society that denies opportunity to those who are not born into wealthy families, one that resembles a third-world dictatorship more than an advanced democracy.

The "Occupy Wall Street" protests that began in New York in September 2011, and then rapidly spread around America and the world, were initially somewhat unclear in their goals. But the protesters were deeply right about one thing: over the last thirty years, the United States has been taken over by an amoral financial oligarchy, and the American dream of opportunity, education, and upward mobility is now largely confined to the top few percent of the population. Federal policy is increasingly dictated by the wealthy, by the financial sector, and by powerful (though sometimes badly mismanaged) industries such as telecommunications, health care, automobiles, and energy. These policies are implemented and praised by these groups' willing servants, namely the increasingly bought-and-paid-for leadership of America's political parties, academia, and lobbying industry.

If allowed to continue, this process will turn the United States into a declining, unfair society with an impoverished, angry, uneducated population under the control of a small, ultrawealthy elite. Such a society would be not only immoral but also eventually unstable, dangerously ripe for religious and political extremism.

Thus far, both political parties have been remarkably clever and effective in concealing this new reality. In fact, the two parties have formed an innovative kind of cartel—an arrangement I have termed America's political *duopoly,* which I analyze in detail below. Both parties lie about the fact that they have each sold out to the financial sector and the wealthy. So far both have largely gotten away with the lie, helped in part by the enormous amount of money now spent on deceptive, manipulative political advertising. But that can't last indefinitely; Americans are getting angry, and even when they're misguided or poorly informed, people have a deep, visceral sense that they're being screwed. Both the Tea Party and the Occupy Wall Street movements are early, small symptoms of this.

So I'm not going to spend much time describing ways to regulate naked credit default swaps, improve accounting standards for off-balance-sheet entities, implement the Volcker rule, increase core capital, or measure bank leverage. Those are important things to do, but they are tactical questions, and relatively easy to manage if you have a healthy political system, economy, academic environment, and regulatory structure. The real challenge is figuring out how the United States can regain control of its future from its new oligarchy and restore its position as a prosperous, fair, well-educated nation. For if we don't, the current pattern of great concentration of wealth and power will worsen, and we may face the steady immiseration of most of the American population.

Before getting into the substance of these issues, I should perhaps make one comment about where I'm coming from. I'm not against business, or profits, or becoming wealthy. I have no problem with people becoming billionaires—if they got there by winning a fair race, if their accomplishments merit it, if they pay their fair share of taxes, and if they don't corrupt their society. The people who founded Intel became very rich—and that's great. They got PhDs in physics. They worked very hard. They treated their employees fairly. And they gave us a thousand times more than they took. Within a decade of its being founded, Intel invented microprocessors and the three most important forms of semiconductor memory. One of Intel's founders—Robert Noyce, whom I once had the honor to meet—*personally* coinvented the integrated circuit. I have no problem at all with the fact that Bob Noyce, Gordon Moore, and Andy Grove made a lot of money. Same for Larry Ellison at Oracle, Steve Jobs and Steve Wozniak of Apple, the founders of Google, eBay, Craigslist, Amazon, and Genentech, and, for that matter, Warren Buffett.

But that's not how most of the people mentioned in this book became wealthy. Most of them became wealthy by being well connected and crooked. And they are creating a society in which they can commit hugely damaging economic crimes with impunity, and in which only children of the wealthy have the opportunity to become successful.

That's what I have a problem with. And I think most people agree with me.

The View from the Bottom 99 Percent

THE 2008 FINANCIAL crisis was the worst economic setback for America, and for the entire globe, since the Great Depression. In 2007, when the financial bubble ended, U.S. economic growth slipped to an anemic 1.9 percent. In 2008 GNP actually declined 0.3 percent—followed by a decline of 3.5 percent in 2009. The year 2010 finally saw a "recovery" with 3 percent GNP growth. But this hasn't helped much. The recovery has been weak and nearly jobless; GNP growth was achieved largely through investments in technology, not by hiring people.[1]

The post-crisis U.S. recession officially ended in June 2009. Yet in the subsequent two years, during the "recovery," median household income in the United States actually fell by nearly 7 percent. The official unemployment rate in early 2012 remained over 8 percent, while the best estimates of America's *real* unemployment rate ranged upward from 12 percent. Poverty, especially child poverty, was at record levels.

Since the crisis began, ten million Americans have spent more than six months out of work, and two million have been unemployed for more than two years. Many of the unemployed have exhausted their benefits, and even more would have done so were it not for temporary extensions—which were agreed to by congressional Republicans only on the condition that Democrats agree to an expensive tax break that mostly benefits the wealthy.

Forced unemployment is damaging for anyone, but long-term unemployment is morale-breaking. Skills deteriorate, people lose their self-confidence, and many of them just give up. Long-term unemployment also, of course, contributes to foreclosures and homelessness. There are no reliable numbers, but America's homeless population is clearly rising fast—especially in warmer climates hit hard by the housing crash, like Florida, but even in relatively prosperous areas like Seattle. The banks of the American River in Sacramento were covered with Hoovervilles in the 1930s. Today, Sacramento officials and organizations like Safe Ground are struggling with a whole new generation of the homeless who are living in the same areas as they were during the Depression.[2]

At the same time, more than two million homes were foreclosed upon in the United States in 2011. American school districts report an upsurge of homeless children due to foreclosures. Newspapers from around the country have reported on adults, often married couples with children themselves, moving back in with their parents, sometimes reduced to living on their parents' social security checks. America's poverty rate is up sharply, to over 15 percent in 2011, including more than sixteen million children. Since the crisis began, the number of people using food stamps has jumped by eighteen million, a 70 percent increase. At the same time, however, the upper 1 percent of the American population has continued to increase its share of America's total income and wealth, to the highest levels since the late 1920s.[3]

Corporate balance sheets are just fine; American companies are sitting on two trillion dollars in cash. But America's governments are *not* fine. The crisis and recession, together with the emergency spending needed to prevent a financial holocaust, caused a 50 percent increase in America's national debt. The federal deficit remains out of control, and many state and local governments have cut essential services, including education and public safety, because they are out of money.

Meanwhile, Europe is suffering from a *new,* and chronic, financial crisis driven by European government debt. As with America, the European debt problem was greatly worsened by the emergency spending that had been needed to prevent the crisis of 2008 from causing a twenty-first-century Great Depression.

In the nations most severely affected by the European debt crisis—Greece, Ireland, Portugal, and Spain—living standards have declined sharply. By early 2012 Spain's official unemployment rate was 23 percent; Portugal's unemployment rate was 12 percent; Ireland's was 14 percent; Greece's was 22 percent. Greece, whose prior government had hired Goldman Sachs to help it fake its national accounts and conceal its budget deficits from the European Union, could no longer pay its $300 billion in government debt. Starting in 2011 (and as a condition for easing the repayment terms on Greece's debts), the European Union, the European Central Bank, and the International Monetary Fund (IMF) forced Greece to institute new taxes and draconian cuts in public sector salaries and pensions. Greece has an enormous, hugely expensive patronage system, but it has thus far remained untouched; instead, most of the pain has been borne by the hardworking and honest. Teachers and university professors have suffered pay cuts of 30 percent or more, unemployment has soared, and GDP declined by 6 percent in 2011. Riots broke out in England, Italy, and Greece, and major protest movements arose in those countries as well as Spain, Germany, and France.[4]

But in many ways, it is America that has changed the most. For most Americans, both salaries and total household income have been flat or declining for many years. The financial crisis, recession, and jobless "recovery" that America has experienced since 2008 are just the latest and worst installment of a process that began many years before. In fact, even during the artificial prosperity of the 2001–2007 financial bubble, the wages of average Americans had been flat or declining, while the incomes of the wealthy were soaring.

No other developed country, even class-conscious Britain, comes remotely close to the extreme income and wealth inequalities of the United States in 2012. Between 2001 and 2007, the years of the great financial bubble, the top 1 percent of U.S. households captured half of the nation's total income growth. This is not the way it used to be; the change started in the 1980s. The top 1 percent's share of taxable income, including capital gains, rose from 10 percent in 1980 to 23 percent in 2007. This is the same percentage as it was in 1928, and about three times the share held by the top 1 percent during the 1950s and 1960s, when America had far higher economic growth, and no financial crises. With the sharp drop in stocks since the financial crash, the top 1 percent's share fell to "only" 17 percent in 2009, but has since risen again to about 20 percent. American wealth is now even more concentrated than income—the wealthiest 1 percent of Americans own about a third of the American people's total net worth, and over 40 percent of America's total financial wealth. This is more than twice the share held by the entire bottom 80 percent of the population.[5]

Consequently, not everyone has suffered over the last decade; CEOs, the financial sector, the energy sector, lobbyists, and children of the already wealthy did just fine. Since 2000, America's four largest oil companies have accumulated more than $300 billion in *excess* profits, defined as profits over and above their profit rate in the prior decade. Investment banking bonuses were similarly enormous—an estimated $150 billion over the decade. The *average* annual salary of New York bankers, which is now $390,000, stayed approximately constant even after the sector collapsed in 2008.

The flip side of the growth in American inequality is an obscene, morally indefensible decline in the fairness of American society—in education, job opportunities, income, wealth, and even health and life expectancy. With the exception of wealthy families, children in America are now less educated than their parents, and will earn less money than their parents. Even worse, the opportunities and lives of young Americans are increasingly determined by how wealthy their parents are, not by their own abilities or efforts.

Many Americans no doubt still believe in the American dream. One wonders how long they can maintain that illusion, for America is transforming itself into one of the most unfair, most rigid, and least socially mobile of the industrialized countries. In the United States, parental income now has about a 50 percent weight in determining a child's lifetime economic prospects. Germany, Sweden, and even class-ridden France are now fairer and more upwardly mobile societies than the United States—on average, parental incomes have only about a 30 percent weight in determining the next generation's outcomes. The truly equitable, high-mobility societies are Canada, Norway, Denmark, and Finland, where parental income accounts for only about 20 percent of a child's lifetime earnings. Even many "developing" nations, such as Taiwan and South Korea, now have levels of opportunity and fairness that exceed America's. For example, someone born into a poor family in South Korea or Taiwan now has a *much* higher probability of graduating from high school, and exiting poverty, than someone born into a poor family in America. Many of these nations' citizens also have longer life expectancies than Americans.[6]

And now the day is past when even a college education in America is either financially available to everyone or a sure ticket to a good life. Technology, globalization, and corporate decisions have been compressing wages and outsourcing many white-collar jobs, much as they have been squeezing blue-collar employment. Now to make your way securely into the upper middle class, you need a degree from an elite institution and/or a graduate degree. And the students who can attend those elite schools come overwhelmingly from the wealthiest families in America. In fact, higher education of all kinds—college and graduate school, private and public, elite and average—has been getting sharply more expensive, and access to it sharply more unequal. With the squeeze on state and local government budgets, even state and community colleges are getting very expensive, so children from working-class or poor families must increasingly choose between not attending college or graduating with mountains of debt. As a result, American college graduation rates have stagnated, and now trail those of many other nations.

Now, having squandered trillions on mismanaged wars, tax cuts designed especially for the rich, a gigantic real estate bubble, and massive bailouts for its banks, the United States is confronting major fiscal problems. At the same time, America's fundamental economic competitiveness has declined severely, as its physical infrastructure, broadband services, educational system, workforce skills, health care, and energy policies have failed to keep pace with the needs of an advanced economy. However, as we shall see later, this is not solely, or even primarily, a matter of money; it is a matter of policy and priorities. In some areas, insufficient government spending is indeed an issue. But in many areas, such as health care, the United States as a society is actually spending far *more* than other nations, without, however, obtaining the same results.

The principal reason for this is that politically powerful interest groups have been able to block reform: the financial services, energy, defense, telecommunications, pharmaceutical, and processed-food industries; the legal, accounting, and medical professions; and to a lesser extent, several unions—these and other groups, including, of course, lobbyists and politicians, have ferociously resisted efforts to improve America's future at their expense.

Meanwhile, both political parties are ignoring, lying about, and/or exploiting the country's very real economic, social, and educational problems. This process is starting to generate an additional danger: demagoguery. As America deteriorates, religious and political extremists are beginning to exploit the growing insecurity and discontent of the population. Thus far, this has principally taken the form of attacks on the federal government, taxes, and social spending. However, sometimes it is also taking more extreme forms: antiscientific fundamentalist Christianity; attacks on education, the teaching of evolution, vaccines, and scientific activity; and demonization of various groups such as immigrants, Muslims, and the poor.

Presiding over all this is an impressive, though utterly cynical, innovation on the part of American politicians: the political duopoly. Over the past quarter century, the leaders of *both* political parties have perfected a remarkable system for remaining in power while serving America's new oligarchy. Both parties take in huge amounts of money, in many forms—campaign contributions, lobbying, revolving-door hiring, favors, and special access of various kinds. Politicians in both parties enrich themselves and betray the interests of the nation, including most of the people who vote for them. Yet both parties are still able to mobilize support because they skillfully exploit America's cultural polarization. Republicans warn social conservatives about the dangers of secularism, taxes, abortion, welfare, gay marriage, gun control, and liberals. Democrats warn social liberals about the dangers of guns, pollution, global warming, making abortion illegal, and conservatives. Both parties make a public show of how bitter their conflicts are, and how dangerous it would be for the other party to achieve power, while both prostitute themselves to the financial sector, powerful industries, and the wealthy. Thus, the very intensity of the two parties' differences on "values" issues enables them to collaborate when it comes to money.

Since the 2008 financial crisis, federal policy has subsidized banks and bankers enormously, while extending the Bush administration's tax cuts for the wealthy. With their bonuses and their industry restored, the fake humility of the bankers who begged for federal assistance has now been forgotten. So, unfortunately, has the fact that when the banks were desperate and dependent in 2008 and 2009, the federal government had an unparalleled opportunity to finally bring them under control—an opportunity that both the Bush and Obama administrations completely wasted and ignored. These same bankers are now among the first to warn about federal deficits, to insist on more tax cuts to stay competitive, and to warn darkly that any further regulation will strangle the "innovation" that made them rich, even as it destroyed the world economy.

But they can be expected to behave that way. Over the last thirty years, the economic interests of the top 1 percent, who now control the country's wealth, businesses, and politics, have diverged sharply from those of other Americans.

The Canopy Economy

CANOPY ECOSYSTEMS ARE worlds of flora and fauna that occur at the tops of very tall trees and exist largely apart from the multiple biosystems layered beneath them. They do this in part by getting the best access to sunlight, but in so doing they block the sun from reaching everything below.

The vast income accumulated by the narrow slice of super-elite at the top of the wealth pyramid has created a kind of global "canopy economy" that has lost its connections to the nations and people they sprang from. At the very top, the most senior executives, rainmakers, and traders at global banks and corporations routinely pull down eight-figure pay packages. These are people with four or five mansions around the world, yachts, private jet services anywhere at any time, limousines, servants, access, power. They are able to indulge any little personal whim—like Blackstone chief Steve Schwarzman's penchant for having $400 stone crab legs flown to him wherever he's on vacation.

The economic impact of this inequality is now astonishingly high. The wealth and power of America's new elite is both a clue to and a cause of America's very tepid recovery from the financial crash. Companies are wallowing in cash, but average Americans don't have money to spend. Labor productivity has improved dramatically, growing by an almost unheard-of 5.4 percent in 2009. So why won't American companies start to hire, and why are average wages declining?

In part, the answer is that the education and skills of the American population are losing two races—one with technological progress, and another with the skill levels of workers in other, lower-wage nations. Education is the critical variable here. In the Internet age, America can be a high-income, full-employment nation only if most of its workforce has education and skills superior to those available in India, China, and elsewhere at far lower wages. And indeed, Americans with master's degrees in computer science from Stanford or MIT still do very well. But most Americans can't participate in the high-technology economy because most of America's educational system is a mess. High school and college graduation rates are vastly inadequate, trailing those of not only most European countries but also Asian nations such as Taiwan, Singapore, and South Korea. (America's high school graduation rate is around 80 percent, and probably declining; South Korea's is over 95 percent.) And as immigrants can tell you, high school in America is a joke compared with high school in South Korea or Taiwan.

But another huge reason for the decline of the American economy, and of average American wages, is the shifting balance of power between America's new oligarchy, the federal government, and the rest of the population. Investment decisions, wage rates, and government policies are determined largely by people in the canopy economy. This has two very deep consequences.

The first is that well-run, successful American companies are indeed investing, but not in people, and not in the United States. CEOs see far better opportunities in purchasing information technology systems and in using inexpensive overseas labor.

Large companies like GE, Boeing, Caterpillar, Ford, and Apple now have, on average, about 60 percent of their sales overseas. (For Intel, it's 84 percent.) Since the days when Ronald Reagan was its spokesman, GE has seemed like the quintessential American company. But more than half of GE's employees, revenues, and assets are on distant shores.

Caterpillar's foreign revenues are about 68 percent of its total. Its recent major acquisitions and investments include two engine plants, a backhoe plant, and a mining equipment factory, all in China; an engine plant in Germany, a truck plant in India, and a pump and motor factory in Brazil. Ford, GM, IBM, and almost any other top manufacturing or services company have much the same profile. Of the $2 trillion in cash sitting on American corporate balance sheets, about $1 trillion is actually parked overseas.[7]

GE was a pioneer in outsourcing, starting with data-processing services, using low-cost vendors like India. President Obama's choice of Jeffrey Immelt, the company's CEO, to head a new White House economic advisory council in early 2011 came just a few months after Immelt had shut down a string of American lightbulb factories to shift production to China. Like many other American firms, GE has also used its global operations to shield income from taxes, helping it to pay no U.S. corporate income taxes for the last several years despite having billions of dollars per year in profits.

Over the last decade, moreover, what is still called "outsourcing" has become something else. The shift to overseas purchasing and investment has spread from low-wage, labor-intensive activities to extremely high-technology, high-skill activities in both manufacturing and services. This development has serious implications for the economic future of the United States.

It would probably not surprise many Americans to learn that most personal computers, laptops, tablets, and smartphones are now manufactured in Asia. However, most of those devices are also now *designed* in Asia, and by Asian firms, not American ones. The United States retains its high-technology lead in advanced research, systems design, software, and systems integration, but has largely lost the capability to design and manufacture information-technology hardware. The employment and competitive implications of this development are profound. For example, Apple has about 70,000 employees worldwide, including its retail stores. But its largest supplier, Foxconn, a Taiwanese company, has *1.3 million* employees. The United States has already become a net importer of high-technology goods, and high technology actually employs a smaller fraction of the total workforce in America than it does in many other nations.

But canopy-economy executives don't care about any of that. They see the whole world not only as their market but also as a source of products, services, labor, and components. For them, the workforce available to nominally American companies is much bigger, and much less expensive, than it was ten or twenty years ago. The canopy is a world of calculation: Indian and Chinese workers have much lower living standards than Americans, so they will work for lower wages. Increasingly, many nations also have broadband systems and logistics infrastructure (such as ports, airports, and rail systems) superior to those of the United States. But it doesn't make sense for American CEOs, either personally or professionally, to lobby for government policies that would improve America's educational or infrastructure systems, particularly if this would also increase their taxes. The benefits of such public investment are society-wide and long-term, not specific to the elite or their companies. And CEOs and bankers have the money and connections to send their children to expensive private schools, to use private jets, to invest their assets globally, and to otherwise avoid the problems of American economic decline.

But how did America's new financial oligarchy get so amazingly rich, particularly during a period of relatively low economic growth and stagnant income for most Americans? Here we come to the second profound consequence of America's new power structure.

The full answer involves a series of economic and political processes that began in the 1970s and are the subject of the final part of this book. But in one regard the answer is very clear. With a few major exceptions—most notably high technology—we can say with great confidence that the principal source of the new canopy elite's wealth was *not* providing greater value to society. In fact, a significant fraction of America's economic decline can be attributed directly to the entrenched power of American executives who destroyed their own industries. Thanks to many excellent studies, some of which I describe in this book, we now know beyond any doubt that for most of the last forty years America's automobile, steel, mainframe computer, mini-computer, and telecommunications industries were very incompetently run. Their oblivious and/or self-interested senior management was protected from replacement by complacent boards of directors, lax antitrust policy, political influence, and outdated, ineffective systems of corporate governance.

And then there's the financial services industry. What do we think of the quality of management in an industry that not only destroys itself but nearly brings down the world economy with it? Do we think that these people deserve great wealth for their achievements? And how about their lobbyists, lawyers, and accountants?

In other words, America's new elite has obtained much of its extreme wealth not through superior productivity, but mainly via forced transfers from the rest of the American, and world, population. These transfers were frequently unethical or even criminal, and were enormously aided by government policies that reduced taxes on the rich, allowed industrial consolidation through lax antitrust enforcement, protected inefficient firms, impeded protests from unions, kept workers' wages low, permitted massive financial sector frauds, bailed out the financial sector when it collapsed, and shielded corporate crime from law enforcement action. Those government policies were, with varying degrees of subtlety, bought and paid for by their beneficiaries.

In this process, one industry stands above all others: financial services. In no other industry has the amorality, destructiveness, and greed of the new elite been so naked. Much of the new wealth of the U.S. financial sector was acquired the old-fashioned way—by stealing it. With each step in the process of deregulation and consolidation, American finance gradually became a quasi-criminal industry, whose behavior eventually produced a gigantic global Ponzi scheme—the financial bubble that caused the crisis of 2008. It was, literally, the crime of the century, one whose effects will continue to plague the world for many years via America's economic stagnation and Europe's debt crisis.

The majority of this book is devoted to describing and explaining this pillaging in considerable detail, but a short overview is in order.

The Greatest Bank Robbery

ALTHOUGH SEVERAL LARGE, concentrated, and politically powerful industries have benefited enormously from deregulation and political corruption, the 2000s were undeniably the decade of the banker. The era of deregulation pioneered by the Reagan and Clinton administrations had removed virtually all restrictions on trading, mergers, and industry consolidation; the few remaining restrictions were then quickly stripped away by the Bush administration, along with any threat of sanctions from either criminal prosecution or civil suits to recoup illicit gains.

Many steps of the deregulatory process were taken openly, often even proudly, for a majority of academic economists and finance experts were insisting that, once freed from obsolete regulatory constraints, the bankers would allocate the world's capital flows with such skill and precision as to usher in a new golden age. Many of the professors doubtless believed in their recommendations, although as we shall see later, many of them also were paid handsomely to support the bankers' positions. Doctors who are on retainer with drug companies may also believe in the products they are pushing, but the money doubtless counts too, and it is wise to be skeptical.

And in fact, bad things started to happen almost immediately. Beginning in the 1980s, the United States began to experience financial crises and scandals on a scale not seen since the 1920s. But deregulation continued, culminating in major laws passed in 1999 and 2000. Once completely freed, the bankers very quickly ran their institutions off the cliff, taking much of the global economy with them. Not only did they create and sell a huge amount of junk, but they turned the financial system into a gigantic casino, one in which they played mainly with other people's money. Consider the position of six large banks at the end of 2007—Citigroup, JPMorgan Chase, Goldman Sachs, Lehman Brothers, Bear Stearns, and Merrill Lynch. Their own proprietary trading accounts, in which traders and financial executives were risking their banks'—or more properly, their shareholders' and bondholders'—money for their own profit, were in excess of $2 trillion. Indeed, their assets had grown by $500 billion in 2007 alone, almost all of it financed with borrowed money.

Leverage—the use of borrowed money to expand the investment banks' businesses—roughly doubled between 2000 and 2007. Three of the largest banks—Lehman Brothers, Bear Stearns, and Merrill Lynch—were leveraged at more than thirty to one at year-end 2007. This meant that only 3 percent of their assets, many of which were very risky or even fraudulent, were paid for with their own money. This *also* meant that a mere 3 percent decline in the value of their assets would wipe out all of their shareholders' wealth and throw these firms into bankruptcy. And, indeed, by early 2008 Bear Stearns was within days of bankruptcy and sold itself to JPMorgan; in September, Merrill sold itself to Bank of America, and Lehman Brothers went bankrupt. Many others failed too—Countrywide, New Century, Washington Mutual— and other even larger institutions, such as Citigroup and AIG, survived only by virtue of massive bailouts. Even Goldman Sachs, one of the strongest of the banks, could not have survived if the government had not saved AIG, and then forced AIG to pay its debts to Goldman and other major banks.

How could so many bankers be so reckless? Money and impunity, is the answer. The structure of personal compensation in the financial system had become completely toxic, and bankers correctly assumed that they would not be prosecuted, no matter how outrageous their conduct. Until the 1980s a combination of tradition, reputation, and tight regulation governed bankers' compensation and prevented major systemic abuses. For example, investment banks were structured as partnerships, with the partners required to invest their own personal money, which constituted the firm's entire capital. In fact, until 1971, *only* partnerships were allowed to join the New York Stock Exchange.

But starting in the 1980s, all that began to change, and by the 2000s, both the structure of the financial sector and its compensation practices would have been unrecognizable to a banker of 1975. At every level from individual traders to CEOs to boards of directors to transactions between firms, people and companies were now rewarded immediately (and usually in cash) for producing short-term profits, with no corresponding penalties for producing subsequent losses. This was fatal. In finance, it is extremely easy to create transactions that are initially profitable, but are disastrous failures in the longer term. But by the 2000s, the bankers didn't have to give any money back if that happened, so they didn't care. In fact, they were *actively incented* to be destructive—to their customers, to their industry, to the wider economy, even frequently to their own firms.

While the party lasted, it made banking look like paradise. During the bubble of the 2000s, financial sector profits soared to nearly 40 percent of all U.S. corporate profits. The average pay of people working at U.S. investment banks jumped from about $225,000—already an amazingly high number—to over $375,000, where it has stayed, even after the crisis. And that was just the cash; those numbers do not include stock options.

And that's the *average*. Consider what happened to the pay of "named executive officers," or NEOs, the highest-paid senior officers (although in any given year, the hottest traders may make more). According to their 2008 proxy statement, the top five officers at Goldman Sachs averaged $61 million *each* in compensation in 2007. Pay levels like that disorient moral compasses; so did the private elevators, the private jets, the partners' private dining rooms and personal chefs, the helicopters, the cocaine, the strip clubs, the prostitutes, the trophy wives, the mansions, the servants, the White House state dinners, the fawning politicians and charities, and the multimillion-dollar parties. There is no denying that in chasing all these things, many bankers not only destroyed the world economy but also sabotaged their own institutions and, in some cases, even themselves.

Nor has financial sector compensation changed greatly since the crisis. In 2008, when all banks were gasping for their last breath, the average NEO compensation dropped back only to the 2005 level, and in January 2009, in the depths of the crisis that they had caused, the New York investment banks awarded their employees over $18 billion in cash bonuses.

But the banks are also guilty of two other, even larger, crimes. The first of these is that they used their wealth to acquire and manipulate political power, to their own advantage but to the nation's enormous, long-term detriment. It was in large measure the financial sector's political activities (through lobbying, campaign contributions, and revolving-door hiring) that gave us deregulation, abdication of white-collar law enforcement, tax cuts for the wealthy, huge budget deficits, and other toxic policies.

And the bankers' final crime was that, far from channeling funds into productive uses, the financial sector has become parasitic and dangerous—a semicriminal industry that is a drag on the American economy. The banks have destabilized the financial system, wasted huge sums of money, plunged millions of people into chronic poverty, and crippled economic growth throughout the industrialized world for many years to come. The proper job of bankers is to allocate capital efficiently by assembling savings from households and businesses, and to place that money into the investments that produce the highest long-term returns for the economy. That is how the financial sector creates jobs and prosperity—or so economic theory says it *should*.

But the housing boom of the 2000s, which was based on a combination of unsustainable consumption and outright fraud, brought no real economic improvement. The financial system deliberately shifted its focus toward people who were either bad credit risks or easy victims, creating new products to entice and defraud them.

By the fall of 2005, Merrill Lynch estimated that half of all U.S. economic growth was related to housing—including new construction, home sales, furniture, and appliances. Much of the rest came from the Bush administration's enormous deficit spending. America was living in a fake economy. Finally, in 2008 the banks ran out of victims, and the bubble collapsed.

NONE OF THE FINANCIAL destruction wreaked by the bankers was an act of God. Nor was it unforeseen. Voices were raised in warning early in the 2000s, and in greater and greater volume, as the bankers plunged into ever more exotic universes of risk. Some of them are in my film *Inside Job*—Raghuram (Raghu) Rajan, Charles Morris, Nouriel Roubini, Simon Johnson, Gillian Tett, William Ackman, Robert Gnaizda, the IMF, even the FBI. They were all ignored, even ridiculed, by those who were profiting from the situation. To a great degree, of course, the outlines of this story are now known, and I will spend relatively little time on it. Most of this book is therefore devoted to two issues: first, the rise of finance as a criminalized, rogue industry, including the role of this criminality in causing the crisis; and second, an analysis of the wider growth of inequality in America.

The book therefore proceeds as follows: Chapter 2 offers a short history of the twenty-year period that led to the rise of a deregulated, concentrated, destabilizing financial sector, including the reemergence of financial crises and criminality.

Next, I describe the available evidence about banking behavior during the 2000s, including the role played by criminal behavior in the bubble and crisis. Chapter 3 examines mortgage lending; chapter 4, investment banking and related activities; chapter 5, the coming of the crisis and the behavior it produced. Chapter 6 surveys the rise of financial criminality, and the case for criminal prosecutions. Not all of the bankers' actions were criminal, of course, but many were—especially if we apply the same standards that sent hundreds of savings and loan executives to prison in the 1990s, not to mention what happened to people not lucky enough to be working for major investment banks when they committed fraud or laundered criminal money.

The last four chapters of the book are a wider analysis of America's recent changes. Starting with financial services, and then turning to academia, other economic sectors, and the political system, I discuss America's descent over the last generation into an economically stagnant, financially unstable, highly unequal society. I begin in chapter 6 by examining the financial sector's transformation into a parasitic industry that increasingly confiscates, rather than creates, national wealth.

In chapter 8, I turn to academia. Many viewers of *Inside Job* commented that the most surprising and shocking element of the film was its revelations about academic conflicts of interest. Here I provide a far more detailed and extensive examination of how the financial sector and other wealthy interest groups have corrupted American academia, changing its role from independent analysis to an additional tool for corporate and financial lobbying. In chapter 9, I consider the broader decline of America's economic and political systems. Chapter 10 concludes the book with a discussion of the alternative futures facing the United States and Europe, the large-scale policy changes required to reverse American decline, and finally the potential avenues for achieving these ends through social and political action.

This last task will not be easy. The conduct of the Obama administration provides a painfully clear example. For reasons described in the final chapters of this book, America's political duopoly is now highly entrenched and resistant to change. Despite their populist pretensions, both parties depend on the money that flows to them because they, and only they, control electoral politics, and both parties would fiercely resist any challenge to this arrangement.

And there is a final problem. To some extent, it must sadly be admitted, America's decline has been tolerated by the American people. Over the last thirty years the American population has become less educated, less inclined to save and invest for the future, and, understandably, far more cynical about participating in politics and American institutions. Consequently, it has proven disturbingly easy for the new American oligarchy to manipulate large segments of the population into tolerating, even supporting, policies that worsen the nation's condition. And, of course, many young Americans have simply given up on politics, particularly after Obama's betrayals.

For now, I still have faith in the American people's essentially good instincts. Many Americans clearly hoped and thought that electing Barack Obama in 2008 would solve these problems; and many are now profoundly disturbed that Obama turned out to be more of the same.

But it is not clear that the American people understand what is happening to them yet, or know how to avert it. For America to reverse its decline, it will be important to do several difficult things. First, it will be necessary to reverse the consolidation of economic power now wielded by highly concentrated industries, the financial sector, and the extremely wealthy. In addition, it will be necessary to shift America's economic priorities toward education, saving, and long-term investment, and away from excessive reliance on military power and cheap energy. And finally, it will be necessary to profoundly change the role of money in American politics—in campaign contributions, political advertising, revolving-door hiring, lobbying, and the enormous disparities between public and private sector salaries.

There are three alternative routes for achieving deep systemic reform: a successful insurgency in one of the existing political parties; a third-party effort; and a nonpartisan social movement perhaps analogous to the civil rights or environmental movement. All of these paths are difficult. But Americans have done difficult things before, even when they faced powerful opposition. Often America's remarkable achievements came in part because it produced equally remarkable leaders. Let us hope it happens again.

CHAPTER 2

OPENING PANDORA'S BOX:
THE ERA OF DEREGULATION,
1980-2000

T WAS IN THE 1970s that the United States first encountered many of its current economic problems. But it was in the 1980s that America began to harm itself in earnest. The Reagan administration provided an eerie sneak preview of the Bush administration, complete with politically popular tax cuts, resultant budget deficits, widespread unemployment, and a sudden rise in economic inequality.

It was in the 1980s that declining American industries and their complacent, outdated, but politically clever CEOs first noticed that paying off lobbyists, politicians, boards of directors, and academic experts was much less expensive, and much easier, than improving their actual performance. And it was also in the 1980s that America's newly deregulated financial sector got back in touch with its dark side, starting a thirty-year phase of consolidation, financial instability, large-scale criminality, and political corruption. In the late 1980s, America experienced its first financial crises since the Great Depression, although by current standards they seem quaint. One crisis was caused by deregulation and rampant criminality; the other, by a complex financial innovation that supposedly *reduced* risk, but that actually increased it. Sound familiar?

Even though hundreds of financial executives went to prison, dozens of financial firms were bankrupted by their executives' corruption, and America endured its first serious postwar financial crises, by the end of the 1980s the financial sector was wealthier and more politically powerful than ever. It was a genie that America hasn't yet been able to return to the bottle.

America Embattled

THE DECADE BETWEEN 1972 and 1982 was a very rough period for the United States. Between 1973 and 1975 alone, America went through the Watergate hearings, Richard Nixon resigning in disgrace to avoid impeachment, the Yom Kippur war, the first OPEC oil embargo, the fall of South Vietnam, and a sudden recession caused by the first OPEC oil shock. Just as the effects of the first oil shock had receded, an Islamic revolution deposed the Shah of Iran and OPEC tripled oil prices again in 1979, yielding an unprecedented combination of recession, inflation, and high interest rates. Then, for the icing on the cake, the Soviet Union invaded Afghanistan.

But it was also in the 1970s that America first encountered its more fundamental economic challenges: the long-term costs of its military when it was misused in distant, poorly managed wars; the complacency and internal decay of America's largest companies and industries; Asian competition based on the "just in time" or "lean" production model; the growth of outsourcing permitted (even driven) by information technology; the declining market value of American unskilled labor; and the need to raise the educational level of the entire American population.

By 1980 it was increasingly clear that the long, lazy, global dominance of American industry was over. American productivity growth declined, from 3 percent per year in the 1950s and 1960s to less than

1 percent in the 1970s and 1980s. Cars imported from Japan were not only less expensive and more fuel efficient than those from Detroit but also *better*—fewer assembly defects, longer lifetimes, less expensive to maintain. Similar effects were seen in consumer electronics, machine tools, steel, even semiconductor memories and IBM-compatible mainframe computers, high-technology markets that Japanese firms entered aggressively in the late 1970s. American specialists noticed that Japanese firms often adopted new technologies faster than their American rivals, even technologies that had been invented in America. Similarly, although Japan was far more dependent on imported oil than the United States, its economy recovered much faster from the 1970s oil shocks.

In America this unfamiliar combination of low growth, two oil shocks, recessions, and rising foreign challenges led to sudden anxiety and rising anger. In 1980 MIT professor Lester Thurow published an imperfect but very prescient book, *The Zero-Sum Society,* arguing that America had entered a painful phase of low growth and distributional conflict. In policy circles, an intense debate started. Some argued in favor of protectionism, others for aggressive government investments and industrial policy.

Many economists dismissed both Thurow's book and the entire issue. Others argued that increased savings and investment, together with a gradual depreciation of the dollar, would take care of America's trade deficits and "competitiveness" problem. All mainstream economists (including some who now say otherwise) denied that the entrenchment of incompetent management, globalization, low-wage Asian competition, or Asian national strategic industrial policies could cause a decline in American living standards. To be sure, it was a confusing time; America had never experienced anything like it before. (As a young academic I participated in some of those debates, and I didn't get everything right, either.)

America's political leadership seemed adrift. And unfortunately, Americans were not, at that moment, ready to be told that America's easy domination of the world economy was over, and that America needed to refocus on saving, improved education, information technology, tougher antitrust policy, energy conservation, and greater understanding of other nations.

Or perhaps, actually, Americans *would* have listened, if their political leaders had told them the truth. But they didn't. They lied, and with occasional exceptions they have continued to lie ever since. By 1980 America was ripe for a simplistic, reassuring story about how everything would be better if only taxes were lower, government regulation scaled back, and the American military strengthened.

With those crude ideas Ronald Reagan sailed into office, on little more than his grin and his optimism, in part because President Jimmy Carter did not offer a coherent alternative. Carter was sincere, but he seemed ineffectual and timid. In contrast, and to the surprise of many, Reagan proved a strong president who accomplished much of his agenda—sometimes for good, often for ill. Tax cuts and deregulation became the order of the day. Even from the start, though, there was a big element of dishonesty in Reagan's strategy. He cut taxes, but *not* government spending, so America's economic recovery came in part from unsustainable deficits. Administration officials claimed that tax cuts would pay for themselves, which they knew was a lie. And what they called "deregulation" was often simply political corruption. Lobbyists and industry executives were appointed to run government agencies, and several industries sharply increased their spending on political donations, lobbying, and revolving-door hiring.

Nowhere was this clearer than in finance. It was in financial services that the Reagan administration initiated America's descent into criminality, financial crisis, political corruption, inequality, and decline.

Banking in 1980

WHEN REAGAN TOOK office, the American financial sector was still organized according to New Deal laws enacted in response to the Great Depression.

Banks and bankers had compiled a terrible record in the 1920s—creating financial bubbles, misdirecting deposits for their own personal benefit, and off-loading bad loans onto their customers in the form of fraudulent investment funds.[1] Excessive leverage, fraud, and Ponzi-like behavior were widely regarded as having contributed to the 1920s bubble and the Great Depression.

The New Deal laws were intended to remove such temptations, or at least limit their damage. The 1933 Glass-Steagall Act forbade any bank accepting customer deposits to also underwrite or sell any kind of financial securities.[2] The Securities Act of 1933 and the Securities Exchange Act of 1934 required extensive financial disclosure by public companies and investment banks, and created the SEC to police them. Also in response to the Depression, in 1938 the federal government created Fannie Mae to purchase and insure mortgages issued by banks and savings and loan institutions (S&Ls), once again under strict regulation. The Investment Company Act of 1940 regulated asset managers such as mutual funds.

As late as 1980, this structure remained in place. Commercial banking, investment banking, residential mortgage lending, and insurance were distinct industries, tightly regulated at both the federal and state levels, and also very fragmented, with no single firm or even group of firms dominating any sector. American commercial banking was a stable, dull industry. Most bank branches closed at 3 p.m.; "banker's hours" allowed for lots of time on the golf course. There were strict limits on branches outside a bank's home state; interest rates were tightly regulated. The industry was divided roughly between a few big "money center" banks, headquartered primarily in New York and Chicago, and thousands of small local and regional banks scattered across the country.

And then there were the S&Ls, small, usually local firms in the sole business of taking savings deposits and selling fixed-rate long-term residential mortgages. As late as 1980, most S&Ls were trusts—they had no stockholders, but rather were cooperatively owned by their local passbook depositors. (The same was true of credit unions and most large insurance companies.) Like banks, the S&Ls were tightly regulated, and their retail deposits were insured. They were explicitly permitted by regulators to pay slightly higher interest rates on savings accounts than commercial banks, in order to encourage mortgage lending.

The world on the other side of the Glass-Steagall wall—the securities industry—was divided between retail brokerages and investment banks. Brokerage firms, the largest of which was Merrill Lynch, sold stocks and bonds to wealthy individual customers. Merrill Lynch was a large firm for this period. It was also one of the first to go public, in 1971.

True investment banks, such as Goldman Sachs, Morgan Stanley, Bear Stearns, Dillon Read, and Lehman Brothers, provided financial advice to big companies and managed and distributed new issues of stocks and bonds. It was a fragmented but still clubby industry, informally divided between Protestant and Jewish firms, with women and minorities welcomed by neither. There were dozens of firms, all of them small but very stable, with low personnel turnover. In 1980 Goldman Sachs, the largest, had a total of 2,000 employees (versus 34,000 in 2011); most of the others had only a few hundred, some only a few dozen. They were all private partnerships, and the capital they used was their own. If they underwrote (guaranteed the sale of) a new issue of stock, the partners were literally risking their own personal money, which constituted the entire capital base of the firm. Their franchises depended on reputation and trust—though also, realistically, on golf, squash at the Harvard Club, and old-school ties.

Regulation, Bankers' Pay, and Financial Stability

BANKERS' PAY HAD reached stratospheric levels in the 1920s but then contracted sharply with the Depression and, even more important, with the tightening of regulation in its wake. After passage of the New Deal reforms, pay in the American financial sector settled down. For forty years, average financial sector pay stayed at about double the average American's income. Executive compensation, while comfortable, was hardly exorbitant; nobody had private planes or gigantic yachts.[3]

Equally important was the *structure* of financial sector pay. Most commercial bankers were paid straight salaries. Investment bankers lived well and received annual bonuses, but through deliberate policy practiced universally within the industry, most of the partners' total wealth was required to remain invested in their firm, usually for decades. Partners could only take their money out when they retired, so partners and their firms exhibited very long time horizons and a healthy aversion to catastrophic risk taking.

All of this—the industry structure, regulation, culture, and compensation practices—remained in place until the early 1980s. Then the wheels came off.

Drivers of Change

IN THE EARLY 1980s, three forces converged in a perfect storm of pressure and opportunity: the upheavals of the 1970s, which destabilized and devastated the financial markets, forcing bankers to seek new forms of income; the information technology revolution, which integrated previously separate markets and vastly increased the complexity and velocity of financial flows; and deregulation, which placed the inmates in charge of the asylum.

The first driver of change was severe financial pressure. In the wake of the 1973 and 1979 oil shocks, the stock market and all financial institutions suffered badly. Inflation grew so severe that in 1981 three-month Treasury bills briefly paid 16 percent interest.

The second driver of change was technology. The U.S. financial sector did need some deregulation, or more accurately, different and modernized regulation, in the computer age. The tight control over interest rates on consumer deposits, the somewhat artificial division between banks and S&Ls, and the prohibition on interstate banking caused significant inefficiencies. Information technology and the rise of electronic financial transactions created opportunities for productivity gains through nationwide and global integration of previously distinct markets.

At the same time, however, information technology posed dangers that required *tighter* regulation in some areas. The advent of frictionless, instant electronic transactions introduced new volatility and market instability. Information technology also made it easy to construct and trade increasingly complicated and opaque financial products, through increasingly complex financial supply chains. But that same complexity also made it easier to hide things—things like risk, or fraud, or who really stood to gain and lose.

In this context—oil shocks, recession, inflation, new technologies and financial products—much of America's staid, rigid financial sector performed badly. In particular, by the early 1980s the regulators were faced with the potential collapse of the entire S&L industry.

The S&Ls had been destroyed by the interest-rate volatility and inflation caused by the second oil shock. Their business of collecting deposits and financing long-term, fixed-rate mortgages assumed an environment of steady, low interest rates. By the early 1980s, depositors fled low-interest S&L accounts for money market funds. At the same time, the value of the S&Ls' low-interest, fixed-rate mortgage loans declined sharply as a result of inflation and higher interest rates.

The Reagan administration's publicly stated response to the S&L problem was to make the S&L industry a star test case for deregulation. But what *really* happened was that deregulatory economic ideology was used as political cover for a highly corrupt process of letting the S&Ls, and their investment bankers, run wild. What followed was a movie we've been seeing ever since.

Deregulatory Fiasco at the S&Ls

HAD THE GOVERNMENT simply shut down the S&L industry, the cost to American taxpayers would have been in the range of $10 billion. But the industry was politically well connected, and was one of the first to make aggressive use of campaign contributions and lobbying. Senator William Proxmire, chairman of the Senate Banking Committee, later called it "sheer bribery" on national television. But it worked. With bipartisan support, a supposed "rescue" bill, the Garn–St. Germain Act, was quickly passed by Congress and signed by Reagan.

The real killer was the appointment of Richard Pratt, an industry lobbyist, as head of the Federal Home Loan Bank Board, the S&Ls' regulator. Pratt proceeded to gut the regulations against self-dealing. For the first time, an S&L could be controlled by a single shareholder, could have an unlimited number of subsidiaries in multiple businesses, and could lend to its own subsidiaries. Loans could be made against almost any asset. S&Ls could now raise money by selling federally insured certificates of deposit (CDs) through Wall Street brokers. The shakier the S&L, the higher the interest rates paid by their CDs, and the larger the investment banking fees.

It was a license to steal. The people running S&Ls started to play massively with other people's money. They loaned money to themselves, they loaned money to gigantic real estate projects that they owned, they loaned money to their relatives, they bought cars, planes, mansions, and assorted other toys.

From 1980 through mid-1983, an operator named Charles Knapp ballooned a California S&L's assets from $1.7 billion to $10.2 billion, and then kept going at an annual rate of about $20 billion until he finally hit the wall in 1985. When the government moved in, the assets were worth about $500 million. The Vernon Savings Bank in Texas ran its assets from $82 million to $1.8 billion in about a year. The owner bought six Learjets, and when the Feds finally looked, they found that 96 percent of its loans were delinquent. As late as 1988, 132 *insolvent* Texas S&Ls were still growing rapidly.

Charles Keating was another S&L pioneer—an expert hypocrite, famous for being an antipornography crusader. He claimed that pornography was part of "the Communist conspiracy," and made really bad movies about the horrors of perversion for profit. The SEC had charged him with fraud in the 1970s, but Keating was still allowed to take over a relatively healthy S&L in 1984. He quickly racked up $1 billion–plus in costs to the government, while making (or rather, taking) a fortune for himself. Keating played Congress and the regulators like a violin, fending off investigators with eighty law firms and the famous Keating Five—the five senators he persuaded to help him, via $300,000 in campaign contributions. (They were Alan Cranston, John Glenn, John McCain, Donald Riegle, and Dennis DeConcini.) For $40,000, Keating also hired Alan Greenspan, then a private economist, to write letters and walk around Washington, DC, with him, telling regulators about Keating's good character and solid business methods. Noting Greenspan's excellent judgment, Reagan later appointed Greenspan to be chairman of the Federal Reserve. Keating was eventually sent to prison.

Then there was Silverado, on whose board of directors sat Neil Bush, son of George H. W. Bush and brother of George W. Bush. Bush approved $100 million in loans to Silverado executives, and loans to himself too. Silverado's collapse cost the taxpayers $1.3 billion. Bush was sued by two federal regulators; he paid fines and was banned from banking but avoided criminal prosecution.

There were many others. The federal government established the Resolution Trust Corporation to take over bankrupt S&Ls and sell off their assets. The cost to the taxpayers was about $100 billion, which seemed like an enormous amount at the time.

But there was one important regard in which the United States system had not yet been totally corrupted. Although many perpetrators got away with it—particularly those who worked for major investment banks, law firms, and accounting firms—many did not. As a result of the S&L scandals, several thousand financial executives were criminally prosecuted, and hundreds were sent to prison. Altogether, the episode was a pointed, but in retrospect very mild, foreshadowing of the outbreak of massive financial criminality in subsequent decades.

But it wasn't just the S&Ls who partied hard in the 1980s. The investment bankers, leveraged buyout firms, lawyers, accountants, and insider trading people had a good time too.

Indeed the first truly disturbing signal about deregulation was that the proudest names in American investment banking, law, and accounting had eagerly participated in the S&Ls' looting. Merrill Lynch earned a quick $5 million by shoveling more than a quarter billion dollars in high-rate deposits into two S&Ls in the six months before they were shut down. The law firms that later paid multimillion-dollar settlements included Jones, Day, Reavis, and Pogue; Paul, Weiss, Rifkind; and Kaye Scholer. The accounting profession was just as bad. Ernst & Young and Arthur Andersen (later of Enron fame) paid especially big settlements for having allowed the S&Ls to fake their books; Ernst & Young alone paid more than $300 million. The total taxpayer cost, of course, was many, many times the recoveries.[4]

But the real party was with the boys who played with junk bonds.

Junk Bonds, Leveraged Buyouts, and the Rise of Predatory Investment Banking

PRIOR TO THE 1980s, only a very few highly rated companies could raise capital by issuing corporate bonds. But years of research convinced an ambitious young man named Michael Milken that ordinary companies could also do so, and in 1977 he and his employer, the investment bank Drexel Burnham Lambert, began to underwrite bond issues for previously unrated companies. Interest rates were higher than in the blue-chip bond market but compared favorably with bank loans. Initially, the availability of so-called junk bonds was a useful service to midsize companies that needed capital for growth. But then things got crazy.

What happened first was that predatory investment firms started to use junk bonds to buy companies. This often made financial sense, for two reasons. First, the stock market had fallen so severely, and often irrationally, that many public companies were cheap to acquire—if you had the cash, which the junk bond market provided. But the second reason for the junk bond boom was that many American companies were grotesquely mismanaged by complacent, entrenched executives. Until junk bonds, they had nothing to fear, because they were supported by their equally complacent, entrenched boards of directors.

But then, suddenly, there was a way to get rid of entrenched management, even if the board supported them. Someone could go to Michael Milken and, nearly instantly, raise billions of dollars on the junk bond market to finance a hostile takeover. In some early cases, this produced real efficiencies as incompetent managers were forced out by new owners. But then the financiers noticed two important things. The first was that once they took over a company, they could do anything they wanted. They could break the company up, sell off its pieces, cut employee benefits, pay themselves huge fees, and, quite often, loot whatever remained. They could also "flip" the company. Early in the leveraged buyout (LBO) cycle, the stock market was severely depressed. But as the market started to recover in the 1980s, it became almost trivial to buy a company in an LBO, cut some expenses, and take it public a few years later.

William Simon, treasury secretary in the Nixon and Ford administrations, put up $1 million of his own money and borrowed another $80 million to buy Gibson Greeting Cards in 1982. Less than a year and a half later, with a stock market recovery under way, he took the company public at a value of $290 million. Ted Forstmann's firm even more spectacularly bought and flipped Dr Pepper. The simplicity and profitability of the early deals led to a bubble, one that Michael Milken and his friends then perpetuated through fraud, of which more shortly.

But the financiers' next insight was much more fun. They realized that actually, they didn't even need to buy the company, and then go through all the messy work of fixing it, running it, selling it. All they needed to do instead was to *threaten* to buy the company. In response, the company's terrified, inept executives and board of directors would pay them enormous sums simply to go away. And thus was born "greenmail." Michael Milken and Drexel's junk bonds started to finance greenmail on a large scale, which was primarily conducted through specialized firms created by the likes of T. Boone Pickens, Ronald Perelman, and Carl Icahn.

Milken and his junk bonds also financed a number of the most corrupt S&Ls, as well as the arbitrageurs, or "arbs," who gambled on the existence and outcome of takeover battles. Of course, making money that way was a lot easier if you actually *knew* what was about to happen, so the rise of LBOs, greenmail, and speculative arbitrage also caused an epidemic of insider trading. People like Ivan Boesky developed networks of informants and paid serious bribe money for leaks; Boesky would then raise money through Milken, buy stock, and sell it as soon as the takeover was initiated or completed. Boesky made a fortune, but in 1986 the SEC and federal prosecutors nailed him. He pled guilty, turned informant on Milken and others, and was sentenced to three years in federal prison.

The first wave of junk-bond-backed LBOs was mostly good for the economy. But it didn't take long for the early deals, plus recovery from the second oil shock, to push up stock prices. This made the early LBOs look insanely profitable, which led to a new wave of LBOs, forcing stock prices up even more. Then came greenmail and speculative arbitrage. In the rational, "efficient" world fantasized by academic economists, buyouts should have tapered off once stock prices reached reasonable levels. In the real world, junk bonds created a bubble, both in the stock market and in the bonds themselves. The Decade of Greed, as it came to be called, lasted until the late 1980s. Once the hysteria broke, collapse rapidly followed. Milken tried to prolong the bubble by "parking" stock through secret side agreements, and by encouraging self-dealing. His clients would buy junk bonds for their company's retirement plans, invest in junk bonds with money he raised for them, and so forth. Milken was indicted on more than ninety counts, pled guilty to six, and was sentenced to ten years in prison, fined $600 million, and banned from the securities industry for life. The fine left him still a billionaire, and he was released from prison after two years. He has since tried to rehabilitate himself through a series of foundations, one of which is now a major source of funding for pro-business academic economists.[5]

The junk bond–LBO-takeover-greenmail-arbitrage craze of the 1980s was a key milestone in Wall Street's metamorphosis from a tradition-bound enclave to the cocaine-fueled, money-drugged, criminalized casino that wreaked global havoc in the 2000s. One major consequence of the LBO craze was to break down the traditional culture of investment banking. LBOs and related activities required lots of capital, particularly as the size of takeover deals increased to billions, even tens of billions, of dollars. They also were inherently driven by short-term, one-time transaction fees. So investment banks started to go public to raise capital, pay short-term cash bonuses, and abandon their quaint old notions of ethics and customer loyalty.

The LBO boom also radically changed Wall Street's compensation structures, in both structure and size. The bankers on LBO deals soon were paid a percentage of the deal, regardless of long-term results, and Wall Street pay soared, as did incomes for the CEOs involved in LBOs, their law firms, their accountants, and their consulting firms. (For several years, Michael Milken was paid over $500 million per year.) It was the beginning of the shift toward the extraordinary inequality and financial sector wealth that characterizes America today.

Financial Innovation, Derivatives, and the 1987 Market Crash

THE BOOM ON Wall Street was accompanied by enormous growth in institutional stock portfolios and also by the first wave of the modern IT revolution, driven by powerful microprocessors and personal computers. The result was the rise of sophisticated computer-driven innovations in portfolio management.

By the summer of 1987, stock indices had racked up years of spectacular gains, signs of a bubble were everywhere, and institutional managers were nervous. But financial innovation was there to help, with a marvelous new product called "portfolio insurance." The idea was this: if a fund manager was worried that the market would fall, he could limit his losses by selling stock-index futures (a form of financial derivative). If the market suddenly plunged, losses would be covered by the futures you sold.

Executing such a strategy was impossible for a mere human being, but two Berkeley finance professors, Hayne Leland and Mark Rubinstein, developed software that would trade automatically. A portfolio manager could pick a desired price floor, and the computers took it from there. Futures selling would be minimal if the portfolio was performing well, but would accelerate as markets fell. Fund managers loved the idea; by the fall of 1987 some $100 billion of stock portfolios were "insured," and the professors had made a fortune.

There was just one little problem. If this strategy was *generally* adopted, it would have exactly the opposite effect from the one intended, because any substantial market fall would automatically generate a huge burst of futures selling. And a sudden wave of selling in the futures market would almost surely trigger panicky selling in the stock market—which could trigger more futures selling, and so on.

And that's more or less what happened. The effect was worsened by the fact that the stock market was in New York while the futures market was in Chicago, and the computer links between them were extremely primitive.

It started on Wednesday, October 14, 1987, but the real carnage hit on the following Monday, October 19, forever dubbed Black Monday. The stock market fell 23 percent, the largest one-day percentage drop in history.[6] The markets eventually stabilized, with the help of a flood of new money from Alan Greenspan's Federal Reserve—one of the first appearances of what Wall Street came to call the "Greenspan Put." Get into whatever trouble you may, Uncle Alan will bail you out.

The episode was a clear warning of the inherent dangers of financial "innovation." Professors Leland and Rubinstein were obviously extremely smart men, as were the bankers using their tools. Some of them had to know that if enough people were using this "insurance," any sizable downturn would trigger large-scale selling and thereby cause the very event they were supposedly trying to prevent. Credit default swaps and other financial derivatives often carry similar risks. Their use therefore requires *regulation*—particularly disclosure of positions to a regulator who can look across the whole market, and limitations on the total level of risk. But derivatives were too profitable for Wall Street, which instead pushed in precisely the opposite direction.

Deregulation Triumphant: The Clinton Administration

THE 1990S WERE, it turns out, the best of times and the worst of times. The economic outlook entering the 1990s was extremely gloomy. In the late 1980s the LBO-takeover–stock market bubble deflated, and America's long-term economic problems once again began to bite.

But in the end, America's economic performance in the 1990s was superb. The reason was the Internet revolution, together with America's venture capital and start-up systems. Starting with the invention of the World Wide Web in 1990, Internet-based innovation and entrepreneurship generated sharply higher economy-wide productivity growth for the first time since the 1960s. Even though the Internet was globally available and the World Wide Web had been invented in Europe, America spawned every major Internet company—Amazon, eBay, Yahoo, Google, Craigslist, Facebook—and thousands of smaller ones. Clinton administration policy helped by privatizing the Internet in 1995, reforming parts of the telecommunications sector, and taking antitrust action against Microsoft.

At the same time, however, the Clinton administration created the regulatory environment that gave us the financial bubble and crisis of the 2000s. Clinton let the financial sector run wild. Economic and regulatory policy was taken over by the industry's designated drivers—Robert Rubin, Larry Summers, and Alan Greenspan. It was during this period that America's financial sector assumed its current form—

highly concentrated, frequently criminal, and systemically dangerous. Its growing criminality even affected the Internet industry, via a stock market bubble that Wall Street deliberately inflated, often with outright fraud. The pervasive level of fraud in "dot-com" stocks was nakedly obvious to everyone in the industry (including me), but the Clinton administration did nothing about it. For the first time, investment bankers were given clear signals that they could behave as they wished.

Equally dangerous, however, were several other developments in the U.S. financial sector during the 1990s. The first was far-reaching deregulation, in both law and practice, championed by the Clinton administration, Congress, and the Federal Reserve. The second was the structural concentration of the industry, much of which would have been illegal without the deregulatory measures. With astonishing speed, the financial sector's major components—commercial banking, investment banking, brokerage, trading, rating, securities insurance, derivatives—consolidated sharply into tight oligopolies of gigantic firms, which often cooperated with each other, particularly in lobbying and politics.

The third change in the industry was the rise of the "securitization food chain," an elaborate industrywide supply chain for generating mortgages, selling them to investment banks, and packaging them into "structured" investments for sale to pension funds, hedge funds, and other institutional investors. The result was an extremely complex, opaque process that integrated nearly every segment of the financial system.

The fourth change in financial services was growth in unregulated, "innovative" financial instruments. Once again enabled by continued deregulation, the industry invented clever new things like credit default swaps, collateralized debt obligations, and "synthetic" mortgage securities.

In principle, these changes created major efficiencies; but they also made the entire system more fragile, interdependent, and extremely vulnerable to both fraud and systemic crises.

But the final change in the financial sector was the most fatal. By the end of the nineties, at every level of the system and at every step in the securitization food chain, all of the players—from lenders to investment banks to rating agencies to pension funds, from mortgage brokers to traders to fund managers to CEOs to boards of directors— were compensated heavily in cash, based on short-term gains (often as short as the last transaction), with built-in conflicts of interest, and with no penalties for causing losses. Almost nobody was risking their own money. In short, nobody had an incentive to behave ethically and prudently. By the time George W. Bush took office, the explosives had been planted; all it took was for someone to light the fuse.

Taming Mortgages but Creating a Monster

IT ALL BEGAN with a clever, sane idea: the mortgage-backed security. In order to allow S&Ls to lend more money, banks could buy mortgages from S&Ls—which would give the S&Ls immediate cash—and then the bank would package the mortgages into securities, which it would sell to investors.

In 1983 Larry Fink and his investment banking team at First Boston invented the CMO, or collateralized mortgage obligation. (Fink is now CEO of BlackRock, the big investment manager.) Fink's innovation was that his CMOs were sliced into several distinct classes, or "tranches," with different credit ratings and yields. The top tranche had first claim on cash flows from the mortgages, while the bottom tranche absorbed the brunt of prepayment and default risk.

Demand was high. These new products started to change the whole structure of housing finance. Now, mortgage brokers sourced deals for a new group of "mortgage banks." The mortgage banks bought loans from brokers, and held them only until they had enough for Wall Street to securitize. By the mid-1990s, this model dominated the market.

But even in the first several years of their existence, collateralized mortgage obligations produced an interlude of craziness ending in a mini-crisis, in the early 1990s. Though tiny by current standards, with estimated losses of $55 billion, it was a warning of the damage that could be inflicted by uncontrolled, or perversely incented, bankers.

There were other dark signs. One was the entry of "hard money lenders" like Beneficial Finance and Household Finance into housing finance. They specialized in high-risk, high-yield lending, and were aggressive in going after defaulting borrowers. By the end of the 1990s, the high earnings of the hard-money housing spin-offs like the Money Store, Option One, and New Century made them darlings of the stock market. Riskier housing lending, although still a small fraction of the market, was growing.[7]

High-risk mortgages were extremely profitable, particularly if their risks could be disguised, because they carried high fees and interest rates. They were also perfect for a Ponzi-like bubble, which would temporarily conceal fraud. If housing prices were rising, then the loans could be paid off by flipping houses or by taking out additional home equity loans, based on the supposed appreciation of the house.

The gradual rise in high-risk lending exploited the fatal flaw of securitization, namely that it broke the essential link between credit *decisions* and subsequent credit *risk and consequences.* If people pumped out bad loans just to sell them, trouble would eventually follow, but it would be *other* people's trouble. In principle, one could adjust for this, for example by requiring sellers of loans to accept a fraction of subsequent losses. But nobody did that; in fact, compensation practices were moving in the opposite direction, and fast.

Securitization spread from high-quality mortgages to so-called subprime mortgages, and also to other classes of loans. Wall Street started securitizing portfolios of credit card receivables, car loans, student loans, commercial real estate loans, and bank loans used to finance leveraged corporate buyouts. Initially, again, only high-quality loans were used; but, again, quality declined steadily over time.

At the same time, the securitization food chain became ever more complex and opaque. Its growth and increasing complexity caused a gradual, disguised rise in system-wide leverage and risk. Many buyers of securitized products were hedge funds and other highly leveraged, unregulated "shadow banking" entities. Securitized mortgage products were increasingly insured by specialized ("monoline") insurance companies and/or via credit default swaps, a market dominated by a London-based unit of AIG (AIG Financial Products). These were unregulated derivatives that generated potentially huge payments in the event of credit downgrades or defaults. But nobody knew the total size or distribution of these risks.

During the same period, the increasing criminality and systemic danger of finance was showing itself, even as the industry successfully pressed for more deregulation. The most visible signs were the Internet bubble, the huge frauds at WorldCom and Enron, the Asian financial crisis, and the implosion of Long-Term Capital Management (LTCM), which at the time was the world's largest hedge fund.

The Internet revolution was very real, and certainly justified a sharp spike in venture capital investment, start-up activity, and initial public offerings, as well as in the stock prices of established companies well positioned to exploit Internet technology. What actually happened, however, was insane, and went far beyond rationality. Companies with almost no revenues, losing huge sums of money, and with no plausible way to reach profitability, received enormous equity investments and then went public at extraordinary valuations. The Nasdaq index, a good proxy for technology stocks, went from under 900 in 1995 to over 4500 in January 2000.

Then the bubble collapsed. Eighteen months later, in mid-2002, the Nasdaq was back down to 1100. Certainly much of the bubble was driven by general public overexcitement, but much of it was also driven by fraud, on the part of both entrepreneurs and Wall Street. Dozens of Internet companies spent lavishly, paid lavishly, told lies, went public, and then went bankrupt by 2001. Wall Street firms and their star analysts gave these companies high investment ratings in order to obtain their business, often while privately deriding them as junk.

In addition to start-ups, several established companies, including Enron and WorldCom (which had acquired MCI, a large telecommunications provider), had exploited and thereby contributed to the stock

frenzy by using accounting fraud and claims of Internet-related innovation. Enron also relied on its political connections, which helped keep
regulatory oversight lax. The company contributed heavily to sympathetic candidates, and one member of its board of directors was Wendy
Gramm, who was not only a former chairperson of the Commodity
Futures Trading Commission (CFTC), but also the wife of Texas senator Phil Gramm, then chairman of the Senate Banking Committee.

The Next Wave of Financial Deregulation

THE CLINTON ADMINISTRATION became the driver of financial deregulation, with frequent assistance from Alan Greenspan and
Congress. The result was a wave of new laws, regulatory changes, and
a sharp deceleration in both civil and criminal law enforcement. Issuance of regulations, monitoring, criminal investigation and prosecution of financial offenses, and IRS audits of financial executives
declined sharply. Ironically, these deregulatory changes were preceded
by the one piece of positive regulatory legislation enacted by Clinton.
In 1994 Congress passed and Clinton signed the Home Ownership and
Equity Protection Act (HOEPA), intended to curb abuses in the emerging market for high-interest subprime loans, particularly for home equity lines of credit (HELOCs). The law gave the Federal Reserve Board
broad authority to issue regulations covering mortgage industry practices. But Alan Greenspan refused to use the law. In fact, the Federal
Reserve issued no mortgage regulations at all until 2008, which was
just a little late, and during the bubble Greenspan made several public
statements encouraging use of "innovative" mortgage products.

Rules against interstate banking were dropped in 1994. The Glass-
Steagall Act, mandating strict separation between investment banks
and commercial banks, was substantially weakened in 1996, and completely repealed in 1999. Citigroup actually violated the law by acquiring an insurance company and investment bank before Glass-Steagall
was repealed; Alan Greenspan gave them a waiver until the law was

passed. Shortly afterward, Robert Rubin resigned from the administration to become vice chairman of Citigroup, where, over the course of the next decade, he made more than $120 million.

Then came the fight over derivatives. One of the Clinton administration's final acts, with strong support from Larry Summers, Alan Greenspan, and Senator Phil Gramm, was a law banning any regulation of over-the-counter (OTC) derivatives, including all the complex securities that were at the heart of the 2008 crisis. Large sections of the bill were drafted by ISDA, the industry association for derivatives dealers.[8]

The total ban on OTC derivatives regulation actually started with a move *toward* regulation. Brooksley Born, chair of the CFTC, had observed the rapidly growing derivatives market and concluded that it posed significant risks. She initiated a public comment and review process, which immediately triggered ferocious combined opposition from Rubin, Summers, Greenspan, and SEC chairman Arthur Levitt. Larry Summers telephoned Born, telling her that he had thirteen bankers in his office who were furious, and demanding that Born desist. (The phone call may have been illegal, since the CFTC is an independent regulatory agency.) Shortly afterward, the administration introduced legislation to ban all regulation of OTC derivatives, supported heavily by Phil Gramm.

Remarkably, the deregulation drive was utterly unaffected by a concurrent wave of scandals involving derivatives and other new instruments. A Bankers Trust trading subsidiary, BT Securities, marketed derivatives in a quite predatory way, usually to hedge against interest rate risk. A simple interest-rate swap for Gibson Greeting Cards on a $30 million debt was constantly tweaked, until a series of twenty-nine separate "improvements" ended up costing Gibson $23 million. When Gibson finally sued, seven more BT clients came forward with similar claims. Procter & Gamble said it had lost $195 million; Air Products and Chemicals, $106 million; Sandoz Pharmaceuticals, $50 million. A BT trader reflected—on tape—"Funny business, you know? Lure people into that calm and then just totally fuck 'em."[9]

Nor was the Bankers Trust episode an isolated one. Merrill Lynch coaxed the treasurer of Orange County, California, into a derivatives deal that caused a $1.5 billion loss, bankrupting the county in 1994. (Merrill and several other banks later were forced to cover more than half the loss.) The centuries-old Barings Bank was destroyed by a rogue trader in Singapore; Daiwa Bank lost $1 billion on treasury derivatives; a copper trader cost Sumitomo Bank $2 billion.

Then in September 1998, in the midst of the Asian financial crisis, the hedge fund Long-Term Capital Management collapsed, largely as a result of its derivatives positions. Just days earlier Alan Greenspan had told Congress that derivatives regulation was unnecessary because "market pricing and counterparty surveillance can be expected to do most of the job of sustaining safety and soundness."[10]

LTCM had been founded in 1993 by John Meriwether, a famed trader, along with a glittering array of partners including Myron Scholes and Robert Merton, who received the Nobel Prizes in Economics for developing the models underlying derivatives pricing. But LTCM had used derivatives to make highly leveraged bets on bonds. When these bets went badly wrong because of the Asian crisis and Russia's 2008 sovereign bond default, LTCM found itself with $100 billion in potential losses. The Federal Reserve feared a systemic crisis and organized an emergency rescue involving a dozen large banks. Forced to defend the rescue, Greenspan testified to Congress:

> Had the failure of LTCM triggered seizing up of markets, substantial damage could have been inflicted on many market participants, including some not directly involved with the firm, and could have potentially impaired the economies of many nations, including our own.[11]

But that didn't stop Greenspan from continuing to press for a complete ban on derivatives regulation. And thus, with continued advocacy from Greenspan, the Clinton Treasury Department, and congressional leaders, Brooksley Born was overruled and the Commodity Futures Modernization Act was passed and signed in late 2000.

Nothing changed Greenspan's mind. In 2003, at a Chicago investment conference, he said:

> Critics of derivatives often raise the specter of the failure of one dealer imposing debilitating losses on its counterparties, including other dealers, yielding a chain of defaults. However, derivative markets participants seem keenly aware of the counterparty credit risks associated with derivatives and take various measures to mitigate those risks.[12]

After the global financial crisis, the collapse of AIG, and at least $10 trillion in losses, Greenspan finally, barely, admitted that there had been "a flaw" in his model.[13]

The Clinton administration also exhibited increasing nakedness in revolving-door hiring. Robert Rubin came to the Clinton administration from Goldman Sachs, and upon resigning as treasury secretary in 1999, became vice chairman of Citigroup, whose mergers had been legalized by legislation that he had supported. Laura Tyson, chair of the National Economic Council, joined the board of Morgan Stanley shortly after leaving the administration. Tom Donilon, the State Department chief of staff, became the chief lobbyist of Fannie Mae shortly after his departure. Franklin Raines, head of the Office of Management and Budget, became CEO of Fannie Mae, where he became deeply embroiled in its accounting frauds. Michael Froman and David Lipton, two senior economic policy analysts, went to Citigroup. After serving as Clinton's final treasury secretary, Larry Summers became president of Harvard, while consulting for a major hedge fund, Taconic Capital. After two no-confidence votes from his faculty, Summers was forced to resign as president of Harvard, at which point he joined another, larger hedge fund, D. E. Shaw, and began giving speeches to financial institutions that made him millions of dollars per year.

Structural Consolidation

IN PART ENABLED by deregulation, in part driven by technological change and the increasing capital intensity of highly computerized operations, and in part to seek greater profits derived from market power, the financial sector consolidated sharply in the 1990s. This consolidation was both horizontal and vertical, and was so extreme that the financial sector of 2000 was completely unlike that of thirty years before. The only industry segments that remained somewhat fragmented were also largely unregulated—hedge funds that managed money for the wealthy, venture capital, and, fatefully, the new mortgage lenders in the shadow banking system.

Between 1960 and 2000, the combined capitalization of the ten largest investment banks in the United States (of which the largest five dominated the industry) had grown from $1 billion to $179 billion. Employment by the largest five had quadrupled since 1980 to 205,000 in 2000. This structural consolidation was not confined to investment banking; it affected every segment of the financial sector and reached across segments via the creation of enormous financial conglomerates. And the main source of this broader consolidation was not the organic growth of the successful; rather, it was mergers.

In 1997 Morgan Stanley merged with Dean Witter, one of the largest remaining retail brokerage firms. In 1998 Nationsbank acquired Bank of America, at that time the largest bank merger in history. In the same year, however, Citigroup acquired Travelers, which was itself the result of many mergers and acquisitions, including Travelers Insurance, Primerica, and the investment banks Salomon Brothers, Shearson Lehman, and Smith Barney. This created the largest financial services firm in the world. As mentioned earlier, the merger violated the Glass-Steagall Act, and when Glass-Steagall was repealed the following year, the new law was sometimes derisively called the Citigroup Relief Act. Then in 2000, JPMorgan merged with Chase Manhattan to form JPMorgan Chase, which as of 2011 is the world's largest financial services firm. Dozens of smaller investment banks, commercial banks, brokerages, insurance companies, and other specialized firms also merged with or were acquired by the large financial conglomerates and leading investment banks. Even the mutual fund industry consolidated; in 2000, for example, Alliance Capital acquired Sanford Bernstein, resulting in a combined entity that managed $470 billion.

By the time George W. Bush took office, every major industry segment and financial market was dominated by an oligopoly of large firms. By 2000 investment banking was dominated by five firms: Merrill Lynch, Goldman Sachs, Morgan Stanley, Lehman Brothers, and Bear Stearns. Most other investment banking activity was housed in the investment banking subsidiaries of enormous financial conglomerates—the three Americans (Citigroup, JPMorgan Chase, and Bank of America), plus a few Europeans such as Deutsche Bank, UBS, and Credit Suisse. Securities insurance was dominated by two monoline firms, MBIA and Ambac, plus AIG, the world's largest insurance company. Securities rating was dominated by three firms (Moody's, Standard & Poor's, and Fitch); Moody's alone held about 40 percent of the total market. By 2000 five accounting firms dominated the market for corporate auditing. (After the collapse of Enron led to the prosecution and dissolution of Arthur Andersen, five became four.) Five banks, led by JPMorgan Chase and Goldman Sachs, controlled 90 percent of all global derivatives trading. The consumer credit card market was overwhelmingly dominated by Visa, MasterCard, and American Express. NationsBank/Bank of America, Citigroup, and JPMorgan Chase dominated interstate banking. Asset management was increasingly dominated by large firms as well—Fidelity, Vanguard, Alliance Capital, BlackRock, Pimco, Putnam, and a handful of others. (These are enormous firms; in 2011, BlackRock managed $3.6 trillion; Fidelity managed $1.5 trillion.)

Not only was the financial sector highly concentrated, but it was increasingly collusive. The major firms did compete with one another, but they also cooperated extensively—in business, for example, through securities syndication, but also in lobbying and political action through industry associations, and through shared use of lobbying firms, law firms, and academic experts.

Incentives

THE LAST MAJOR development in financial services during the 1990s was its progressive internal corruption. By the time the Bush administration took office, incentives had turned pervasively toxic.

Although the details varied by industry segment and individual profession, the direction was remarkably consistent. Prior to 1971 only private partnerships were allowed to join the New York Stock Exchange, ensuring that investment banks and bankers had the long time horizons and caution associated with partnership money that could only be withdrawn upon retirement. But in 1971 the New York Stock Exchange changed the rule, investment banks started going public, and bankers' incentives started to shift toward annual bonuses and stock options. In principle, it would have been possible to replicate the earlier incentives; for example, by having very long vesting and holding periods for stock. But this was never done, and by 2000 the majority of investment banking compensation was in annual bonuses, mostly cash. Even the stock options rarely required more than five years' vesting. Equally important, the former requirement that senior bankers place the majority of their own money at risk was abandoned.

Several major developments corrupted the structural incentives of firms relative to their customers. One major factor was the securitization food chain. Mortgage lenders no longer needed to care about whether mortgages would be repaid, because they sold them almost instantly to investment banks, which in turn sold them to various structured investment vehicles or to suckers (i.e., customers). In order to generate loans with higher sales prices, the lenders started paying mortgage brokers "yield spread premiums," which were effectively bribes for pushing borrowers into the most expensive loans possible.

The investment banks didn't care about selling trash to their customers for several reasons. First, the former model of relationship banking was largely gone. Second, fee structures carried no penalties for selling junk; the banks and bankers didn't share in any subsequent customer losses. Third, bankers' compensation was overwhelmingly dominated by annual bonuses, which were driven by that year's transaction revenues, so traders and salesmen didn't care what happened later.

The ratings process was corrupted by the shift from buyer to issuer payment, by personnel turnover, and by the rise of ratings "consulting." As late as the 1970s, rating agencies were paid by the *buyers* of the securities they rated, not by the investment banks that created and sold the securities. But that started to change, and by 2000 all three of the major rating agencies were paid to rate new securities almost entirely by the large investment banks that issued them. Since there were only a handful of these issuers, the rating agencies were very cooperative. But conflicts of interest went even further. The rating agencies also rated the debt *of the banks themselves,* a crucial indicator of the banks' stability. But since downgrading a bank would, again, infuriate a major customer, it was never done. Indeed, the rating agencies started consulting to the banks, receiving huge fees for advising how to construct a security such that it would receive a high rating. At the individual level, things were even ickier. Rating agencies paid substantially less than investment banks, so employees of rating agencies tried hard to please the bankers they dealt with, in hopes of getting a job at the bank. Many did.

The securities insurance companies, especially AIG Financial Products, compensated their employees just like investment bankers—annual cash bonuses based on the year's transactions. So, again, they had every incentive to sell insurance, either literal insurance or credit default swaps, in order to get their bonuses. Losses five years later would be the company's problem.

Incentives among the ultimate buyers of securities were dangerous as well. In the case of hedge funds, compensation at the firm level was so-called 2 and 20: clients were charged fees of 2 percent per year of assets managed, and the fund kept 20 percent of all gains, computed annually. However, the fund did *not* participate in losses, so fund managers were incented to take risks. The same was true, to a lesser extent, of other larger institutional investors such as pension funds and mutual funds. They too were compensated annually based on performance, and they too were rewarded for gains but not punished for losses. This incented them to "reach for yield," and made them far less attentive to long-term risks. For example, they started to trust ratings uncritically, rather than examine risks independently.

And finally, there were the external incentives supplied by the regulatory and policy environment. It was the Clinton administration that first signaled, decisively, that it was suspending enforcement of the law when it came to the financial sector and even to individuals with substantial financial assets. In addition to supporting legislation—such as the repeal of Glass-Steagall—that permitted previously illegal activities, the administration stopped enforcing the laws that existed. When Alan Greenspan refused to issue mortgage regulations under HOEPA, nobody complained. When the Internet bubble spawned huge amounts of extremely obvious fraud, nobody investigated and nobody was prosecuted. America was now an open city.

And then George W. Bush became president. He was not elected, and to a significant extent the American people therefore cannot be blamed for what happened afterward. Bush lost by over 500,000 votes, and almost certainly lost the state of Florida, so he should have lost the electoral college as well. But through a well-orchestrated public relations and legal campaign, a Florida recount was avoided and the Supreme Court handed George W. Bush the White House by a 5 to 4 decision.

With the changes of the 1990s, the conditions for a financial disaster were fully in place. Bush's ascent to the presidency was just the final nail in the coffin.

CHAPTER 3

THE BUBBLE, PART ONE: BORROWING AND LENDING IN THE 2000s

THE DOT-COM STOCK MARKET bubble peaked in the winter of 2000. Its inevitable collapse was worsened by the terrorist attacks of September 11, 2001; and yet the resulting recession was short and mild. There were two reasons for this.

First, the Bush administration embarked on a campaign of massive deficit spending. The administration employed tax cuts, particularly for the wealthy, and sharply higher spending, particularly for the military—for the war in Afghanistan, the invasion and occupation of Iraq, and counterterrorism and intelligence efforts. And second, Federal Reserve chairman Alan Greenspan aggressively reduced interest rates. Greenspan cut rates from 6.5 percent at the peak of the Internet bubble all the way down to 1 percent by July 2003, the lowest in fifty years.[1]

The recovery, however, was an anemic one, even if you took it at face value. And the real problem was that you *couldn't* take it at face value. What followed, in fact, was a remarkable alliance of financial sector greed and political calculation. The recovery of the 2000s was fake, driven almost entirely by unsustainable behavior: massive tax cuts and federal deficits, the housing bubble, and consumer spending enabled only by borrowing. While the real economy did continue to benefit from Internet-driven productivity gains, the United States was simultaneously falling behind many other nations in the underlying educational, infrastructural, and systemic determinants of national competitiveness. America's manufacturing sector was quietly decimated. Moreover, most of the benefits of America's productivity gains were now appropriated by the top 1 percent of the population, not by the broader workforce—a major change from prior generations. As a result, during the 2000s, even during the bubble, real wage levels for average Americans stagnated or fell, and on a net basis very few jobs were created. Gains from the fake economy and the (real) Internet revolution were offset by massive job losses both in manufacturing (including information technology products) and in services functions susceptible to outsourcing or automation.

A Marriage of Convenience Produces a Bubble

GIVEN THESE STRUCTURAL problems, a fake recovery driven by a financial bubble was very politically convenient. Most of the growth in consumer spending during the 2000s was driven by the bubble. As house prices rose, homeowners could borrow more against the supposedly higher value of their homes; and by spending the proceeds of their borrowing, they both pumped up the general economy and also perpetuated the housing bubble itself, as borrowed cash was used to finance further home purchases (for second homes, rental properties, etc.).

In fact, much of the 2000s-era subprime lending wasn't about increasing home ownership at all. Fewer than 10 percent of subprime loans financed a first home purchase.[2] Many subprime loans issued during the bubble were devices to take money *out of* a home, to refinance a prior mortgage, or to buy a second home. Some of the loans were for personal consumption (televisions, vacations, cars, home improvements); some were for trading up to a more expensive home; many were speculation driven by the bubble, for the purpose of flipping houses repeatedly; and many more were frauds perpetrated against borrowers, who were tricked into deceptive, overly expensive loans.

But all of them contributed to the bubble. As a result the Case-Shiller U.S. National Home Price Index *doubled* between 2000 and 2006, the largest and fastest increase in history.[3]

Greenspan's rate cuts undoubtedly helped *start* the bubble. Most people borrow heavily to buy a house, and the amount of house they can afford is driven by monthly mortgage payments, which in turn are heavily affected by interest rates. As a result of Greenspan's rate cuts, prime mortgage rates fell by 3 percentage points from 2000 to 2003. Assuming standard fixed-rate mortgage terms, the same monthly debt service that supported a $180,000 home in 2000 would support a $245,000 home in 2003, a 36 percent increase.[4] Not surprisingly, between 2000 and 2003, the Case-Shiller U.S. National Home Price Index went up more than a third.[5] So, yes, interest rates were relevant. But they don't even come close to explaining that doubling of housing prices during the bubble, which continued even after Ben Bernanke started raising rates again.

Over the next four and a half years, from 2003 through mid-2007, America's financial sector churned out some $3 trillion in often fraudulent mortgage-backed securities (MBSs) and even more exotic, risky, and/or fraudulent derivatives tied to those securities. The home loans underlying these securities were mostly sourced through a new breed of largely unregulated mortgage banks, as well as by several leading commercial banks. Investment banks, some of which were subsidiaries of the larger banking conglomerates (e.g., JPMorgan Chase, Citigroup, Deutsche Bank), bought these mortgages and packaged them into *structured investment products*—mortgage-backed securities and collateralized debt obligations (CDOs). These were rated by the ever-cooperative rating agencies, insured through either the monoline bond insurance companies or AIG's credit default swaps, and then sold to pension funds, insurance companies, mutual funds, hedge funds, foreign banks, and many others—even, often, to the asset management arms of the same banking conglomerates that had created them.

More than half of the increase in lending volume during the bubble was accounted for by subprime, Alt-A, Option-ARM, and other high-risk or predatory loans (see Glossary).

An astonishingly large share of these loans and the resultant securities were defective. The borrowers were people under financial pressure, people who were speculating, people committing fraud, and/or people who were being defrauded (a major category, discussed below). And whatever the reason for the defects in the loans, they were pushed all the way through the securitization chain with no regard for quality control—indeed, with *negative* quality control, due to intense pressure to find high-yield loans regardless of risk, and to cover up the risks that existed. Some of it was mere sloppiness, but much of it was conscious and deliberate. There was massive fraud. The deception was so enormous and so obvious that senior management frequently must have known, and indeed there is growing evidence that in many cases they approved or even directed it. And if some of them didn't know, then the enormity of their negligence would be nearly as criminal as pure fraud. It wasn't subtle, and we shall see it was discussed widely and explicitly within the companies involved. Moreover, there is clear evidence that many CEOs and senior executives lied to their investors, auditors, regulators, and the public, both during the bubble and afterward, as their firms started to collapse.

What was going on, of course, was that Wall Street and the lenders were using fraud to create, fuel, and exploit a Ponzi scheme. During the bubble, lending standards basically disappeared. Of course, there are always *some* people in America who want loans to buy a house, or to take out home equity cash, when they can't afford the loan or have no intent to repay. Suddenly, those people had no problem getting loans. Neither did anyone else. There were people who had good incomes and steady jobs, but were stretching to buy houses beyond their means; people who wanted to cash out almost all their equity; speculators buying multiple houses with no intent to occupy or rent them, hoping to flip them at a profit; people who wanted a second home or vacation house they couldn't really afford—all with a high risk of default, especially if prices ever fell. But during the 2000s, none of that mattered. Tax policy helped too; the Clinton administration had enacted a law specifying that the first $500,000 in gains from selling a house was normally tax free if it was rolled into a new house purchase. This encouraged flipping.

But there were also many blameless people, millions of them, who just got screwed. They decided to buy a house toward the end of the bubble, when prices were severely inflated, possibly even using a traditional, conservative mortgage and a large down payment. But a few years later they lost their job, or retired, or got divorced, or had sudden medical expenses, or needed to move for a new job. And when they tried to sell their house, they suddenly discovered that they *couldn't* sell it, because its value had declined by a third, and that they had just lost their life savings.

And finally, there was also massive fraud committed *against* borrowers, in part through the proliferation of highly deceptive loan structures and sales practices. It is no exaggeration to say that the mortgage brokerage, real estate brokerage, and subprime lending sectors became pervasively criminalized during the bubble. Mortgage brokers were usually unregulated, and during the bubble thousands of small-scale shysters put on a suit and sold loans.

The bubble period saw the rise of exotic loan structures designed to make payments artificially low for some initial period, and/or to disguise the real terms of the loan, while actually charging the high interest rates that the banks liked. Mortgage brokers pushed loans with teaser rates heavily, often telling borrowers that when the higher real rate kicked in, the value of their home would have increased so much that they could handle the new payments by refinancing—in other words, by taking out yet another loan.

Mortgage brokers also steered clients into needlessly expensive loans on a massive scale. Several studies have concluded that at least one-third of all people receiving subprime loans during the bubble *actually would have qualified for a prime loan.* But they were placed into subprime loans with higher interest rates and unnecessary fees by mortgage brokers, who were paid explicit cash bonuses by lenders—yield spread premiums—for placing borrowers into more expensive loans. This, of course, also made the loans harder to repay, particularly after teaser rates expired or interest rates adjusted upward, and increased hardship and defaults when the bubble collapsed.

There was also a lot of flat-out fraud, often very cruel, committed against immigrants who didn't speak English and/or had no financial experience. They were simply lied to—about the size of the loan, the size of the payments, the real interest rate—and told to sign documents they couldn't understand or even read. Many mortgage brokers worked with unofficial lenders, sometimes even loan sharks, who provided additional concealed loans to cover down payments or "points." Mortgage brokers paid real estate brokers bribes for referrals to illiterate and/or illegal immigrants. Often the victims trusted their mortgage broker in part because they shared a common language or ethnic background, or had been introduced by a mutual acquaintance.

Illegal immigrants were particularly easy to defraud because they were afraid to go to the police. The presence of large numbers of non-English-speaking illegal immigrants was unquestionably one reason that so much of the bubble was concentrated in California, Arizona, and Florida, as well as parts of New York City populated by recent immigrants. The Bush administration also deliberately made it difficult for subprime borrowers to use civil remedies. In 2001, in one of the Bush administration's first economic policy decisions, HUD interceded in a federal legal case in order to make it extremely difficult for subprime borrowers, including U.S. citizens, to join class-action lawsuits against predatory lenders. This forced borrowers to sue individually, which for many was prohibitively expensive and difficult.

The wave of fraud did not go unnoticed. In 2004 the FBI issued a press release warning of "an epidemic of mortgage fraud," and held press conferences to publicize the problem. In its 2005 *Financial*

Crimes Report to the Public, the FBI noted that "a significant fraction of the mortgage industry is void of any mandatory fraud reporting," and that the Mortgage Bankers Association provided no estimates on fraud levels. The same FBI report also stated that "based on various industry reports and FBI analysis, mortgage fraud is pervasive and growing." Even more interestingly, the FBI report noted that mortgage fraud was *not* usually committed by borrowers alone, stating that "80 percent of all reported fraud cases involve collaboration or collusion by industry insiders"—real estate brokers, mortgage brokers, lenders, or some combination thereof.

But law enforcement was AWOL and/or overwhelmed, at both the local and federal levels. The entire FBI has fewer than fourteen thousand special agents for all categories of crime; only a tiny fraction were assigned to mortgage fraud during the bubble, when the FBI was intensely focused on counterterrorism efforts. In addition, the Bush administration deliberately gutted the investigative and enforcement capacity of financial regulators such as the SEC. With good reason, mortgage lenders and Wall Street felt largely immune from criminal sanctions. There was not a single high-level prosecution during the bubble, and very few arrests even for the most flagrant, low-level frauds.

But why did mortgage banks and Wall Street tolerate massive fraud, push so hard for subprime lending even for trustworthy borrowers, and favor exotic, toxic mortgage structures? Because that's where the money was. Subprime loans paid *much* higher interest rates. They therefore sold for much higher prices to investment banks, because they could be used to construct mortgage-backed securities with much higher yields, which in turn were much easier to sell to investors—at least, until the loans defaulted. An extensive analysis of 250 million mortgage records carried out by the *Wall Street Journal* in 2007 showed that in the previous year "high-rate" mortgages, on average, had spreads of 5.6 percent over comparable Treasury bonds, at a time when spreads on a safe, honest, conventional loan with a real down payment were only about 1 percent.[6]

So how crooked did the lenders become in pursuing this strategy? Very crooked indeed.

The Rise of Subprime Mortgage Lenders
and the Shadow Banking Sector

THE COLLAPSE OF the S&L industry in the late 1980s and early 1990s, combined with the start of the housing bubble, led to the spectacular growth of highly unethical mortgage lenders, many of them in the largely unregulated shadow banking sector. These lenders, who drove the worst excesses of the bubble, were *not* traditional banks that took consumer deposits for savings and checking accounts. They existed solely to feed the securitization food chain, and they got their funding from Wall Street—from the same investment banks and financial conglomerates that bought their loans. Like the investment banks themselves, they relied on very short-term credit, which reduced the interest rates they needed to pay, but which also left them highly vulnerable to interest rate increases and other financial shocks. So when the bubble collapsed, they all collapsed too.

Many of these firms were in California—"mortgage banks" like New Century, Ameriquest, Golden West Financial, Long Beach Mortgage, and Countrywide. All of them made loans primarily to sell them into the securitization chain, and during the bubble their business exploded. For example, from 2000 to 2003, New Century increased its originations fivefold, from $4 billion to $21 billion, while Ameriquest's jumped tenfold, from $4 billion to $39 billion.[7] Both were highly fraudulent, and were the object of many lawsuits. However, both are now bankrupt, so substantial recoveries are impossible, even though their former executives and sales personnel remain wealthy—a story we shall encounter frequently.

As the bubble got under way, several large traditional banks, financial conglomerates, and *all* of the major investment banks acquired predatory or subprime mortgage lenders of their own. Citigroup snapped up Associates First in 2000, acquiring what was then the second-largest subprime lender, one that a consumer advocate called "an icon of predatory lending." Lehman bought six subprime lenders by 2004, Washington Mutual bought eight, and Bear Stearns three. First Franklin, one of the larger subprime lenders, was taken over by Merrill Lynch in 2006. Those that remained independent formed tight relationships with the investment banks that purchased their loans and also supplied them with general financing, managed their stock and bond offerings, and invested the personal wealth of their executives. For example, a group of banks led by Morgan Stanley made large financing commitments to cement ties with New Century.

As we now know, the whole industry was extremely unethical. Here is a short survey.

WaMu/Long Beach

Washington Mutual, or WaMu, was a longtime federally chartered savings and loan. Its CEO, Kerry Killinger, joined WaMu in 1982, and served as CEO from 1990 until the organization collapsed, was taken over, and then sold to JPMorgan Chase in 2008. Long Beach Mortgage Corporation was a California mortgage bank that was acquired by WaMu in 1999. Long Beach was just one of twenty originators acquired by WaMu in the 1990s, but was the only one allowed to continue to operate under its own name more or less independently. It had a terrible reputation, which it deserved. Losses on securities backed by Long Beach loans were among the country's highest. The delinquency rate on Long Beach MBSs in 2005 was the worst in the country.[8]

WaMu's reputation was not much better. It had grown by helter-skelter acquisition of smaller originators, without ever managing to create a well-integrated management system. But the booming housing market more than made up for executive incompetence. Killinger's total compensation for the period 2003 through 2008 was more than $100 million.

WaMu made a decisive turn toward riskier lending in 2005 after Killinger called for a "shift in our mix of business, increasing our Credit Risk tolerance." In a later board presentation, he said the objective was to "de-emphasize fixed rate and cease govt [Fannie/Freddie conforming loans]." While 49 percent of new originations in 2005 were already in the higher-risk categories, the objective was to achieve 82 percent higher-risk originations by 2008.[9]

Killinger's board presentations carefully specified the "strong governance process" that would be required for the higher-risk strategy. But the control processes never were really implemented. Capital-based high-risk lending ceilings were violated almost from the start.

A more accurate picture of WaMu's management style might be inferred from the "I Like Big Bucks" skit performed by the Kauai Kick It Krew at the President's Club 2006 celebration of top loan "producers" (sales personnel) in Hawaii.[10] The company had spared no expense for the event; the awards presentation was hosted by Magic Johnson, the Hall of Fame basketball star. At the event, the Krew, all top producers, backed up by a local cheerleading group, performed a rap number:

> I like big bucks and I cannot lie
> You mortgage brothers can't deny
> That when the dough rolls in like you're printing your own cash
> And you gotta make a splash
> You just spends
> Like it never ends
> Cuz you gotta have that big new Benz.

WaMu's compensation system reflected the rhetoric on Kauai. Loan officers were paid on a volume-based point system geared to loan product priorities. Of the sixteen products in the schedule, only the very last one was a traditional mortgage. The top priority was an Option-ARM product, one of the most dangerous of recent inventions. Borrowers could defer principal or interest payments during the first five years of a loan, accumulating unpaid balances that would later be added to principal. The higher principal payments would kick in at the same time as the permanent interest rate, which was much higher than the initial teaser. WaMu bragged that they were in second place in Option-ARMs, and gaining fast on the market leader, Countrywide.

WaMu's Long Beach subsidiary was the worst. WaMu's chief operating officer, Steve Rotella, reported to Killinger in the spring of 2006, when the bubble started to slow down: "Here are the facts: the portfolio (total serviced) is up 46 percent... but delinquencies are up 140 percent and foreclosures close to 70 percent.... First payment defaults are way up and the 2005 vintage is way up relative to previous years. It is ugly."[11] But the problems went far beyond Long Beach. WaMu sold almost all forms of high-risk loans—80/20 piggyback loans in which a first and a second mortgage covered the purchase price, the down payment, and the settlement costs; subprime loans; Option-ARMs; and subprime home equity loans. All of those were combined with "stated income" loans—loans with no income verification. Half of WaMu's subprime loans, three-quarters of its Option-ARMs, and almost all of its home equity loans were stated income. High-risk loans with stated income were used for properties that were obviously being bought for speculation. Nobody seemed to blink when babysitters claimed executive salaries. To top it off, like most high-risk lenders, WaMu required that income be adequate only against the initial teaser rate, not the far higher permanent rate.

Two high-production centers in poor sections of Los Angeles were found to have high levels of fraud—of eighty-five loans reviewed at one center, 58 percent had confirmed fraud; in forty-eight reviewed at another, *all* were fraudulent. The two managers were deeply involved in the frauds. Both of them, of course, were longtime President's Club honorees. The frauds included straw purchasers, forged documents, and the like. An investigation conducted in 2005 was brought to the attention of senior management but never followed up, and the managers continued their President's Club run. A high level of fraudulent activities was disclosed in a third center—mostly production officers forging borrower data—but another investigation went nowhere. WaMu, of course, never notified investors who had purchased loans from these centers that the documentation was fraudulent.[12]

Former WaMu employees, who are serving as confidential witnesses in various civil suits, have testified that every originator was required to underwrite nine loans a day, with cash bonuses beyond that; that lending standards were changed almost daily; and that loans that combined FICOs* (credit scores) in the 500s (very low), Option-ARM structures, and high loan-to-value ratios (LTVs) were sometimes treated as prime. A senior underwriter testified that loans she had turned down frequently reappeared as approved by higher management. Dozens of former employees have testified in the same vein. The New York State attorney general has also sued WaMu for using financial pressure to cause appraisers to inflate property values.[13]

Even in 2007 and 2008, Killinger wanted to ramp up high-risk lending. In late 2007 he announced that WaMu was "adding some $20 billion in loans this quarter, increasing its loan portfolio by about 10 percent." This at a time when losses on Option-ARMs in its portfolio had jumped from $15 million in 2005 to $777 million in the first half of 2008.[14] Then the firm collapsed and was sold to JPMorgan Chase. Afterward, when asked at a Senate hearing why he had adopted a high-risk lending strategy, Killinger blandly answered that he had done no such thing.[15]

In March 2011 the FDIC sued Killinger and two other senior WaMu executives for $900 million, alleging that they had taken excessive risk for purposes of short-term personal enrichment. In December 2011 the executives agreed to settlements totaling $64 million. However, all but $400,000 was covered by their insurance; their personal assets remained nearly untouched, and they were not required to admit any guilt. Earlier in 2011, the Justice Department had already announced that it was closing its criminal investigation of WaMu, stating "the evidence does not meet the exacting standards for criminal charges."[16]

New Century

New Century Financial Corporation was founded in 1995 as an independent mortgage lender concentrating on the subprime segment of

---

*FICO is the stock ticker symbol for the Fair Isaac Corporation, the company that pioneered the three-digit credit score.

the market. It was listed on the Nasdaq exchange in 1997. Its annual originations had grown to $3.1 billion by 2000, and shot up to $20.8 billion in 2003, making it the second-largest subprime originator. By 2006, its originations had grown to $51.6 billion. Three-quarters of its loans were purchased by Morgan Stanley and Credit Suisse, who also provided much of its financing.[17]

In early 2007 it announced both that it would restate its earnings from the first three quarters of 2006, previously announced as $276 million, and that for the full year, 2006 would show a loss. Securitizing banks withdrew their finance lines in March, effectively shutting down the business, and the company filed for bankruptcy in April. The salaries and bonuses of its three senior officers in 2005 were approximately $1.9 million each, and that same year each of the three cashed out between $13 million and $14 million in vested stock options.[18]

Interestingly, in 2008, a hedge fund manager named David Einhorn became famous for betting against Lehman Brothers, while questioning its finances and conducting a public campaign against it. Einhorn accused Lehman of deceptive accounting and of maintaining falsely high valuations on its real estate holdings. Mr. Einhorn certainly knew his subject; but he had been considerably less vocal about mortgage-related accounting irregularities when he had been a member of New Century's board of directors throughout the bubble. An examiner later appointed by New Century's bankruptcy trustee conducted an extensive investigation of the company and its auditor, KPMG. A 581-page report filed in February 2008 found substantial causes of action against company officers for "improper and imprudent" business practices and against KPMG for "professional negligence" and "breach of its professional standard of care."[19]

The report itself provides many examples of on-the-ground practice during the bubble. New Century's loan-acquisition volume nearly doubled every year from 2000 through 2004, by which time internal warning sirens were screaming. Here are samples of e-mails to senior management:

[Oct. 2004] Stated wage earner loans present a very high risk of early payment defaults and are generally a lower credit quality borrower than our self employed stated borrowers.[20]

[Oct. 2004] Stated Income. This has been increasing dramatically to the point where Stated Income loans are the majority of production, and are teetering on being >50 percent of production. We know that Stated Income loans do not perform as well as Full Doc loans.

[Fall 2004] I just can't get comfortable with W2'd borrowers who are unable or unwilling to prove their income.

[Jan. 2005] To restate the obvious, a borrower's true income is not known on Stated Income loans so we are unable to actually determine the borrower's ability to afford a loan.

An internal memo said:

The most common subprime product is a loan that is fixed for 2 or 3 years and then become[s] adjustable. The initial rate is far below the fully-indexed rate, but the loan is underwritten to the start payment. At month 25 the borrower faces a major payment shock even if the underlying index has not changed. This forces the borrower to refinance, likely with another subprime lender or broker. The borrower pays another 4 or 5 points (out of their equity), and rolls into another 2/28 loan, thereby buying 2 more years of life, but essentially perpetuating a cycle of repeated refinance and loss of equity to greedy lenders.

Inevitably, the borrower lacks enough equity to continue this cycle (absent rapidly rising property values) and ends up having to sell the house or face foreclosure.[21]

Despite the sharp deterioration in loan quality, compensation plans stayed firmly focused on volume. In the end, it was sheer sloppiness that pushed New Century into bankruptcy, well before the full extent of its loan defaults and fraudulent behavior became clear. When an auditor discovered that accounting for loan repurchases required restating, it wiped out profits for 2006. The committee of Wall Street banks that financed New Century (chaired by Morgan Stanley) stopped providing money, and the company was effectively out of business.[22]

Countrywide Financial Corporation

Countrywide, at first glance, was not the typical subprime lender. Founded in 1969 by David Loeb and Angelo Mozilo, it grew to become the nation's largest and most profitable mortgage lender. Mozilo was famous for being obsessively hands-on as well as a terrifying boss. For many years the company had a reputation for conservative lending and excellent cost controls. In 2003 *Fortune* extolled it as one of the most successful American companies, with 23,000 percent stock appreciation since 1982.[23]

Mozilo was ambivalent toward the subprime strategy, and sometimes internally warned of its dangers. But in the end some combination of ego, greed, laziness, and perhaps fatigue (he underwent spinal surgery several times during the bubble) won out over both ethics and caution. As Mozilo approached retirement age in the midst of the bubble, he announced an absurdly ambitious goal for Countrywide: a 30 percent share of the whole U.S. mortgage market. This required aggressive expansion into the whole spectrum of toxic loan products, which Mozilo pressured Fannie Mae to buy. The rest he sold to Wall Street, which didn't have to be pressured at all.

Countrywide also lobbied intensively and used techniques verging on bribery. Mozilo created a special "Friends of Angelo" VIP unit to provide vastly improved customer service and favorable mortgage terms to dozens of Fannie Mae executives, members of Congress, congressional staff members, and various prominent people (one recipient was *Tonight Show* host Ed McMahon, who defaulted on his $4.8 million loan).[24] Recipients included House Speaker Nancy Pelosi and Senator Chris Dodd, chairman of the Senate Banking Committee, as well as three successive CEOs of Fannie Mae.

By 2006 Countrywide and its practices had become pervasively fraudulent. In September 2005, Countrywide hired a woman named Eileen Foster as First Vice President, Customer Care, in Countrywide's Office of the President. In mid-2006 she was promoted to Senior Vice President. Then, on March 7, 2007, she was promoted again—to Senior Vice President for Fraud Risk Management. In this position she was *supposedly* in charge of Countrywide's fraud reduction policies and she also directly managed several dozen fraud investigators.

Naively, she began to investigate fraud, and to do something about it. She rapidly uncovered massive frauds, in multiple regional loan offices, perpetrated by loan officers and managers. As usual in the industry, loan officers were being compensated based on "production" volume regardless of quality, and indeed, as was also common, they were incentivized to produce loans with the highest possible interest rates and fees. They could only do this at high volume through fraud.

Nearly immediately, Foster and her organization identified a massive organized fraud operation run by Countrywide personnel in the Boston area, including a regional and division manager.[25] Foster and her unit developed evidence that forced Countrywide to close six of its eight branch offices in Boston and to terminate over forty employees. Foster and her unit were told about, and developed evidence regarding, a number of other organized frauds and senior loan personnel involved in fraud. In December 2007 Foster started to warn her management that there was systematic, widespread fraud within Countrywide. Her immediate manager agreed with her.

In December 2011 *60 Minutes* broadcast an excellent two-part report entitled "Prosecuting Wall Street," exploring the *lack* of criminal prosecution related to the bubble and crisis. Foster is interviewed on camera by *60 Minutes* correspondent Steve Kroft. Here are excerpts:

STEVE KROFT: Do you believe that there are people at Countrywide who belong behind bars?

EILEEN FOSTER: Yes.

KROFT: Do you want to give me their names?

FOSTER: No.

KROFT: Would you give their names to a grand jury if you were asked?

FOSTER: Yes.

KROFT: How much fraud was there at Countrywide?

FOSTER: From what I saw, the types of things I saw, it was—it appeared systemic. It, it wasn't just one individual or two or three individuals, it was branches of individuals, it was regions of individuals.

KROFT: What you seem to be saying was it was just a way of doing business?

FOSTER: Yes.

KROFT: Do you think that this was just the Boston office?

FOSTER: No. No, I know it wasn't just the Boston office. What was going on in Boston was also going on in Chicago, and Miami, and Detroit, and Las Vegas and, you know—Phoenix and in all of the big markets all over Florida. I came to find out that there were—that there was many, many, many reports of fraud as I had suspected. And those were never—they were never reported through my group, never reported to the board, never reported to the government while I was there.

KROFT: And you believe this was intentional?

FOSTER: Yes. Yes, absolutely.

Foster *also* began to see evidence that Countrywide's corporate Employee Relations department was protecting fraudulent activity. It did this in several ways, including not reporting it to Foster's organization; reporting fraud allegations to the perpetrator; identifying informants and whistle-blowers to the perpetrators; failing to act on complaints of retaliation against whistle-blowers; and by retaliating directly against them itself. (She told *60 Minutes* that a senior Countrywide executive had ordered the ER to circumvent her department.[26]) Foster complained to the senior executives in charge of Employee Relations, at which point Countrywide's ER department began to investigate *her*. In May 2008 Foster spoke to the executives in charge of Countrywide's Internal Affairs unit, describing both the pervasiveness of fraud and also ER's conduct. As we shall see shortly, this did not go well.

When the bubble peaked and everything at Countrywide started to go bad, Angelo Mozilo resorted to various forms of deception, both personal and corporate. First, he intensified efforts to get rid of dubious loans fast, so that Countrywide wouldn't be caught holding them when they failed. Throughout the e-mail trails, he crassly urges his subordinates to "comb the assets" and sell off the riskiest ones while there is still time. As he well knew, however, the documentation of every loan sale or securitization states that the instruments being sold are representative of all loans of that type in possession of the seller—that they have not been selectively chosen to off-load risk. So this remedial strategy was itself fraudulent.

Then Mozilo protected himself financially, as many executives did. As Countrywide started to fail, Mozilo used $2 billion of Countrywide's borrowed money to repurchase its own stock, in order to prop up the stock price. Mozilo also repeatedly made representations to analysts and investors with respect to the high quality of Countrywide's credit and control processes, the good performance of its products, and the company's financial soundness. One lawsuit lists some three dozen separate occasions in which Mozilo made or confirmed statements about the company's lending and credit oversight policies. Based on what we now know, all of them were false.

However, at the same time that Countrywide was buying back its stock and Mozilo was telling the world that everything was fine, Mozilo was actually selling *his own* Countrywide stock—over $100 million in the year before the firm collapsed. His total compensation during the bubble was more than $450 million, and as a result of his stock sales over the years he remains extremely wealthy, with a net worth estimated at $600 million.

When collapse could no longer be postponed, Countrywide sold itself to Bank of America; the deal was signed in January 2008 and finally completed in July. The acquisition was to prove a very costly mistake for Bank of America, causing many billions of dollars in further losses. By 2012 Countrywide's losses and legal liabilities were so severe as to threaten Bank of America's continued viability.

In July 2008, when Bank of America officially took over Countrywide, Eileen Foster was offered the position of Senior Vice President, Mortgage Fraud Investigations Division Executive, which she accepted. However, the Employee Relations organization continued to investigate Foster and question her colleagues, one of whom warned Bank of America executives, including its general counsel and its chief operating officer. On September 8, 2008, Eileen Foster was told by senior Bank of America executives that she had been terminated. She filed a whistle-blower lawsuit, which she won; OSHA ordered her reinstatement and awarded her damages of over $900,000. In her interview with *60 Minutes,* Foster stated that the immediate cause of her firing was that she refused to be coached appropriately about what to say to federal regulators. She also stated on camera that as of the time of the interview in 2011, she had never been interviewed by any federal law enforcement official.

Other Subprime Lenders

While WaMu, New Century, and Countrywide were among the largest subprime lenders, there were many others just as bad. Fremont, for example, was one the country's largest, and sold its loans to the top banks in securitization—Goldman Sachs, Merrill Lynch, Bear Stearns, Deutsche Bank, Credit Suisse, Lehman Brothers, Morgan Stanley. That is, it did so until March 2007, when the FDIC forced it out of business, and into bankruptcy, for multiple violations of law and regulations. In 2008 the Massachusetts Supreme Court, on an action brought by the state attorney general, affirmed a prohibition on foreclosures of many Fremont mortgages, on the ground that they had been designed to be predatory.[27]

In lawsuits, a long list of confidential witnesses drawn from former employees recited the usual frauds. Allegedly, underwriters were instructed "to think outside the box," and "make it work."[28] If borrowers' actual incomes were not sufficient to support a mortgage, loans were converted to stated income loans at whatever level was necessary. A series of forty loans was allegedly accepted from one broker even though all of them had identical bank statements.

WMC was yet another. It was the sixth-largest subprime originator in the country in 2004, when it was sold to GE Capital (yes, General Electric) by its owner, the private equity investment firm Apollo Management, whose CEO, Leon Black, spent $1 million to have Elton John play at his birthday party. For several years GE made lots of money, but it shut the company down in September 2007, swallowing a $400 million charge.

WMC's lineup of Wall Street securitizers was much like Fremont's— the largest and most prestigious firms on Wall Street. Yet WMC was fourth on the Comptroller of the Currency's 2010 "Worst Ten in the Worst Ten" list—the ten worst lenders in the ten most decimated housing markets in the country. A postmortem conducted as part of a civil fraud suit by PMI, Inc., a mortgage insurer like MBIA, found the usual story—widespread breaches of securitization warranties, missing or obviously falsified documentation, and so forth.[29]

Ameriquest was yet another, and the U.S. leader in subprime lending in 2003, having driven its volume to $39 billion, up from just $4 billion in 2000. An assistant attorney general in Minnesota requested Ameriquest files in 2003, and was amazed to see file after file list the applicant's occupation as "antiques dealer." Borrowers told of signing a loan application and finding at closing that an entire financial record—tax forms and everything—had been fabricated for them. Ameriquest, too, was on the "Worst Ten in the Worst Ten" list. It speaks volumes for the cluelessness of Citigroup senior management that it purchased Ameriquest in the summer of 2007, even as the subprime bubble was collapsing.[30] Ameriquest was the object of major lawsuits filed by more than twenty state attorneys general during the bubble, while federal regulators and law enforcement agencies did nothing. In 2005 its CEO, a major Republican donor, was appointed ambassador to the Netherlands by President Bush.

Another subprime lender, Option One, was a subsidiary of H&R Block, the tax preparer. Tax preparers were incented, in effect, to say, "Your interest on that mortgage seems high, why don't you visit our mortgage consultant before you leave. We may be able to find you a better deal."[31]

So the lenders wanted everyone to borrow ever more, and actively *preferred* borrowers who didn't understand mortgages, shouldn't have them, could be defrauded, and/or couldn't fight back after being screwed. For a while, the bubble covered all this up, at least to naive investors outside the industry. Ironically, the huge increase in lending and the collapse of lending standards made subprime loans and mortgage securities seem much safer than they really were because it kept driving up home prices. Rising home prices allowed even unemployed, fraudulent, and/or delinquent borrowers to avoid (or simply *postpone*) default through refinancing, home equity loans, or selling at a profit. As the bubble progressed, teaser rates, deception, and/or unsustainable mortgages became normal. A standard broker sales pitch was "Don't worry about the high post-teaser payments." When it was time, the broker would refinance you—at another teaser rate—because the value of your home would already have gone up.

This kept money flowing through the system to naive investors such as municipal pension funds and small overseas banks, which collected high returns without any defaults for a few years until the music finally stopped. In the meantime these high returns led them, of course, to purchase even more of the same junk. The same mechanism also allowed fully knowledgeable but unethical investment managers—hedge funds, private wealth managers within investment banks—to do the same thing. The temporarily high returns kept their clients happy for several years, and kept their annual bonuses high. When the music stopped, the fund managers closed the fund or resigned, taking their money with them and leaving the losses to their clients.

Fannie Mae and Freddie Mac

Fannie Mae and Freddie Mac are not, of course, literally mortgage lenders. They purchased, insured, and securitized loans sourced from mortgage lenders; Countrywide was their largest single source of loans. They also bought and held enormous portfolios of mortgage-backed securities for investment purposes, which caused a major fraction of their losses during and after the crisis.

Fannie and Freddie are both government-sponsored enterprises (GSEs) created by the federal government to support home owner-ship and affordable mortgage lending. But over the three decades prior to the crisis, Fannie and Freddie had gradually freed themselves from regulatory constraint in the pursuit of profits. They went public and, more important, masterfully neutered both congressional over-sight and Office of Federal Housing Enterprise Oversight (OFHEO), their ineffective and understaffed regulator. They accomplished this through a combination of extraordinarily aggressive lobbying, pa-tronage, revolving-door hiring, and flat-out deceit. Their hires ranged from Newt Gingrich ($1.6 million from Freddie Mac's chief lobbyist for "strategic advice" and "outreach to conservatives") to Tom Donilon, who was Fannie Mae's chief lobbyist for years and is now President Obama's national security advisor. Both firms also neutered effective corporate governance by stacking their boards of directors with the compliant and the politically connected, who were overpaid and who were expected to keep quiet. And they instituted the same compen-sation structures found universally in the financial sector, which pro-vided large bonuses based upon short-term performance.

And, just to leave no stone unturned, they also engaged in massive accounting fraud to ensure that their publicly reported performance enabled them to *collect* those bonuses.

Concerns about Fannie and Freddie's accounting were first publicly raised in congressional hearings in 2000, before a subcommittee of the House Financial Services Committee. In those hearings, Fannie Mae and its then-CEO, Franklin Raines, were defended by congressional

Democrats, including Barney Frank. Other defenders included Representative Maxine Waters and other members of the Black Caucus, in part because Raines was a well-connected African American (Clinton's former budget director), and in part simply because Fannie Mae was so politically powerful in urban congressional districts where it operated, lobbied heavily, and was a major campaign contributor.

The first major allegations of accounting fraud came in 2003, when OFHEO sued the executives of Freddie Mac. Freddie Mac paid a $125 million fine. (Later, in 2006, Freddie Mac was also fined $3.8 million by the Federal Election Commission for making illegal campaign contributions.) In 2004, OFHEO and the SEC both released extremely critical reports on Fannie Mae. Then, in 2006, OFHEO sued Raines and two other former executives of Fannie Mae in an attempt to recover bonuses linked to the accounting frauds. Raines alone had received more than $90 million; he was also one of many executives and government officials who received favorable loans from Countrywide's VIP program. Later settlements for all three executives allowed them to keep the majority of their bonuses, and did not require any of them to admit guilt. Fannie Mae paid a $400 million corporate fine to settle the SEC lawsuit. No criminal cases were brought.

Both Fannie and Freddie certainly contributed to the bubble, although they were late to the party. In part due to the discovery of their accounting frauds, in the early years of the bubble they remained fairly conservative with regard to the loans they were willing to purchase and/ or insure. Starting in 2004, however, they began to increase the number of Alt-A loans they purchased, and to relax their credit standards. They remained a minority of the market for junk loans, and such loans constituted only a small percentage of their total loan purchases. However, they were such large firms that their losses were huge, comparable to those of the worst firms in the purely private sector.

Fannie and Freddie also contributed to the bubble in another way— as massive investors in mortgage-backed securities. From 2004 through 2006, Fannie and Freddie purchased $434 billion in mortgage-backed securities that had been created by Wall Street.[32] They did this primarily because their executives had the same toxic incentives as everyone else, and these securities paid high interest rates. Both Fannie and Freddie had AAA credit ratings, of course, and so they could borrow money at very low interest rates and use it to purchase much higher-yielding mortgage securities. It was insanely easy and insanely profitable—until it wasn't. In the end, the two firms' investment losses were almost as large as their losses on mortgages that they had purchased or insured.

They started losing money in 2007. By the end of 2010, between them Fannie and Freddie had $71.9 billion in investment losses and $75.1 billion in mortgage credit losses, for a combined total of $147 billion. They have continued to lose money since then. Even in 2012 they were still losing money, because the Obama administration has forced them to provide mortgage payment relief for unemployed homeowners.[33]

In 2011 the SEC sued the former CEOs of both firms and four other former senior executives for securities fraud, charging that both firms had misrepresented their exposure to subprime mortgages to investors.[34] The complaint alleged that both firms started purchasing larger quantities of high-risk loans in order to meet short-term profit targets related to the executives' annual bonus payments. At the same time, the SEC entered into nonprosecution agreements with both firms. No criminal charges have ever been filed against either the firms or any of their former executives.

Did Fannie and Freddie Cause the Bubble?

Republican conservatives, firmly supported of course by Wall Street banks, have asserted that the housing boom was caused by federal overregulation, which forced Fannie and Freddie to subsidize unwise mortgage lending to unqualified borrowers, by which they mean poor people, minorities, and immigrants. The usual villains in this story are liberal Democrats in Congress and the Community Reinvestment Act, a federal law that sets targets for mortgage lending to disadvantaged groups and neighborhoods. But that story doesn't hold up, for many reasons.

First, the numbers simply don't support this argument. It was not Fannie and Freddie, but rather the pure private sector, especially its least-regulated shadow banking components, which drove the bubble. In fact, the default rate on loans that the GSEs bought or guaranteed remains lower than those created and packaged by the mortgage lenders and Wall Street.

It wasn't overregulation that pushed Fannie and Freddie into their disasters. In fact, if anything Fannie and Freddie's regulator slightly *reduced* the damage the GSEs did, by stopping at least one of the ways that they had been gaming the system, namely their massive accounting frauds. Until those scandals, and even to a great extent after them, Fannie and Freddie behaved largely as they pleased, their conduct driven far more by thoroughly private-sector forces (i.e., annual bonuses and stock options) than by regulation or affordable housing goals. Moreover, their worst behavior occurred at a time when the Republicans controlled the White House and both houses of Congress, making it unlikely that liberal Democratic pressure affected them very much.

Furthermore, almost half of their eventual losses came from being *investors,* not loan buyers, insurers, or securitizers. Fannie and Freddie didn't buy those securities out of social responsibility or liberal political pressure; they bought them because their executives and traders had the same toxic incentives as everyone else, based on short-term performance, and with no "clawbacks" if things went bad later. For the same reasons, they started buying higher-risk, higher-yield mortgages after the bubble was under way. Political pressure probably played a small role in their mortgage purchases, but it wasn't the primary factor.

So the bubble wasn't caused by too many poor people buying houses because of do-gooder federal regulators. Fannie and Freddie were certainly major participants, but they neither started the bubble nor were its major beneficiaries. Merely because of their size, however, they did a lot of damage.

What started and drove the bubble, in short, was a combination of very low interest rates, pervasive dishonesty throughout the financial system, massive lending fraud, speculation, demand for high-yield securities, and, not insignificantly, a squeezed American consumer desperate to maintain living standards and told by everyone—including George W. Bush and Alan Greenspan, as well as the brokers and banks—that home borrowing was the way to do it. From 2000 through 2007, net cash extractions from homes pumped $4.2 trillion into the U.S. economy,[35] and by 2005 half of all American GDP growth was related to housing.[36] By the end of the bubble in 2007, American household debt had jumped to 130 percent of GDP, a historical record, up from just 80 percent in 2000.

All of this could happen only because of the securitization food chain, combined with the collapse of ethics and the spread of toxic incentives throughout the entire financial sector. In fact, once the investment banks had invented the CDO, they didn't even need to confine themselves to mortgages—any kind of loan could be fed into CDOs, and the result sold as an utterly safe "structured product." There were parallel but smaller bubbles, showing equal levels of dishonesty, in other credit assets such as car loans, student loans, credit card debt, Icelandic bank debt, commercial real estate, and private equity (aka leveraged buyouts). These loans, too, were sold and fed into Wall Street's securitization machine, sometimes placed into the very same CDOs that contained subprime mortgages. Indeed this is further evidence that it was the greed and dishonesty of the financial sector, rather than a general mania for housing or do-gooders pressuring Fannie and Freddie, that drove the bubble.

Of course, none of this would have been possible if Wall Street's largest and best financial institutions had refused the business. The lenders were wholly dependent on the wholesale corruption of the core of the financial system—the Wall Street banks, the rating agencies, the mortgage insurance companies, the industry analysts, and, of course, the regulators. Let us now turn to them.

CHAPTER 4

WALL STREET MAKES
A BUBBLE AND
GIVES IT TO THE WORLD

Investment Banking During the Bubble:
World Without Limits

WE HAVE JUST SEEN what mortgage lending was like during the bubble. What was Wall Street thinking when they bought these loans and turned them into trillions of dollars of supposedly ultrasafe, but actually quite toxic, products? Assuming that most investment bankers were not cretinously stupid, they were either: 1) innocents, being defrauded by brilliantly evil mortgage bankers; 2) stunningly complacent and oblivious, not bothering to look at or understand what they were buying and selling; and/or 3) in on the scam.

Well, it wasn't door number one. For most of them, it wasn't door number two, either, although there *was* some staggering obliviousness, particularly among very senior management and boards of directors; this is an interesting subject explored later. But the people actually doing the work, as well as many senior managers, knew perfectly well that they were dealing in manure. Often they simply didn't *care* what it was, or what damage it might cause, as long as they could sell it. But they were not innocent. Quite often they actively pressured the mortgage lenders to supply even more manure that smelled even worse, lied about its known characteristics when they sold it, and profited again by betting against it.

But defenders of the banks (and rating agencies, and insurance companies, and hedge funds) raise one seemingly powerful objection to this view: many of the banks collapsed, causing CEOs, senior executives, and board members to lose their jobs and a lot of money. Even many traders and department heads were fired or laid off. This supposedly demonstrates that they couldn't have realized what they were doing since they were hurting themselves, too. Joe Nocera of the *New York Times,* Laura Tyson (on the board of Morgan Stanley), and C. Michael Armstrong (a former board member of Citigroup, during the bubble) all have made this argument to me personally. Richard Parsons (Citigroup's chairman during the bubble) and Angelo Mozilo both made this argument in their congressional testimony—Parsons described the crisis as "when they hit this iceberg." How on earth, they and others have asked, could bankers possibly have been knowingly committing fraud when it was so clearly contrary to their self-interest? After all, they destroyed their institutions, lost their jobs, and their stock became worthless almost overnight. They—er, *we*—wouldn't knowingly do that, would we? Even if we're selfish, that's just not logical, is it?

Well, actually, it *is* logical, and quite often it *wasn't* contrary to their rational self-interest. Stunningly enough, Wall Street was set up in such a way that for many bankers, destroying their own firms was completely rational, self-interested behavior. Consider the following.

First, the money. If you created, sold, or traded fraudulent junk securities, indeed even if you *bought* them for your institution, you got paid huge annual bonuses, mostly in cash, based on your performance that year. How long will a major bubble last? Five to seven years seems to be the recent average: the S&L and junk bond bubble lasted from 1981 or 1982 until 1987 or 1988; the Internet bubble lasted from about

1995 until the middle of 2000; the housing bubble went from roughly 2001 until 2006 or 2007. (Some last even longer: Japan's property and stock market bubble lasted nearly the full decade of the 1980s, and Bernard Madoff's Ponzi scheme lasted over twenty years.) Until the collapse, not only are you making money, but your firm is making money too, lots of it. The more you contribute to the bubble, the more money you make. When the crash comes, even if your firm goes under, you're still rich. You don't have to give back any of the money; very possibly, you can retire or change careers. But even if you want another job, your track record won't disqualify you—quite the contrary, as we shall see.

Second, there is the "public goods" problem—in this case, however, a public *bad*. Suppose you're one of the twenty or forty (or five hundred) people creating, trading, selling, buying, insuring, or rating mortgage-backed junk at Merrill Lynch, Morgan Stanley, Lehman, Moody's, AIG, wherever. You see a horrific train wreck in the making, with all your coworkers contributing to it. But they are all making a fortune, and their manager—who is *your* boss too—is making *even more* money by keeping it going. Quite obviously, they're going to keep doing it whether you participate or not; so even if you refuse to participate, the firm will be dead anyway. You can try to stop it by going over your boss's head to the CEO; but your boss won't like that at all, and he and the entire department will tell the CEO whatever they need to tell him in order to keep it all going. And if—speaking purely hypothetically— your CEO is an oblivious, selfish, obnoxious egomaniac nearing retirement age, heavily focused on his golf game and art collection, with a few hundred million in cash already stashed away, scheduled to rake in another $50 million this year, whose contract guarantees him another $100 million *if he loses his job*—well, then *he* probably won't be very sympathetic to you, either. You could try going to the board of directors, but even if you could reach them, it will turn out that they are old pals of the CEO, often stunningly clueless, picked largely so that they won't rock the boat.

So if you try to stop the party, you'll probably get marginalized or fired, as happened to a number of serious, ethical people who tried to warn their management and curtail unethical and illegal conduct at Merrill Lynch, Lehman, Citigroup, AIG, and elsewhere. So you'd gain nothing by acting ethically—quite the contrary, you'd ostracize yourself and lose your chance to build (or, rather, transfer to yourself) some real personal wealth—possibly a once-in-a-lifetime opportunity.

Third, consider the partitioning of information. Many people knew that they were doing something dishonest and taking advantage of a bubble, but often they *didn't* know its scale or impact on the industry or even their own firm. How much stuff did the firm hold, how was it being valued, did they intend to keep it or sell it, had they hedged it already, and so forth—many people in investment banks, even at a fairly high level, did not have access to enough information to know how much damage their firm would suffer. Nor did they know when the bubble would end; but they *did* know that as long as it continued, they could keep making a lot of money.

They certainly didn't know the size of the entire industry's exposure, nor the distribution (or concentration) of risk across firms. This last consideration was an important one even for CEOs. There was no single institution anywhere—the regulators and the Treasury Department very much included—that possessed a comprehensive view of the financial system's positions and exposures. Only very late in the bubble did it become clear that so much fraudulent junk had been created, with so many deep interdependencies across firms, that it could threaten the entire global financial system; even then, it was not publicly known (or knowable) until the crisis itself how much further risk had been created through totally unregulated, opaque derivatives transactions.

Fourth, there is the "getting a little bit pregnant" problem: once you're in, no matter how you got there, you might as well *stay* in. Say you're a senior trader, department head, or even CEO, and after a completely blameless life, you wake up one day to find that you're stuck with a pile of fraudulent junk that was created by your department or company over the previous several years. What do you do at that point?

You probably *don't* call a press conference to announce that your firm is built on sand and is doomed to collapse. Rather, you keep the machine going as long as you can—to maximize your own income, try to work your firm out of its hole, or simply, as in Bernard Madoff's case, to delay the inevitable day of reckoning as long as possible. Maybe you try to wind down your positions, or hedge them. Or maybe you can start trying to profit by betting against the bubble, including your own customers. If you sense that the bubble is about to end, you can make serious money by betting on the failure of your own securities—and yes, people did this, in a huge way.

But finally, there is the problem of reality—both in general, and specifically in relation to this bubble. The fact is that people do commit fraud, even when they know that it is personally risky for them. To take an extreme example, we *know* that people still perpetrate literal Ponzi schemes (Allen Stanford, $8 billion; Bernard Madoff, $20 billion), even though every Ponzi scheme is mathematically guaranteed to collapse at some point, with inevitable imprisonment to follow. And now, thanks primarily to private lawsuits and secondarily to a few government investigations, we also know that during the housing bubble many people were, in fact, consciously committing fraud and selling defective products.

Moreover, in the case of the housing bubble—and unlike isolated noninstitutional Ponzi schemes—everyone got away with it. The people responsible for the bubble are still wealthy, out of jail, socially accepted, and either retired or not, as they prefer. Even those who really did lose something—CEOs, eminences on boards of directors, business unit heads, people such as Richard Fuld, Robert Rubin, Angelo Mozilo, Stan O'Neal, or Joseph Cassano—are still enormously wealthy as a result of having taken lots of cash out during the bubble, and/or from their severance payments.

In fact on a net basis, many of these people made far more money by creating and participating in the bubble than they would have made by staying out of it, even though they destroyed their firms. It is true that they lost the value of whatever stock they owned when their firms collapsed in 2008. But over the previous seven years their incomes had been hugely inflated by the bubble, and they cashed a lot of it out—behavior, incidentally, not suggestive of deep faith in (or concern for) their firms' futures. Some of them also received enormous severance payments when they were fired, even *after* the nature and effects of their conduct became known. To a remarkable extent they have avoided social disgrace, and still occupy positions of prestige, even power. So the defenders of the banks are in effect saying: who are you going to believe, me or your own lying eyes?

During the bubble, the Bush administration and the Federal Reserve were essentially AWOL; if anything, they made matters worse. In 2004 the SEC voted unanimously to allow the five largest investment banks to calculate their own leverage limits, based on their internal risk models. This meant that by the time the party ended, several of them were leveraged at more than thirty to one, meaning that if the value of their assets declined by just 3 percent, they would be bankrupt. As a result, when the crisis occurred, three of the banks, Bear Stearns, Lehman Brothers, and Merrill Lynch, were insolvent by 2008. Only Goldman Sachs and Morgan Stanley survived, and that by grace of federal rescue operations.[1] During this time, the SEC and other federal regulators reduced their risk analysis and enforcement staffs, and basically left the investment banks unsupervised. The same was true of the industry's several "self-regulatory" organizations, such as the Financial Industry Regulatory Authority (FINRA), the Securities Investor Protection Corporation (SIPC), and others. FINRA, for example, describes its mission thus on its website:

> FINRA is the leading non-governmental regulator for all securities firms doing business with the U.S. public—nearly 4,495 firms employing nearly 635,515 registered representatives. Our chief role is to protect investors by maintaining the fairness of the U.S. capital markets. We carry it out by writing and enforcing rules, examining firms for compliance with the rules, informing and educating investors, helping firms pre-empt risk and stay in compliance.[2]

Well, FINRA didn't do too well. (The head of FINRA during the bubble? Mary Shapiro, who became chair of the SEC in 2009, appointed by President Obama.) As a result of the failure of both government and private regulation, during the entire bubble the inmates were in charge of the asylum. Given their incentives, a massive fraud was entirely rational for most of them, even if they had known in advance of all the damage it would cause.

Was it all really that naked? Yes, it was. Some of what follows might be a little dry. But I ask readers to bear with me because later in this book, I will be saying some rather strong things—things like, these people should be in jail, they should have their wealth taken from them and given to people whose lives they destroyed, they should live in disgrace for the rest of their lives, it is shocking that they have not been prosecuted, and it is obscene and dangerous that they still occupy prominent positions in government, universities, companies, and civic institutions. So in the next couple of chapters, there will be some rather detailed stuff, because when we come to the punch line, I want it to be convincing.

Let us start our survey of the investment banking industry's conduct with a lawsuit filed by the discount brokerage and asset management firm Charles Schwab, Inc. The case provides an unusually broad statistical picture of the securities that Wall Street produced, and also helps provide context for some of the truly stunning conduct we shall encounter later.

The Schwab Complaint

SCHWAB SUED THE broker-dealer arms of twelve major financial institutions. The suit is based on the representations made in the offering materials for thirty-six securitizations—mortgage-backed securities—that were purchased from these banks by various units of Schwab between 2005 and 2007. The defendants are BNP Paribas, Countrywide, Bank of America, Citigroup, Credit Suisse, Deutsche Bank, Goldman Sachs, Greenwich Capital, HSBC, Wells Fargo, Morgan Stanley, and UBS.

Investors in residential mortgage-backed securities do not have access to individual loan files when they make the purchase; they are shown only summary data for each mortgage on the "loan tapes" that accompany a sales prospectus. But when Schwab sued, it analyzed the summary data for 75,144 loans included in the securitizations it had purchased. While not a random sample, it is a broad one.[3] If anything, the sample is probably substantially above average in quality, because Schwab invested conservatively, and the defendants in this lawsuit do not include Bear Stearns and Merrill Lynch, two firms that produced much of the worst junk. As we'll see shortly, some of it was *much* worse.

Still, Schwab's analysis estimated that 45 percent of the loans violated the representations made in selling the securities. Schwab used four separate tests; most of the suspect loans failed more than one of them.

1. Loan-to-Value Representations. The prospectus for every security that Schwab had purchased contained detailed representations about the average loan-to-value ratio (LTV) of the mortgages supporting the security. All but one of the prospectuses stated that no individual loan had an LTV greater than 100 percent. Schwab tested those statements with a model that is widely used in the industry, based on 500 million home sales, in zip codes covering 99 percent of the population.

The results of Schwab's tests suggest that all securitizers significantly understated LTV ratios, and that all of the securities included substantial numbers of loans with LTV ratios of more than 100 percent—in other words, loans for more than the home was worth. In one security comprising 1,597 loans, the model estimated that 626 loans were overvalued by more than 5 percent, with only 69 undervalued by as much. The pool's weighted-average LTV rose from a represented 73.8 percent to 90.5 percent, and the model estimated that 196 loans had LTVs of more than 100 percent, although the documents represented that none did. Roughly similar outcomes applied to all the other pools. A second test was applied to properties that were subsequently sold. The sales prices were consistently below the values implied by the claimed LTVs, in a pattern consistent with the model. Schwab notes that given the average leverage of the loans, a 10 percent LTV overstatement implies an 80 percent reduction in stated equity.*

2. Stated Liens. All of the securities' offering materials stipulated that all property liens were fully disclosed. No mortgage loan, supposedly, is ever funded without a title search to spot any lien that might be senior to the bank's lien. Schwab did new title searches on the properties. In one pool of 2,274 loans, 669 had undisclosed liens that, on average, reduced stated equity by 91.5 percent. In some pools, as many as half the loans had undisclosed liens.

3. Occupancy Status. Owner-occupied homes have lower default and foreclosure risk than second homes or investment properties. For this reason, all of the securities' offering materials contained representations as to the percentage of loans in the security that were for owner-occupied (primary) residences. Schwab researched the properties listed as primary residences for indications that they were really not, including:

- Does owner have a different property tax address?
- Does owner not take advantage of local homestead tax exemptions?
- Does owner have three or more houses?
- Is there a shorter-than-normal time lapse from current pay to foreclosure?
- Has owner not updated personal billing addresses six months after closing?

Using these tests, in one pool of 1,498 loans, in which only 99 were alleged to be nonprimary residences, the correct total was estimated to

---

*That calculation was across all the securities. In the pool example used here, the 73.8 percent LTV implied equity of 26.2 percent. If LTV was really 90.5 percent, the equity falls to 9.5 percent, which is 64 percent lower.

be 598, with most of those failing more than one test. Roughly similar results prevailed throughout all the securities.

4. Internal Guideline Compliance. Schwab collected data on early payment defaults (EPDs) on all securitized loans issued by the originators of the mortgages in these securities from 2001 through 2007. In well-underwritten mortgages, the rate of EPDs, defined as default during the first six months of the loan, should be vanishingly small. Schwab investigated whether and when EPD rates changed during the bubble, and if so, whether stated credit guidelines changed at the same time.

None of the lenders changed its represented credit guidelines during this period. Despite this, *every* lender experienced a sharp upward break in its EPD rate at some point, a trend that persisted thereafter in every case. But the date at which the break occurred was different for *each originator.* For Countrywide, for example, EPDs suddenly quadrupled starting in the first quarter of 2005 and stayed at consistently high rates from then on. All the other lenders showed comparable upward EPD breaks; the starting dates ranged from mid-2003 to mid-2007.

Since the breaks occurred at different times for different originators, they were not likely to have been caused by general economic conditions. Rather, they probably reflected an internal policy change; but those policy changes were never reflected in the lending guidelines officially represented to investors. (Credit guideline representations were usually detailed and specific.) The obvious interpretation is that, one by one, originators chose to go aggressively down-market to make more money, while officially denying that they had done so.

The banks, of course, could allege—and indeed have alleged—that they were scammed, just as Schwab was. But in their securities prospectuses all the securitizers also claimed that they carefully underwrote the loans they purchased from originators. The representations they made were about the quality of their *own* credit processes, not those of the originators. And, unlike final investors like Schwab, they did have access to all the detailed backup records. Furthermore, most of them were deeply in bed with several major lenders—they provided the lenders' financing, managed their securities offerings, and so forth.

And finally, in order to justify the representations made to investors, all of the securitizing banks hired outside firms to review the quality of the loans they bought. The largest and most comprehensive reviewer was Clayton Holdings, which examined 911,000 mortgages for twenty-three different securitizing banks, including all of the largest securitizers, between January 2006 and July 2007. In testimony and documents provided to the Financial Crisis Inquiry Commission (FCIC), senior Clayton executives revealed that 28 percent of the loans they examined did not meet even the securitizers' own internal guidelines. Despite this, 39 percent of all loans that failed the securitizers' guidelines were purchased and securitized anyway, a fact never disclosed to the investors purchasing the final securities.[4]

But were the banks just sloppy passive conduits, or active co-conspirators? Did they understand the full implications of their actions? To understand that, we need to look inside them. This has not been done nearly enough, because the federal government hasn't really tried. There have been no criminal prosecutions using large-scale subpoena power and sworn testimony. All we have are civil suits, in which the banks ferociously (and often successfully) resist subpoenas and often succeed in keeping records sealed. Even the FCIC established by the Obama administration had extremely limited subpoena power, and a tiny budget. If there ever were to be a truly serious investigation, I have no doubt that we would learn much, much more than we currently know.

But what we currently know is still quite impressive.

Bear Stearns

BEAR STEARNS WAS one of the most experienced mortgage players on Wall Street. In the three years from 2004 through 2006, Bear securitized nearly a million mortgage loans with a total value of $192 billion—serious money, even for Wall Street.

Bear Stearns had been in the mortgage-backing business for nearly two decades, mostly securitizing high-quality loans. But in 2001 it created a new mortgage conduit, EMC Mortgage, to securitize Alt-A loans. In 2003 EMC started to securitize subprime, stated income, and "no doc" loans, then in 2005, second-lien loans, of the type that even Angelo Mozilo called the "most toxic" he had seen in his entire career.

Bear Stearns gives us a lurid peek at a white-shoe investment bank turned boiler room, using a succession of strategies to extract money from the bubble in every possible way. We know about it because of a lawsuit filed by the Ambac Financial Group, a bond insurer now in bankruptcy. Ambac's suit against Bear Stearns and its successor company, JPMorgan Chase, is one of the few cases in which plaintiffs were able to obtain the internal documents, e-mails, and loan files of defendants to use in evidence.[5]

The history of the lawsuit indicates the banks' strategy, and their ferocious opposition to every attempt to shed light on their conduct. Ambac filed suit in November 2008, and as of this writing—February 2012— the case has still not come to trial. Bear Stearns and its new owner, JPMorgan Chase, have used a long succession of procedural tricks to delay the case. They also tried hard to prevent Ambac from being able to subpoena records and depose witnesses, but eventually lost. They are still trying to delay the trial, presumably hoping that Ambac's bankruptcy trustee will eventually give up or run out of money to pursue the case.

Of course, what follows is a partisan account based on materials assembled by Ambac's attorneys. During the bubble, Ambac and the other major insurers (MBIA and AIG) were not angels themselves; their former executives and salespeople (now long gone) had the same toxic incentives and destroyed their own firms, just like everyone else. But now, an independent bankruptcy trustee appointed by the courts is trying to recover as much as possible. Ambac's lawsuit is part of a gigantic post-crisis food fight in which dozens of firms are trying to recover money, often while being sued themselves for their own highly unethical behavior. And JPMorgan's answer to the Ambac suit, when it becomes available, may cast some of the quotes below in a different light. But the accuracy of the quotes has not been challenged, and they make for interesting reading.

Ambac is suing to recover losses from payouts it made on failed Bear Stearns securitizations; Ambac argues that it agreed to insure them only due to gross misrepresentations by Bear Stearns. Many of the loans in the securitizations came from a wonderful company called American Home Mortgage, Inc. (AHM), also now bankrupt. We can get a taste of AHM's enthusiastic approach to home lending from the official description of its "Choice" loan programs:

> Offering financing for borrowers with more serious credit issues, these programs provide solutions for multiple mortgage lates, recent bankruptcies or foreclosures, little or no traditional credit, and FICO scores as low as 500. These programs are also offering 100 percent financing on all doc types for borrowers who do not meet the credit criteria of the standard Choice programs.[6]

Now, over to Bear Stearns. Its mortgage securitization program was run by four executives: Mary Haggerty and Baron Silverstein, coheads of Mortgage Finance, and Jeffrey Verschleiser and Michael Nierenberg, coheads of mortgage trading. Haggerty and Silverstein underwrote the suitability of mortgages from originators, and pushed them through the steps to get to a sale. Verschleiser and Nierenberg traded loans in and out of Bear Stearns's portfolio and also constructed the securitizations. These people were emphatically *not* obscure file clerks whose machinations went unnoticed by management. All four were senior managing directors—in all of Bear Stearns, a fourteen-thousand-person company, only ninety-eight people were at that level. They would have all been paid millions of dollars per year.

The first thing they did, of course, was simply to package and sell a lot of trash (while concealing this fact). The record shows that loan delinquencies were already rising sharply in early 2005. John Mongelluzzo, the due diligence manager in Mortgage Finance, and therefore junior to Haggerty and Silverstein, was pushing for stricter standards and tighter underwriting reviews. The response to his actions indicates the futility of being ethical in American investment banking during the bubble. Instead of tightening standards, in February 2005 Mary Haggerty ordered a *reduction* in due diligence "in order to make us more competitive on bids with larger sub-prime sellers." She reduced the size of the loan samples used to test compliance and, most important, postponed the due diligence review until *after* Bear had bought the loans, and often even after the loans had been bundled into securities.[7]

This change in procedure was made almost by stealth. A year later, in March 2006, a conduit manager wrote that "until yesterday we had no idea that there was a post close dd [due diligence] going on." Loans "were not flagged appropriately and we securitized many of them which are still to this day not cleared." In other words, loans were going out with no due diligence at all.[8]

Later that spring, Mongelluzzo wrote to Silverstein, "I would strongly discourage doing post close [due diligence] for any trade with AHM. You will end up with a lot of repurchases"—a "repurchase" was a buyback from a sold securitization, and was always expensive. The advice was ignored. Two pools of 1,600 loans were purchased from AHM and quickly securitized. A review the following year showed that 60 percent were delinquent, and 13 percent had already defaulted.[9]

At the same time, Verschleiser was pushing hard for more volume. One of the conduit managers e-mailed her staff:

> I refuse to receive any more e-mails from [Verschleiser]...questioning why we're not funding more loans each day. I'm holding each of you responsible for making sure we fund at least 500 each and every day....If we have 500+ loans in this office we MUST find a way to underwrite them and to buy them....I was not happy when I saw the funding numbers and I knew that NY would NOT BE HAPPY.

Later that year, the same executive e-mailed her staff: "I don't understand that with weekend overtime why we didn't purchase more loans....Our funding needs to be $2 billion this month....I expect to see ALL employees working overtime this week to make sure we hit the target number."[10]

An early warning of declining quality was a 2005 spike in EPDs, which Bear Stearns defined as a missed payment in the first ninety days. Bear Stearns's policy had previously been to hold purchased loans in inventory for ninety days before securitizing them, in order to ensure their quality. But in 2005 the team decided to shorten the holding period, so loans could be pushed into securities before an EPD occurred. Verschleiser told the unit that he wanted all "the subprime loans closed in December" to be in securitizations by January—in effect, within a month of purchase. He confirmed that policy in mid-2006, reminding staff "to be certain we securitize the loans with 1 month epd before the epd period expires." Later, he demanded to know why specific loans that experienced early delinquencies "were dropped from deals and not securitized before their epd period expired."[11]

The predictable consequence was a flood of EPDs in securitized loans. Bear assured its investors that they would diligently police EPDs, because these usually indicated a seriously defective loan. In their presentations to Ambac, Bear Stearns had touted their aggressive follow-up to assert claims on behalf of investors if a securitized loan went bad soon after the close of a securitization deal. The usual protocol was to buy back the bad loan from the investor and force the originator either to replace it with a good equivalent or to return the cash.

But you can't keep a good investment banker from innovating, and in 2006 Bear Stearns came up with another bright idea, initiating a second scam. Whenever Bear Stearns learned of a loan default, instead of repurchasing the defective loan, it made a cash settlement with the originator at a discount, *without informing the investors* of either the breach or the cash settlement. So Bear kept the settlement cash, leaving the investors to discover the default later, which likely did not occur until after the investors' contractual option to return the loan had expired. When a Bear Stearns manager specifically asked her boss if the policy was to make settlements with lenders without checking for violations of the representations and warranties that Bear Stearns had made to the investors, she confirmed that it was.[12]

At first Bear Stearns was overwhelmed by the flood of loan defaults, but it soon created a system to process them efficiently, generating $1.25 billion in settlements. Bear kept it all, and investors later learned that they owned securities backed by thousands of loans that Bear had officially listed as defaulted. The entire EPD process and the cash gains from the settlements were reported in detail to the most senior managers in the firm, so they were fully aware that investment agreements were being flouted and knew how bad the underlying loans were. Both the Bear Stearns auditor and legal counsel eventually insisted on stopping the one-sided settlements, although it seems that they continued for some months after the order.[13]

Underscoring that Bear managers well understood what they were selling, the deal manager on an August 2006 securitization called the deal a "shitbreather" and a "SACK OF SHIT." In deposition, he said he intended those phrases as "a term of endearment."[14]

All of the investment banks tried to maintain an appearance of propriety for a combination of legal and sales reasons. So, like all of them, Bear Stearns did not entirely ignore due diligence on the loans it bought, and as usual, had contracted with outside reviewing firms. But internal Bear Stearns e-mails mocked the low quality of the reviews, and managers consistently blocked proposals for tightened reviews. The head of one of the reviewing firms said in deposition that in a 2006 review, up to 65 percent of his rejection recommendations were ignored. Another reviewer said that about "75 percent of the loans that should have been rejected were still put in the pool and sold."[15]

In 2006 Bear hired a third outside firm to check a sample of loans that had already been securitized. The review was subject to strict limitations: do not count occupancy violations (i.e., a declared prime residence not owner occupied); there could be no employment check; no credit report verifications; and no review of appraisals. Even with all those restrictions, 42.9 percent of the sampled loans were found to be in breach of the securitization conditions. Bear Stearns did not notify investors of those findings.[16]

By mid-2007 the impending collapse of the subprime housing bubble was becoming apparent. This initiated the third phase of the mortgage unit's strategy. Instead of warning customers and investors, the unit went on an all-out drive to clear out its inventory—"a going out of business sale," one manager called it. A rule against securitizing loans from suspended or terminated lenders was summarily dropped, without this fact being disclosed. Verschleiser railed about one $73 million batch of loans, three-quarters of which did not meet securitizing guidelines. He couldn't understand "why any of these positions were not securitized...why were they dropped from deals and not securitized before their epd period." And another senior trader demanded to know "why are we taking losses on 2nd lien loans from 2005 when they could have been securitized?????"[17]

In late 2007 Ambac managers became aware of the growing number of defaulted loans in the portfolios they had insured and requested a delivery of detailed loan files. Without telling Ambac, Bear Stearns hired one of its outside credit reviewers to look at the loans. The review found that 56 percent had material breaches. Bear did not share this information with Ambac.[18]

Then came the fourth phase of Bear Stearns's mortgage strategy—one practiced on a far larger scale by others, as we shall see. Verschleiser realized that as the bubble ended, the resulting avalanche of loan defaults would have a catastrophic effect on Ambac, their insurer. Far from being a disaster, this was an enormous opportunity. Verschleiser realized that he could make a fortune—*by betting on Ambac's failure by shorting its stock*. As he recounted in his 2007 self-evaluation:

> [At] the end of October, while presenting to the risk committee on our business I told them that a few financial guarantors were vulnerable to potential writedowns in the CDO and MBS market and we should be short a multiple of 10 of the shorts I had put on....In less than three weeks we made approximately $55 million on just those two trades.[19]

Bear Stearns took his advice, and by 2008 Verschleiser was consulting with other traders on other banks' exposure to Ambac, so Bear Stearns could profit from its bad loans coming and going. In fact, the worse the loans, the more money Bear Stearns made. In mid-2007 Bear Stearns stock peaked at $159 a share, its all-time record.

But all good things must end. On March 16, 2008, Bear Stearns was facing bankruptcy, and its board agreed to sell the company to JPMorgan Chase for $2 a share (later revised to $10 after shareholder protests).

But if these guys were so good at being devious, why did Bear Stearns fail? At one level, the answer is simple: Bear Stearns ran out of money. It is very difficult to forecast with precision the end of a bubble, or the exact rate at which various market participants—banks, rating agencies, investors, insurers, executives—will catch on. So Bear Stearns got caught holding a lot of junk—bad loans, pieces of securitizations, stocks and bonds of other institutions also being decimated by the crisis—and couldn't get rid of it fast enough, at high enough prices, because everybody else was waking up (and going down the drain) at the same time. Moreover, like all the investment banks, Bear Stearns was very heavily leveraged, dependent on huge quantities of dangerously short-term loans from money market funds and large banks. This funding needed to be rolled over weekly or even daily. When these funding sources sensed trouble, they stopped lending, and Bear Stearns ran out of cash very fast.

But *why* was the firm so dangerously exposed? Knowing the risks, knowing that a huge bubble would inevitably end, why had the firm continued to buy and hold so much junk, and why was it so reliant on such huge amounts of short-term funding? Well, the working-level people directly exploiting and profiting from the bubble didn't have much incentive to end it, or warn anyone. As long as they could sell junk, they made money. When it started to go bad, many of them even made money by betting against it—by betting against specific securities, against indexes of mortgage-backed securities, and against firms likely to fail in the crash. And while they shared in the gains, all of the losses were someone else's problem.

But that logic mainly applies to those who were most directly profiting from annual cash bonuses and could move to other firms. What about senior management and boards of directors, not just of Bear Stearns but of the others that collapsed—Lehman, Merrill Lynch, AIG, Citigroup, and even the lenders (WaMu, Wachovia, Countrywide, etc.)? In the event of failure, the CEOs and boards of these firms would unquestionably lose jobs and wealth not easily replaced. The answer to this question reveals a great deal, and we will consider it shortly. For now, let us continue our tour of Wall Street conduct.

We know more about Bear Stearns than we do about most other banks, due to the lack of federal investigation and because the civil suits are being delayed. But sufficient material is available on other lenders to confirm the generality of bad behavior. Some examples follow.

Goldman Sachs and GSAMP

GOLDMAN SACHS IS the other major bank for which there is a substantial internal record, thanks to documents obtained by the Senate Permanent Subcommittee on Investigations. The most interesting parts of Goldman's behavior are considered in the next chapter, because they pertain to what happened after the bubble ended. For now, I will simply provide one example to make the point that Goldman created junk like everyone else.

In the October 15, 2007, issue of *Fortune* magazine, Allan Sloan published his superb article "House of Junk," which focused on a series of securities, the GSAMP Trust 2006-S-3, totaling $494 million out of the $44.5 billion in mortgage-backed securities that Goldman Sachs sold in 2006. The GSAMPs were issued in April 2006 (during Hank Paulson's final months as CEO before becoming treasury secretary), having been assembled from second mortgages sourced from among the worst subprime lenders, including Fremont and Long Beach. Since they were all second mortgages, the lender could not foreclose in the event of default. The average loan-to-value ratio of the pool was 99.29 percent, meaning that borrowers had essentially zero equity in the homes, and 58 percent of the loans had little or no documentation. Despite this, 93 percent of the securities were rated investment grade, and 68 percent were rated AAA, the highest possible rating, by both Moody's and Standard & Poor's, the two largest rating agencies. Yet by October 2007, 18 percent of the loans had already defaulted, and all of the securities had been severely downgraded.[20]

So it was junk. But did they *know* it was junk? They most certainly did; they started betting against it in late 2006, and by late 2007 they were already making net profits on their bets against mortgage securities. We'll return to Goldman Sachs later in discussing how the financial sector handled the end of the bubble, the crisis, and the post-crisis environment. It's interesting, and hasn't been sufficiently publicized.

Morgan Stanley

MORGAN STANLEY WAS one of the leading global securitizers. In the first quarter of 2007 alone, MS created $44 billion of structured securities backed by mortgages and other assets. One modest deal sold to an unsophisticated institutional investor, the pension fund for Virgin Islands government employees, is a good illustration of banking ethics in the twenty-first century.[21]

The security in question was a particularly toxic thing called a synthetic CDO. A synthetic CDO is a kind of virtual, imitation CDO, not backed by actual loans or debts, but essentially a collection of side bets on other securities, constructed to track their performance. As with any bet, it takes two parties—someone betting that the securities will work, and someone else betting that they will fail.

The synthetic CDO in question here, Libertas, referenced, or made side bets on, some $1.2 billion of mostly mortgage-backed securities, a large share of them sourced from New Century, WMC, and Option One, all of them notoriously bad subprime lenders. The Virgin Islands pension fund bought $82 million worth of AAA-rated notes forming part of Libertas. The deal closed in late March 2007, and before the year was out, the securities were nearly worthless. But it gets better.

Morgan Stanley owned the short side of the entire deal—in other words, the people who created and sold these securities were betting that they would fail. So they did very well indeed when the pension fund's notes defaulted, as they did within months. Since Morgan Stanley owned the short side, they kept the entire $82 million principal of the Virgin Islands pension investment. Nice work. You sell a deal, collect your sales commission, then you get to keep the customer's entire investment when the securities fail.

That much is not in dispute. But, stunningly enough, it is not per se illegal to create and sell a security with the intention of profiting from its failure—a state of affairs that the investment banking industry is in no rush to publicize, much less change. So the question in the Virgin Islands lawsuit is whether Morgan Stanley knowingly misrepresented the quality of the securities. Here is the pension fund's side of the story.

Morgan Stanley had long been New Century's largest "warehouse" lender—supplying funds for New Century to assemble loans for securitization. As such, it carefully monitored conditions at the lender. We saw in the previous chapter that as the bubble ended and accounting problems surfaced, New Century rapidly declined into bankruptcy.

Morgan Stanley disclosed in the Libertas prospectus that New Century had been accused of trading and accounting violations, but did *not* mention the mounting claims for breaches of warranties. They also mentioned that "several published reports also speculated that [New Century] would seek bankruptcy protection or be liquidated." Still, like all securitizers, they claimed they had vetted the loans and that they met standard quality guidelines.[22]

But Morgan Stanley knew a great deal more than it had disclosed. It had participated in a March 6 conference call with New Century and its creditors. After the call, Citigroup decided to invoke its default rights against New Century. About a week after the Libertas deal closed, Morgan Stanley seized $2.5 billion in New Century assets; New Century declared bankruptcy soon thereafter. The bankruptcy examiner later wrote: "[The] increasingly risky nature of New Century's loan origina-tions created a ticking time bomb that detonated in 2007."[23]

The question in the lawsuit is whether Morgan Stanley deliberately withheld material information. But that was habitual for them. Like those of all the other securitizers, Morgan Stanley's loans had been ex-amined by Clayton Holdings, which, as usual, found that many of them violated even Morgan Stanley's internal guidelines, and that many de-fective loans were securitized anyway.

In June 2010 Morgan Stanley agreed to pay $102 million to settle a lawsuit brought by the attorney general of Massachusetts. While not admitting wrongdoing, Morgan Stanley executed an "Assurance of Discontinuance" specifying a long list of improper acts and referencing a long list of past bad practices.

According to the settlement, when Morgan Stanley had been faced with a choice of maintaining its credit standards or continuing to source New Century loans, it chose to jettison standards. Morgan Stanley began to accept loans that didn't comply with the Massachu-setts "best interest" law, and progressively discarded its remaining in-ternal quality rules. Even after Morgan Stanley declared New Century to be in default, it continued to provide funding for its mortgages—as long as the money was wired deal by deal to settlement accounts with availability only upon mortgage execution.[24]

And what about Option One? They were the H&R Block subsidiary, one of the "Worst of the Worst" subprime lenders. By the first part of 2007, delinquency rates on the loans from Option One that were used for Libertas were more than double the company's earlier default rates even *before* the deal was closed. It does not appear that Morgan Stanley shared that information with the investors.[25]

During the bubble, Morgan Stanley had record profits, like every-one. As for the crisis, well, they survived, despite coming close to col-lapse in 2008. But Morgan Stanley would have done much better had it not been for one man, Howie Hubler, a senior trader whose erroneous bets on the mortgage market cost Morgan Stanley $9 billion.

But the *nature* of Mr. Hubler's bets is far more revealing than the size of the loss, particularly when compared to the rest of Morgan Stanley's behavior. Mr. Hubler didn't lose money because he innocently thought that mortgage securities were good things. Quite the contrary.

Like the people at Bear Stearns, Mr. Hubler was anything but an obscure rogue trader. He ran a fifty-person group, and his decisions were reviewed by senior management. Mr. Hubler realized by late 2004 that the housing market was a huge bubble, that it would burst, and that when that happened, thousands of mortgage-backed securities based on awful subprime loans would fail. Mr. Hubler talked to his management about this, and they agreed with him.

Did Morgan Stanley then warn its customers? No. Did it stop selling tens of billions of dollars of crappy subprime mortgage-backed securities? No. Did it tighten its loan standards? No—indeed, as we have just seen, it lowered them. Did it warn the regulators? No. Did it stop financing the worst subprime lenders? No.

What Morgan Stanley *did* do, however, was give Howie Hubler permission to begin betting *against* subprime mortgage-backed securities, massively. Using credit default swaps—we'll get to them—he placed enormous bets that very low-quality, but nonetheless highly rated, mortgage securities would fail.[26]

But there was a problem. The bubble lasted longer than anyone at Morgan Stanley predicted that it could. And as 2004 became 2005 and then 2006, maintaining Mr. Hubler's bets became expensive. But Mr. Hubler was absolutely certain that the bubble would eventually burst, and he wanted above all to maintain his bets against those really awful subprime mortgage securities.

And so, with Morgan Stanley's knowledge and approval, Howie made a huge mistake. In order to pay for his bets *against* the lowest-quality mortgage securities, he started writing insurance *for* other, supposedly higher-quality mortgage securities—securities that Mr. Hubler thought would not default until much later than the really awful ones. But insurance on these higher-quality securities was much cheaper, so in order to sell enough insurance (to obtain enough premium income) to fund his bets against the obviously crappy securities, he needed to write insurance on *a lot* of them.

For a short time it worked, and in the first quarter of 2007 Morgan Stanley made $1 billion from Hubler's strategy. But when the shit hit the fan, the supposedly higher-quality securities failed rapidly, too. Just as Morgan Stanley had underestimated the size and duration of the bubble, so too it had underestimated the severity of the collapse. Internal politics and/or sexism probably also interfered; an article published in *New York* magazine in April 2008 described power struggles and institutional sexism involving Hubler, other traders, John Mack (the CEO), and Zoe Cruz, Morgan Stanley's highest-ranking female executive. Cruz was not a saint; she too endorsed the idea of secretly shorting the subprime market. But Cruz, to whom Hubler reported, apparently became alarmed about the potential risks of Hubler's strategy.

But Hubler apparently ignored her. And so Howie lost $9 billion for Morgan Stanley. Of course, he kept his previous bonuses—tens of millions of dollars. He was forced to resign but was not officially fired, so he also collected his deferred compensation.

With wonderful irony, during its crisis in 2008, Morgan Stanley's CEO campaigned publicly and angrily against one group that, he said, represented a danger to financial stability and a menace to society. After a tough public fight, Morgan Stanley persuaded the SEC to restrict the actions of this group. Who were these evil people, and what was this dangerous activity that needed emergency regulation?

Short sellers, of course—people betting against Morgan Stanley stock, who therefore had an incentive for the company to fail. In late 2008 Laura Tyson, a member of Morgan Stanley's board of directors whom I have known for twenty-five years, told me with an utterly straight face, in what was probably my final conversation with my former friend, that hedge funds were conspiring against Morgan Stanley, shorting its stock while spreading malicious rumors and withdrawing their money in order to weaken the firm. Laura also told me that she and Stephen Roach, Morgan Stanley's chief economist during the bubble, had both warned senior management that the bubble would burst. When I asked her whether the bonus system had contributed to the crisis, she said no, and told me that those who had caused Morgan Stanley's own losses had themselves suffered greatly. "Those people were *crushed*," she said. "They have lost *everything*."

Laura did *not* tell me that her firm had been constructing and selling securities with the intent of profiting from their failure, nor that Morgan Stanley's losses in 2008 were caused principally by a tactical error in implementing a massive bet against the bubble that it had helped create—a strategy that had provided a huge incentive not to warn its customers, the regulators, or the public of the impending crisis. Did she know about it? I don't know, although during the bubble she had been in frequent contact with Zoe Cruz and Morgan Stanley's senior management.

In early 2009 I also spoke with Stephen Roach, whom I had also known (slightly) for a long time. To his credit, Mr. Roach had warned publicly about America's unsustainable debt levels, and of a coming recession. But he was careful never to blame his firm or industry; the culprit was Alan Greenspan, for keeping interest rates too low. When I asked Mr. Roach if the structure of financial sector compensation had contributed to the bubble, he said no, and argued that regulating compensation would be a bad idea. He didn't mention Morgan Stanley's betting against the mortgage market either. Given that it cost his employer $9 billion, I find it difficult to believe that he didn't know.

The Rest of Them

THE EVIDENCE SUGGESTS that Citigroup behaved as unethically as Morgan Stanley and Bear Stearns did. But they weren't as smart, or at least their senior management wasn't, so when the music stopped they were caught without a chair.

Although Citigroup had earlier applied fairly strict credit standards, when the bubble accelerated they held their noses and accepted whatever the originators sent them. By mid-2006 Richard Bowen, the recently promoted chief underwriter of Citigroup's consumer division, grew seriously alarmed. He discovered that 60 percent of the loans that Citigroup was buying from lenders failed to meet its own internal standards. He warned everyone around him, including senior management. But not only was nothing done, things actually got worse. By 2007 he said, "defective mortgages . . . [were] over 80 percent of production."[27] He testified to the FCIC that he and other credit officers repeatedly complained to the senior executives in the bank. In October 2007 Bowen wrote a very explicit e-mail, marked "URGENT—READ IMMEDIATELY," about the failure and violation of Citigroup's internal controls, and their possible financial consequences. Bowen sent this e-mail message to four senior executives, including Citigroup's CFO and also Robert Rubin, the former treasury secretary who was vice chairman of the board and chairman of the board's executive committee. As a result, Bowen was demoted and his 220-person group reassigned, leaving him with only two employees.

During the bubble, Citigroup purchased and resold huge volumes of mortgages, and also created and sold huge amounts of toxic mortgage securities. It sold many of these to the usual victims, including Fannie, Freddie, and the Federal Housing Administration. But it also retained many of them, even though it pretended that it had not done so. Like the other securitizers, Citigroup made use of highly deceptive accounting. In this case, it used a loophole in the accounting rules governing structured investment vehicles (SIVs). Actually it wasn't a loophole at all, in the sense of being an initially unintentional oversight later used for unanticipated purposes. Rather, it was a provision for which the banks had specifically lobbied hard (and won).

By placing its toxic mortgage securities in SIVs, Citigroup could take current profits and temporarily pretend that the securities weren't on its own balance sheet—that is, until the securities lost money, when it became necessary for Citigroup to pay up. In the meantime, of course, many people collected large bonuses, including Citigroup's senior management. In the end it turned out that Citigroup had ownership or liability for over $50 billion of the stuff, which was why it had to be rescued by the federal government. Late in the bubble, Citigroup's CDO unit did start to bet against the bubble, by creating synthetic CDOs that it could dishonestly sell to fools, thereby profiting by holding the short side of the bet. One such synthetic CDO resulted in a civil fraud lawsuit filed by the SEC.[28] But the profits thereby obtained were dwarfed by losses on Citigroup's holdings and the obligations it had to its SIVs.

Citigroup's CEO during most of the bubble, Chuck Prince, was forced to resign in late 2007, replaced by Vikram Pandit, who remains CEO as of 2012. Rubin resigned in January 2009, forced out when Citigroup became heavily dependent upon federal rescue funds, which gave the government over 30 percent ownership.

UBS is one of Switzerland's three big banks, and one of the largest banks in the world. It was both perpetrator and victim—some parts of UBS purchased huge quantities of mortgage securities and lost billions on them, while others created and sold them to unsophisticated victims. In 2001—quite early—UBS created a hybrid CDO (part real, part synthetic) called North Street 4. UBS sold it to a small, local German bank, HSH Nordbank.

The bank's lawsuit against UBS alleges that contrary to representations, UBS and a subsequent acquisition, Dillon Read Capital Management (a small U.S. investment bank), later used the structure to dump poorly performing assets from its internal books. The last investment made on behalf of the investors was made by Dillon Read in February 2007. This investment was to go long on an index of subprime mortgage CDOs (i.e., bet that they would perform well), so that Dillon Read could take the opposite position, betting *against* them. As of the date of the court filing, HSH had lost half its investment.[29]

Essentially these same patterns of behavior have been alleged against all the other major securitizers—Merrill Lynch, Deutsche Bank, Credit Suisse, Lehman. All of them sold securities backed by high-risk residential mortgages sourced from the same universe of subprime originators. All of them had the same compensation practices.

And all the cases against the big Wall Street firms we have met in this narrative come down to the simple proposition that no competent securitizer could have financed the loan originators, purchased tens or hundreds of thousands of mortgages from them, structured and sold the securities, and made elaborate representations and warranties in their sales material without ever understanding the toxic nature of the instruments they were selling.

In many cases, we have the additional evidence that they started betting against the market and even sometimes their own securities, while continuing to tell customers to buy. For example, late in the bubble, traders at Merrill Lynch went to the extent of creating a new unit within Merrill to buy securities that the real market wouldn't touch. Since that was obviously a losing game, the traders split their bonuses with the fake purchasing group. In effect, the traders were financing bonuses by bribing their fellow traders, and all of them were ripping off the company's shareholders.

But there were two other major sets of players who were essential to the scam—the rating agencies and the insurers.

The Rating Agencies

THE BUSINESS OF rating debt securities was and remains an oligopoly, a quasi-cartel, of three firms—Moody's (the largest); Standard & Poor's (S&P); and Fitch. For many years, they used their power to establish remarkable legal positions for themselves. The SEC recognized a limited number of Nationally Recognized Statistical Ratings Organizations, and many government pension funds could only invest in securities that had high NRSRO ratings. The rating agencies avoided legal liability for their numerous misjudgments by claiming that ratings were merely "opinions," expressions of free speech protected by the First Amendment, and not subject to liability claims. When state legislatures occasionally threatened to reduce their power or increase their liability, the rating agencies threatened to stop rating bonds issued in those states.

For the last quarter century, the rating agencies have been paid by issuers, and as the investment banking industry itself consolidated, the banks increasingly called the tune, and the rating agencies happily danced, all of them joined in corruption, cynicism, and exploitation. For the entire period of the bubble, and through 2007 as the bubble peaked and started to deflate, Wall Street had pretended to ignore the impending crash. The rating agencies carried on issuing their triple-As with abandon.[30]

At both Moody's and S&P, the volume of ratings processed on residential mortgage-backed securities (RMBS) doubled between 2004 and 2007. Mortgage-backed CDO ratings increased tenfold, and each year the instruments grew far more complex. There was a similar boom in other bubble-related debt—instruments such as collateralized loan obligations (CLOs), auction-rate securities, synthetic securities, and even more exotic objects, all of them routinely receiving extremely high ratings. The rating agencies became insanely profitable as a result. The relative stock price gains for Moody's outstripped even those of the best-performing financial services company, Goldman Sachs, by a factor of ten; during the bubble, Moody's was the most profitable company in the Fortune 500.

In the first week of July 2007, S&P rated 1,500 new mortgage-backed securities, or 300 per working day. It was an assembly line. In 2010 the former president of Clayton Holdings testified to the FCIC that in 2007 he had approached all three major rating agencies, asking if they wanted the results of Clayton's reviews of the loans being used by the securitizers. All three declined.

By 2009 more than 90 percent of all 2006- and 2007-vintage AAA subprime-backed securities were rated as "junk."

Even more striking, however, was how the rating agencies treated the investment banks—their principal clients. Did they warn the world when Bear Stearns and Lehman became wildly overleveraged, when the industry shifted to unstable, ultra-short-term borrowing? No. Did they worry about the exposure of AIG and the other bond insurers? No. Even as the crisis deepened, all of the securitizers and insurers, including all of those who failed or were rescued by the federal government, continued to have high-investment-grade ratings—in several cases, AAA.

Here is an excerpt from my interview with Jerry Fons, a former managing director at Moody's who departed in 2007:

CF: And if I recall correctly, Bear Stearns was rated AAA, like, a month before it went bankrupt.

FONS: More likely A2.

CF: A2. Okay. A2 is still not bankrupt.

FONS: No, no, no, that's a high investment grade, solid investment-grade rating.

CF: Tell us about that.

FONS: Not only Bear Stearns. You also had Lehman Brothers A2 within days of failing. AIG, AA within days of being bailed out. Fannie Mae and Freddie Mac were AAA when they were rescued. Citigroup, Merrill. All of them had investment-grade ratings. Even WaMu, the bank that went under, wound up having a BBB- or AA3 rating at the time it was rescued.

CF: How can that be?

FONS: Well, that's a good question. [laughter] That's a great question.

"Protection" and Financial Weapons of Mass Destruction

ONE LAST PART of the system deserves comment: the protection racket, which in this context means selling insurance on mortgage-backed securities, making investors feel even more confident that they were safe. This insurance came in two forms, bad and worse.

The less malignant form was literal insurance, sold by specialized monoline insurance companies, the largest of which were MBIA and Ambac. They depended heavily on their own AAA ratings, helpfully supplied as usual by the rating agencies. As everywhere, their salespeople and executives made lots of money during the bubble, which they kept even after securities started to fail and the companies faced an avalanche of claims; both companies suffered disastrously. But at least they had previously been known principally for writing actual insurance, purchased by the actual owners of actual bonds. For true insanity, one needs to look at the business of selling derivatives called credit default swaps (CDSs), the most famous practitioner of which was, of course, AIG.

Credit default swaps are pure gambling, and they differ from insurance in extremely important ways. You can use CDSs to bet that any security will fail, and you can make your bets as large as you want. The reverse is true as well: if you're crazy enough, you can *sell* as much "protection" as you want, far beyond the real value of the securities in question. AIG sold around $500 billion of it—and it didn't work out too well.

CDSs were (and remain) particularly dangerous for several reasons. First, courtesy of the Commodity Futures Modernization Act of 2000, the law championed by Larry Summers, Robert Rubin, and Alan Greenspan, CDSs were totally unregulated and extremely opaque. *Nobody* knew the total size and distribution of CDS ownership or risk, and the government did not have the legal right to control it. Second, CDSs generated dangerous incentives—if you owned enough of them, then you had powerful incentives to *cause* something to fail, and also to remain silent about risks in the financial system.

CDSs also provided the illusion, and sometimes the reality, of total protection against even the riskiest, most dangerous financial behavior. Real insurance policies guard against irresponsibility and fraud by having deductibles, policy limits, higher premiums for people with bad records, and other constraints. You cannot buy an insurance policy on your house for twenty times its real value, especially if your house has conveniently burned down five times in the last decade. You also cannot buy a home insurance policy if you don't own a home. If you have five convictions for drunk driving, you may not be able to buy automobile insurance at all, and if you can, it will be very expensive.

Unlike real insurance, CDSs had no deductibles or policy limits, and placed no constraints on buyers. As long as you had the money, you could buy as many of them as you wanted, even on securities that you did not own—in other words, you could bet that a security, and/or the company issuing it, would fail. If you were the creator and issuer of such securities, you could therefore profit by creating and selling junk, and then betting against it.

You could also *buy* junk, and ignore its risks, as long as you could buy CDS protection on it. One major additional reason that Wall Street was able to sell so many toxic mortgage securities was that they could point to CDS sellers, especially AIG, and say: Look, this stuff is great. But if you're worried about it, no problem; all you need to do is walk over to those great folks at AIG, pay them a small fraction of your annual returns, and you'll be totally protected.

Moreover, the total amount of risk created in the market was potentially limitless. Consider real insurance again. In the event of a disaster—an earthquake, a hurricane, or a tornado—the total liability of a real insurance company is limited to the actual damage caused by the disaster. But in the case of CDSs, as long as someone was willing to sell them, there was no limit to the size of the liabilities and risks that could be created.

Of course, selling gigantic amounts of such "insurance" on risky, even fraudulent, securities would be unwise. But AIG did it, for three reasons. The first was the complexity and opacity of the market, even—a cynical person might say *especially*—to AIG senior management. The second reason was that AIG's senior management and board of directors were out to lunch. I invite readers to compare AIG's investor presentations from the late bubble era—late 2007 and early 2008 especially—to the post-crisis congressional testimony of AIG's ex-CEO Martin Sullivan. The investor presentations are absurdly optimistic and misleading, but they are also incredibly complex, whereas Mr. Sullivan appears to be rather...simple. He was the handpicked successor to Maurice (Hank) Greenberg, who chose him as a pliable fellow when Greenberg was forced out as CEO by Eliot Spitzer's fraud investigations in 2005. AIG's board, which had also been largely handpicked by Greenberg, was as pliable and clueless as Mr. Sullivan.

But the third reason is that AIG used the same toxic bonus system that destroyed everyone else. The company's CDS business was insanely profitable—until it wasn't—with profit margins of over 80 percent in its "best" years. It was run by a highly autonomous 375-person London-based unit, AIG Financial Products (AIGFP), which was the personal fiefdom of a man named Joseph Cassano. AIGFP kept 30 percent of each year's profits as cash bonuses, passing the rest to the parent company. During the bubble, AIGFP paid itself over $3.5 billion in cash bonuses (Cassano personally made over $200 million) and handed $8 billion to AIG, by 2005 accounting for 17 percent of AIG's total corporate profits.

In 2007, when the bubble started to deflate, the CDS buyers started to come knocking, demanding their money. Cassano resisted, while publicly telling investors in late 2007 that he could not see AIG losing "even one dollar" on the CDSs. Cassano blocked both external and internal auditors from reviewing AIGFP's books. In 2007 AIGFP's vice president for accounting policy, Joseph St. Denis, grew concerned about the CDSs and how they were being valued. Cassano angrily and obscenely denied him access to the information, telling St. Denis that he would "pollute the process." St. Denis eventually resigned in protest, telling AIG's chief auditor in late 2007 that he could not support AIGFP's CDS accounting. Cassano stayed in place until AIG collapsed in September 2008. In response to public pressure, AIG terminated him, but then immediately rehired him as a consultant at the rate of $1 million per month, until that arrangement too was ended after being publicized in congressional hearings.

As of this writing (early 2012), credit default swaps have resurfaced as a factor in the sovereign debt crisis of Europe, and the potential spread of that crisis throughout the United States and European banking sector. Some people never learn....

Financial Culture and Corporate Governance During the Bubble

HAVING CONSIDERED THE investment banking industry's behavior, let us return to the question of how and why CEOs and boards of directors could have tolerated this, and in particular why they could have allowed it to destroy their own companies. In part, the same financial incentives operated for them, and made them indifferent to the fate of their firms, employees, and customers. In some other cases, however, destroying their firms was clearly contrary to their self-interest, at least to some extent. Why did they let it happen? For there is no question that to some extent, the senior management of some of the banks did indeed behave irrationally.

Here, we must leave pure economics and ponder the toxic effects of too much wealth, too much power, the new culture of American investment banking, and a life conducted within the cocoon of America's new oligarchy. Let us consider, for example, Jimmy Cayne. For those who might find what follows just slightly difficult to believe, I invite you to Google a phrase along the lines of "Jimmy Cayne helicopter Plaza Hotel bridge golf megalomaniac marijuana."

Jimmy Cayne became CEO of Bear Stearns in 1993, and assumed the additional role of chairman in 2001, remaining in both positions until he was finally forced out as CEO in January 2008, by which point it was too late to save the company.

Mr. Cayne, who appears to have been very widely disliked, was not someone you were likely to feel comfortable telling that he was destroying his firm and the world economy. Former employees have told me a variety of stories. He would convene early morning meetings in the office, order a nice hot breakfast from a waiter, and consume it during the meeting, offering nothing to his subordinates, who waited for him to finish. He would invite someone into his office, make a show of taking out two cigars, light one up, and then put the other one in his pocket. He insulted subordinates in public, using extreme profanity. His predecessor as CEO of Bear Stearns, Ace Greenberg, described him as "a dope-smoking megalomaniac."

But that's his good side. As Bear Stearns's profits and stock price soared as a result of the bubble, Mr. Cayne became a billionaire, and he went from being merely obnoxious to being seriously disconnected. He routinely took three- and four-day weekends, as well as extended vacations. For his long weekends, he frequently commuted from Bear Stearns headquarters by helicopter to his New Jersey golf club, where he had permission to land his helicopter on the grounds, and where he kept a house. At Bear Stearns, he reserved an elevator for his sole use. A serious bridge player, he paid two Italian professionals $500,000 per year to play with him. He traveled to many bridge tournaments and also spent a great deal of time playing bridge on his computer. Despite being a staunch Republican, he also smoked a lot of marijuana, with bridge partners, fellow hotel guests, and others frequently seeing and smelling it.

When the bubble started to implode in 2007 and Bear Stearns started to come under pressure, Mr. Cayne was frequently AWOL at critical times. Even on weekdays, and even when his company was collapsing in 2007 and 2008, he never carried a phone or pager when he was playing golf or bridge. He traveled repeatedly to bridge tournaments during this period, sometimes remaining away from the office a week or more. He would not participate in conference calls or meetings if they conflicted with his bridge schedule.

Bear Stearns's troubles started for real in mid-2007, with the collapse of two of its investment funds that had been heavily concentrated in real estate. On Thursday, June 14, 2007, when Bear Stearns publicly reported its first worrisome financial results, Cayne was playing golf in

New Jersey; he played the following day as well. One month later, on July 17, 2007, Bear Stearns told investors that the two real estate investment funds were now worthless. The next day, July 18, Mr. Cayne flew to Nashville for a bridge tournament, joined by Bear Stearns's head of fixed-income products, Allen Spector, and stayed there for most of the following ten days, playing bridge. Mr. Cayne was in the office for only eleven days that month. Even when he participated in conference calls, he would sometimes drop off without warning.

This did not seem to disturb the board of directors. Indeed, the impetus for Cayne's removal as CEO seems not to have been his performance, but the increasing publicity, particularly a *Wall Street Journal* article in November 2007 that described his golf and marijuana habits, and his being unreachable while indulging them. Even after being forced out as CEO in January 2008, Cayne remained chairman of the board. In early March 2008, about a week before his firm collapsed and was sold to JPMorgan Chase, Mr. Cayne closed on his purchase of two adjoining apartments in the Plaza Hotel for $24 million. On March 13, when Bear Stearns entered its final death spiral, he was in Detroit, playing bridge again; he joined the board's conference call late so that he could finish his game first.

On May 10, two months after his firm's collapse, Mr. Cayne attended a party held at the Plaza for new residents. The party included caviar and cognac bars, as well as a buffet that replicated paintings from a Metropolitan Museum exhibit, "The Age of Rembrandt."

Mr. Cayne did suffer, of course. He lost his job; but when Bear Stearns collapsed he was seventy-four years old, near retirement age anyway, and it seems likely that in his head, he had already been retired for quite some time. The value of his Bear Stearns stock declined from about $1 billion at its peak to a mere $65 million when JPMorgan Chase bought it. But Mr. Cayne had thoughtfully taken out lots of cash over the previous years, so his estimated net worth remains about $600 million, probably sufficient to support his golf, bridge, helicopter, and marijuana habits. He still lives at the Plaza (at least when he's in

Manhattan—he has several other homes, including the one next to his golf club).

Certainly extreme, I hear you say, but could such behavior possibly be common, much less representative?

Well, yes, actually.

So, yes, it is true that some of the destruction caused by the bubble and crisis cannot be attributed entirely to rational self-interest and fraud. But that doesn't mean that the rest was caused by innocent, well-intentioned error. Rather, it was symptomatic of a culture, and a governance system, that was seriously out of control.

During the bubble, many Wall Street executives constructed surreal little universes around themselves. The essential components of these worlds were physical isolation via private environments off-limits to their employees (limousines, elevators, planes, helicopters, restaurants), sycophantic employees and servants both at work and at home, and a compliant, clueless board of directors. Often their worlds also included trophy wives, mistresses, prostitutes, and/or drugs. Leisure activities were divided generationally. Young traders and salesmen focused on nightclubs, strip clubs, parties, gambling, cocaine, and escorts; New York investment bankers certainly spend over $1 billion a year in nightclubs and strip clubs, much of it charged to their firms as reimbursable, and tax-deductible, business entertainment. The older generation of senior executives, most of them married, tend to favor golf, bridge, expensive restaurants, charity events, art auctions, country clubs, and Hamptons estates.

Jimmy Cayne wasn't the only one with a private elevator and a taste for helicopter commuting; in fact he was comparatively reasonable. After complaints, he eventually agreed to reserve the elevator for his private use only between 8 a.m. and 9 a.m. every day. Richard Fuld, Lehman's CEO, had a different system. Whenever Fuld's limousine approached Lehman headquarters, his chauffeur would call in; a specially programmed elevator would descend to the garage, held there by a guard until he arrived. Then the elevator took Fuld straight to the thirty-first floor, with no stops, so he didn't have to see any of his employees. Here's how a former Lehman employee described it (part of this is in my film):

> This man never appeared on the trading floor. We never saw him. There was a joke on the trading desk. The H. G. Wells series, the *Invisible Man*...Now, a lot of CFOs are disconnected on the Street, but he had his own private elevator. He went out of his way to be disconnected.

Stan O'Neal at Merrill Lynch had a private elevator too—namely, any elevator that happened to be around when he arrived. A security guard would hold the next elevator that appeared, preventing anyone else from entering and, if necessary, ordering others already in the elevator to leave.

Lehman and most of the other banks also had corporate art collections, which sometimes absorbed considerable executive energy. All of the banks maintained chefs for their elegant private dining rooms, usually several of them, with access strictly controlled for executives and guests of differing levels of seniority and wealth. I've eaten in a few of them (Morgan Stanley, JPMorgan Chase); they're *very* nice.

Everyone had limousines and drivers, of course, but there were serious toys, too. When Lehman went bankrupt, it owned a helicopter and six corporate jets. Two of the jets were 767s, which normally seat over 150 people when used by airlines, and cost more than $150 million when purchased new. In addition, however, Joe Gregory, Lehman's president (the number two position under Fuld, the CEO), had *his own* personal helicopter, in which he commuted daily to Lehman from his mansion in the Hamptons. (In bad weather, he sometimes used a seaplane.) Gregory had a household staff of twenty-nine people. Citigroup owned two jets, and tried to take delivery on a new $50 million plane *after* it had collapsed and been rescued by the federal government.

Okay, so they had toys. But what were their financial incentives, how did their boards of directors compensate them, examine their conduct, reward and discipline them? Were others as bad as Bear Stearns and Jimmy Cayne?

Yes, they were. Professor Lucian Bebchuk of Harvard Law School examined the conduct of the most senior executives of Bear Stearns and Lehman Brothers in the years prior to their collapse. In both cases the top five employees had collectively taken out over $1 billion in cash (that is, a billion from *each firm*) in the several years immediately preceding the collapse. This does not suggest that these men (and all ten were men) had unlimited faith in the future of their firms, nor powerful incentives to avoid risk.

Or consider Stan O'Neal. He had been CEO of Merrill Lynch for four years by the end of 2006, and had pushed Merrill aggressively into subprime securities. In 2006 O'Neal's *take-home* compensation was just over $36 million, of which $19 million was in cash. But this was not his *total* compensation. To avoid taxes, much of his compensation was deferred, to be paid upon retirement.

In 2006 Merrill Lynch had revenues of $33.8 billion and pretax earnings of $9.8 billion. In January 2007 Merrill paid its annual bonuses—just under $6 billion, of which one-third went to people involved in mortgage securities. Dow Kim, the head of Merrill's fixed-income unit and therefore in charge of subprime securitizations, received $35 million. As late as the second quarter of 2007, ending June 30, Merrill Lynch was still profitable, reporting earnings of $2.1 billion. But as with Bear Stearns, in the middle of 2007 the bubble started to deflate. In the very next quarter, the third quarter of 2007, Merrill reported a net loss of $2.6 billion caused by over $8 billion in losses on subprime loans and securities. Then the company went off a cliff. For the full year 2007, Merrill's revenues declined by 67 percent and it lost $8.6 billion. It would subsequently lose much, much more, nearly all of it stemming from decisions made while O'Neal was CEO. So what was Stan O'Neal doing during the third quarter of 2007, when Merrill Lynch was falling apart?

He was playing a lot of golf. In the last six weeks of the third quarter, O'Neal played twenty rounds of golf, sometimes with his cell phone switched off. Usually he played on weekends, but not always. Shortly afterward, as Merrill's condition drastically worsened, O'Neal made unauthorized overtures to other banks regarding a potential merger. This, finally, led Merrill Lynch's board of directors to fire him.

Except they *didn't* fire him. They allowed him to resign, thereby enabling him to collect an additional $161 million, representing deferred compensation and severance—$30 million in cash, $131 million in stock. Nor has Mr. O'Neal been banished from the business world; after leaving Merrill, he was invited to join the board of directors of Alcoa, on which he now sits. In fact, he also sits on two committees of Alcoa's board. Which ones? Audit and governance. Rewards for a job well done.

Finally, consider Robert Rubin. As treasury secretary, Mr. Rubin oversaw the elimination of the Glass-Steagall separation between investment banking and consumer banking. This change greatly benefited Citigroup; and shortly after leaving the Treasury, Mr. Rubin became Citigroup's vice chairman. At Citigroup, Rubin displayed disconnection from both reality and ethical standards. In 2001, acting on Citigroup's behalf, he had called his former colleague Peter Fisher at the Treasury Department, asking Fisher for help in preventing Enron's credit rating from being downgraded, very shortly before Enron went bankrupt. (Citigroup was a major Enron creditor, and was later fined for helping Enron conceal its losses.)

During the bubble, Rubin pressed Citigroup to take on more risk, even after being warned of the increasing dangers and dishonesty of housing loans and mortgage-backed securities. He does not seem even to have been aware of his company's financial structure and obligations. In his testimony before the FCIC, Rubin said that it was only post-crash that he learned about "liquidity puts," the contract provisions by which Citigroup was obligated to repurchase CDOs if they lost money or couldn't be sold. These agreements with the structured investment vehicles (that Citigroup itself had created) added over $1 trillion to Citigroup's real balance sheet, and caused billions of dollars in losses during the crisis. It's too bad that Rubin didn't read the footnotes in his own company's financial statements, for he might have noticed the puts and raised an alarm.[31]

After a decade at Citigroup, during which he was paid over $120 million, Rubin resigned under pressure in January 2009. But this does not seem to have interfered with him much. He remains cochairman of the Council on Foreign Relations; is still a member of the Harvard Corporation, the small group that is effectively Harvard's board of directors; and both he and his son were active in the Obama transition team, helping to select a *new* batch of unethical policymakers. (Who turned out mostly to be the *old* batch, recycled; but we'll get to that later.)

Unquestionably, none of these men made a deliberate decision to destroy their firms. But, equally unquestionably, personal incentives and personal risk focus the mind in a way that golf and bridge generally don't. These people had way too much money *outside* of their companies to care as much as they should have about what was going on *inside* them. But the psychological atmospherics were just as important as the direct incentives. They became corporate royalty, with all the absurd arrogance, disconnection from reality, ego poisoning, and cults of personality thereby implied.

However, there were others—most famously, Goldman Sachs—who didn't allow the temptations of helicopter golf to cloud their thinking. These very disciplined and predatory people therefore made money not only from the bubble, but also from the *collapse*. We will now consider them, and the implications of their behavior for financial stability, in looking at the warnings, the end of the bubble, the crisis, its impact, and government responses to it. It is not a pretty, or reassuring, picture.

CHAPTER 5

ALL FALL DOWN:
WARNINGS, PREDATORS,
CRISES, RESPONSES

SOME NOTICED THE BUBBLE quite early. In 2002 a prominent hedge fund manager, William Ackman, discovered that one of the largest bond insurers, MBIA, was actually a house of cards. It had a AAA credit rating (naturally), but was leveraged at over eighty to one, had started to write insurance on risky mortgages, and used questionable accounting methods. Ackman bought CDSs on MBIA, later adding bets against the other major bond insurer, Ambac, as well. Ackman then started an aggressive public campaign to discredit MBIA via meetings with the rating agencies, the media, and the SEC. The rating agencies ignored him, of course. The SEC then spoke with MBIA, which responded that Ackman was spreading false rumors. In fact, MBIA persuaded the SEC to investigate *Ackman,* who, in the end, turned out to be completely right. (After several years losing money while waiting for the bubble to burst, Ackman finally made serious money from his bet.)

In 2004 Robert Gnaizda, a housing and financial policy analyst who ran the Greenlining Institute, a housing NGO, began warning Alan

Greenspan personally. Gnaizda, who met with Greenspan and the Federal Reserve Board once or twice a year, had noticed the proliferation of toxic, highly deceptive mortgages. He provided examples, and urged Greenspan to finally use his power under the HOEPA legislation to rein in mortgage lending. Greenspan wasn't interested.

But the first truly serious, public warning of systemic danger came in 2005, at the Jackson Hole conference of the Federal Reserve, where the world's most prominent central bankers and economists gather annually. The 2005 conference was Alan Greenspan's last one as chairman of the Federal Reserve, and everyone was supposed to admire and celebrate his brilliant record. But Raghuram Rajan, then the chief economist of the International Monetary Fund, rained on the parade by delivering a brilliant, prescient, scary paper.[1] The audience included Alan Greenspan, Ben Bernanke, Tim Geithner, Larry Summers, and most of the Federal Reserve Board.

Rajan's paper was titled "Has Financial Development Made the World Riskier?" And his answer was yes. After some introductory comments, Rajan said: "My main concern has to do with incentives." Rajan discussed the new compensation structures that dominated the financial system, making risk taking so deliciously profitable: "These developments may create more financial-sector-induced procyclicality than the past. They also may create a greater (albeit still small) probability of a catastrophic meltdown" (page 6).

On page 25, he describes a scenario nearly identical to the destruction of AIG by Joseph Cassano's unit: "A number of insurance companies and pension funds have entered the credit derivatives market to sell guarantees against a company defaulting.... These strategies have the appearance of producing very high alphas (high returns for low risk), so managers have an incentive to load up on them. Every once in a while, however, they will blow up. Since true performance can be estimated only over a long period, far exceeding the horizon set by the average manager's incentives, managers will take these risks if they can."

And then, on page 31: "Because they [banks] typically can sell much of the risk off their balance sheets, they have an incentive to originate the assets that are in high demand and, thus, feed the frenzy. If it is housing, banks have an incentive to provide whatever mortgages are demanded, even if they are risky 'interest-only' mortgages. In the midst of a frenzy, banks are unlikely to maintain much spare risk-bearing capacity."

Three pages later: "Linkages between markets, and between markets and institutions, are now more pronounced. While this helps the system diversify across small shocks, it also exposes the system to large systemic shocks."

Starting on page 44, Rajan discusses how to curtail the dangers posed by the new system: "Perhaps the focus should shift to ensuring investment managers have the right incentives"…"Industry groups could urge all managers to vest some fixed portion of their pay…in the funds they manage"…"In order that incentives be to invest for the long term, the norm could be that the manager's holdings in the fund would be retained for several years."

When Rajan finished delivering his paper, Greenspan and most of the audience reacted with sullen, defensive silence. But not so Larry Summers. At the time, Summers was president of Harvard, while also consulting to a hedge fund, Taconic Capital Advisors. One year later, after being forced to resign, he became a consultant to D. E. Shaw, a $30 billion hedge fund, which, in 2008, paid Summers $5.2 million for one day per week of work. Both hedge funds used precisely the incentives that Rajan was warning about in his paper—managers kept 20 percent of annual profits but had no liability for losses.

With his trademark casual arrogance, Summers stood up to put Rajan in his place. If you want to read all of his response, it's on the website of the Kansas City Federal Reserve Bank. Some quotes from Summers's remarks:

"I speak as…someone who has learned a great deal about the subject…from Alan Greenspan, and someone who finds the basic, slightly Luddite premise of this paper to be largely misguided.

"We all would say almost certainly that something…overwhelmingly positive has taken place through this process [of financial innovation].

"While I think the paper is right to warn us of the possibility of positive feedback and the dangers that it can bring about in financial markets, the tendency toward restriction that runs through the tone of the presentation seems to me to be quite problematic. It seems to me to support a wide variety of misguided policy impulses in many countries."

But serious Wall Street insiders already understood what Summers didn't. When did they know there was a really serious bubble, and that they could game it? Many of the smart ones knew it by about 2004, when, for example, Howie Hubler at Morgan Stanley first started to bet against the worst subprime mortgage securities with the knowledge and approval of his management. But you can only make money betting *against* a bubble as it unravels. As long as there was room for the bubble to grow, Wall Street's overwhelming incentive was to keep it going. But when they saw that the bubble was ending, their incentives changed. And we therefore know that many on Wall Street realized there was a huge bubble by late 2006, because that's when they started massively betting on its collapse.

Here, I must briefly mention a problem with Michael Lewis's generally superb financial journalism. In his highly entertaining and in many ways informative book *The Big Short*, Lewis leaves the impression that Wall Street was blindly running itself off a cliff, whereas a few wild and crazy, off-the-beaten-track, adorably weird loners figured out how to short the mortgage market and beat the system. With all due respect to Mr. Lewis, it didn't happen like that. The Big Short was seriously big business, and much of Wall Street was ruthlessly good at it.

To begin with, a number of big hedge funds figured it out. Unlike investment banks, however, they couldn't make serious money by securitizing loans and selling CDOs, so they had to wait until the bubble was about to burst and make their money from the collapse. And this they did. In addition to Bill Ackman, already mentioned, other major hedge funds including Magnetar, Tricadia, Harbinger Capital, George Soros, and John Paulson made billions of dollars each by betting against mortgage securities as the bubble ended. It appears that just those five hedge funds made well over $25 billion, and possibly over $50 billion, shorting the mortgage bubble, and all of them worked closely with Wall Street in order to do so. In fact, as we shall soon see, their bets against the bubble were extremely helpful in allowing Wall Street to *perpetuate* the bubble.

And as we've just seen, many people on Wall Street had huge financial incentives to keep creating and selling junk until the very end, even if it meant knowingly destroying their employers. Without question, thousands of Wall Street loan buyers, securitizers, traders, salespeople, and executives knew perfectly well that it would end in tears, but they were making a fortune while it lasted, with no individual ability to stop the bubble and very little to lose when it ended.

In fairness to Mr. Lewis, it *is* true that in several major cases—most notably Citigroup, Merrill Lynch, Lehman, and Bear Stearns—senior management was indeed disconnected and clueless, allowed their employees to take advantage too long, and therefore destroyed their own firms. Unquestionably, the general atmosphere of adrenaline, testosterone, and money also played a role, infecting many in the banks who should have known better. But even within these firms, there were groups that started dumping bad assets on unsuspecting customers and profiting by betting against their own securities. In 2011 the SEC tried to settle a case against Citigroup in which senior CDO traders profited by holding the "short side" of bad securities. A federal judge rejected the SEC's proposed settlement on the grounds that it was too lenient.[2]

Moreover, cluelessness was most definitely *not* an issue with the senior managements of Goldman Sachs, JPMorgan Chase, and Morgan Stanley. As we saw, Morgan Stanley started betting against the bubble as early as 2004 but made a tactical error in doing so, one that cost them $9 billion. The fact that they underestimated the scale of the collapse does not excuse them, nor does it mean that they didn't realize there was a bubble. They realized it very clearly, and ruthlessly tried to exploit it.

Conversely, JPMorgan Chase just stayed away; they sold some toxic stuff, but mostly just remained prudently above the junk mortgage fray. JPMorgan Chase's senior management sometimes countenanced extremely unethical, even illegal behavior, but they weren't stupid or complacent, and they kept their employees firmly under control. It probably also helped that Jamie Dimon only became CEO of JPMorgan Chase in 2005, and that he had just come from a troubled bank in Chicago that he had needed to rescue.

But it was also clear that Dimon was paying attention. In May 2007 Bill Ackman, the hedge fund manager who was shorting MBIA, delivered a presentation to an investment conference, bluntly entitled "Who's Holding the Bag?" It dissected the bubble and its imminent collapse with devastating thoroughness. I have read it; the presentation was sixty-three pages long and left absolutely nothing to the imagination. It ranged from high-level questions of corporate governance and incentive structures to the conflicts of interest at the rating agencies, to the very fine-grained details of how many hundreds of billions of dollars of adjustable-rate mortgages would reset at higher interest rates in the coming year, with an inevitable wave of defaults to follow. Ackman's presentation was widely circulated among the investment banks. A few months afterward, Ackman encountered Jamie Dimon at the U.S. Open tennis tournament. Ackman said to Dimon, "You should read my presentation," to which Dimon replied, "I already have."

Goldman Sachs, though, was in a class by itself. They made billions of dollars by betting against the very same stuff that they had been making billions selling only a year or two before, profiting from the foolishness of AIG, Morgan Stanley, and, allegedly, Lehman Brothers. We consider them next; but first, a brief digression.

The coming end of the bubble produced one final, wonderfully poisonous financial innovation, whose invention and widening use proves that many people on Wall Street knew *exactly* what was going on.

Creating Something Special
Just for the Innocents and Fools

BY LATE 2005 and certainly by 2006, even the most fraudulent sub-prime mortgages were becoming harder to find. Borrowers had all the financing they could take, and even the most crooked mortgage broker would soon have been reduced to making loans to dead people, pets, and aliens. But there were still so many naively greedy investors out there who were willing to *buy* toxic securities. What to do? Wall Street came up with something brilliant. Once again, derivatives came to the rescue. The bankers' insight was to realize that many investment managers in the world were so innocent, avaricious, and/or foolish that they would buy mortgage securities even when they knew that their interest payments came not from real mortgages, but rather from smart people betting that their securities would collapse.

Enter a new product, the synthetic CDO. (We encountered it earlier, briefly, as the way Morgan Stanley ripped off the pension fund of the Virgin Islands.) Synthetic CDOs permitted banks to generate hundreds of billions in new high-risk paper, out of thin air, when they could no longer find subprime mortgages to buy. All it took was a computer, a flair for math, and complete amorality.

Instead of going to all the trouble of defrauding borrowers, you simply used existing mortgage-backed securities as a reference or index. You then created a two-sided wager. On one side, an investor purchased the "long side" of the synthetic CDO, receiving payments that mimicked the performance of some "real" CDO (or an index of CDO prices). But the payments to the investor didn't come from real mortgages; rather, they came from the opposite side of the bet—someone willing to pay an interest rate, often a surprisingly low rate, in return for the right to collect money *if the referenced securities failed*. So a synthetic CDO basically turned an "investor" into a seller of CDS insurance, on whatever stuff had been used as the reference or index. The investors' "interest payments" were actually the bets being placed by the other side on the reference securities' failure.

What is interesting—and very dangerous—about this is that even as the *housing* bubble ended and the flow of real mortgages dried up, the investment banks were able to prolong the *financial* bubble (and worsen the eventual crisis) by selling synthetic CDOs. They used them to bet against the very securities they had created and sold, as Morgan Stanley did with Libertas and Goldman Sachs did repeatedly; to bet against the market generally; and to collect transaction fees by matching fools with sharks (e.g., hedge funds), structuring and selling both sides of the deal. Since synthetic CDOs can exist only if someone is willing to bet against the "long side," their sharp rise was a clear indication that Wall Street knew not only that there was a bubble, but also that its end was imminent. It was no coincidence that synthetics grew strongly after home price increases leveled out in 2006.

And this was most emphatically *not* a small business catering to a few adorably cranky contrarian individuals. A reasonable estimate is that by the end of 2006, the volume of synthetic, or primarily synthetic, CDOs was approaching $100 billion, while about a quarter of the assets in "conventional" CDOs were also synthetic. By the first half of 2007, just before the market collapsed, synthetic CDOs were almost certainly the majority of the total CDO market.

And nobody knew more about this business than Goldman Sachs, John Paulson, Magnetar, and Tricadia.

Goldman Sachs, the *Really* Big Short, Gaming the Crisis, Lying to Congress

THE NINE-HUNDRED-PLUS PAGES of documents and e-mails gathered by the Senate Permanent Subcommittee on Investigations, supplemented by the Levin hearings of April 2010 and other records, lay out a remarkable narrative of how Goldman Sachs profited from the collapse. Two conclusions dominate.

The first is that Goldman's management was tough and competent. In contrast to Jimmy Cayne, Stan O'Neal, and Chuck Prince (CEO of Citigroup), who had no clue or apparent concern about what their traders were doing, Goldman's executives closely monitored and understood both the wider market and their own position. Helicopter golf and bridge tournaments did not take precedence. They called the end of the bubble accurately, shifted their strategy to betting against it, and implemented their decision with great discipline, speed, and foresight.

The second clear lesson, from the way they dumped their "shitty" assets, gamed the industry, failed to warn regulators of impending crisis, and later lied about their behavior, is that they could be utterly cold-blooded bastards and often strayed well over the line into what, to a layman at least, looks a lot like fraud and perjury. We'll look first at their trading and asset-shedding strategies in 2006–2007, then their brilliant, ruthless manipulation of the industry in 2007–2008, and finally, their not-so-honest Senate testimony in 2010.

E-mail records reveal Goldman's strategic shift. The first step was a full-scale "drilldown" on the company's entire mortgage portfolio, conducted in mid-December 2006. The working group produced a listing of all its mortgage positions and hedges, and a position-by-position list of loss exposures that added up to $807 million in potential losses.

David Viniar, the Goldman CFO, sat down with the entire mortgage team on December 14 and decided on an approach. The objective was to "reduce exposure…distribute [sell] as much as possible on bonds created from new loan securitizations and clean previous positions."

Just four days later, Fabrice Tourre, a thirty-one-year-old senior account manager based in London, made a special inquiry about buying some selected bonds because he was aware that *"we have a big short on"* [italics mine].[3] Goldman reduced its bids on new loans, loaded up on mortgage index shorts, and bought credit default protection on individual bonds. To avoid revealing its strategy, Goldman continued to be active in buy-side markets but deliberately lowered its bids in order to win as few auctions as possible.

Almost immediately afterward, the mortgage market started deteriorating badly. A medium-sized subprime lender, Ownit, filed for bankruptcy in late December, and two big originators admitted to major problems in the first week of February 2007. HSBC announced large subprime losses, while New Century, one of the most important subprime originators, announced it would restate its 2006 earnings—what had appeared to be large profits became substantial losses. New Century's stock went off a cliff, and it filed for bankruptcy soon afterward. The spread, or risk premium, on a widely used subprime mortgage index jumped from 3 percent to 15 percent.

By that time, however, Dan Sparks, the head mortgage trader, could advise his bosses that his "trading position has basically squared"— in other words, the $807 million exposure was almost gone, although "credit issues are worsening on deals and pain is broad (including investors in certain GS-issued deals)." He also advised his management that his group's estimates of the real value of Goldman's holdings was dropping even faster than market prices.

The main reason for this is that most of the other investment banks didn't react the same way; virtually all of them kept their marks (i.e., valuations) much higher than Goldman's, which made Goldman's market exit all the easier.[4] This difference between the behavior of Goldman Sachs and the other banks was the combined result of three forces we have discussed previously. The first was that many traders were gaming the system, keeping the bubble going as long as they could for their own personal benefit. The second was the compartmentalization of information. And the third force, of course, was the obliviousness of the senior management of some of the large banks, which allowed their employees to keep going too long.

Sparks continued his shorting and said that his group had continued to make aggressive markdowns, which were "good for us position-wise, bad for accounts who wrote that [CDS] protection."[5] It appears that Goldman had bought all the CDS protection it could while protection was still cheap, and *then,* as soon as it had protected itself, wrote the securities down and demanded payment from its protection suppliers. (We will see this again, on steroids, when we come to AIG.) A week later, with the market collapsing, Sparks ordered the team to "monetize" their positions. This meant that they locked in a limited but guaranteed profit, which they could start booking immediately for that year's earnings, rather than waiting until their protection contracts ended. "This is the time to just do it, show respect for risk, and show the ability to listen and execute firm directives. . . . You guys are doing very well."[6]

Sparks told his bosses, "We are net short,"[7] but that he was still worried. He needn't have been. Mortgage trading had a record first quarter in 2007, booking $266 million in revenues, at the same time that it accomplished major position reductions. The overall mortgage inventory was down from $11 billion to $7 billion, with the subprime component down by a net $4.8 billion. From that point onward, Goldman was safe—unless the whole financial system melted down, a contingency for which, we shall see, they started to prepare. In late July 2007, after two Bear Stearns mortgage hedge funds had blown up, Goldman Sachs's copresident Gary Cohn commented to David Viniar, Goldman's CFO, on the sudden carnage. Viniar replied, "Tells you what might be happening to people who don't have the big short."[8]

Although Goldman made large profits on its mortgage shorts, it could have made much more. But top management—Viniar, Cohn, and Lloyd Blankfein, the CEO—decided against truly massive short bets. They loved beating their competitors, but they wanted to stay safe, preferring to lock in smaller immediate profits as protection against the risks posed by the fear, uncertainty, and destruction cascading through the entire global financial system as the crisis widened. One of Goldman's traders, Josh Birnbaum, later lamented that his desk could have made more money than John Paulson's fabled "Greatest Ever Trade" if only management had let him.[9] But this would have required making significant investments in buying short positions and also postponing the booking of profits from them, a strategy that carried with it the risk that investors would panic if Goldman reported losses in 2007 or 2008.

As a result of Goldman's foresight and caution, 2007 was the best year ever for its mortgage business. By the end of the third quarter, and as Table 1 below illustrates, mortgage revenues were nearly equal to full-year 2006 revenues, the previous high. The revenue jump came from the shorts, which were concentrated in the structured products desk. The losses in residential mortgages came from Goldman's decision to mark down its remaining long positions.

To be fair, when Goldman managers referred to their mortgage business as "modest," they were telling the truth. Full-year 2007 mortgage revenues were about $1.2 billion. But that is what makes Goldman's performance so impressive; they understood that in the new financial world of derivatives and massive leverage, even a modest business could suddenly generate catastrophic, multibillion-dollar losses if they were caught unprepared. Contrast that with, say, Citigroup's behavior, not to mention Jimmy Cayne's. Even though Citigroup had a much larger position—more than $50 billion of high-risk home mort-

TABLE 1

GOLDMAN SACHS MORTGAGE BUSINESS PERFORMANCE,
2005–2007

| | (REVENUES IN $ MILLIONS) | | |
	FY 05	FY 06	9M 07
Residential mortgages	277	311	(389)
Commercial mortgages	197	167	139
Asset-backed securities	45	40	102
Structured products trading	245	401	955
Other	121	110	210
Total	885	1,029	1,017

Source: Presentation to Goldman Sachs board of directors, Residential Mortgage Business, September 17, 2007

gages on their books—senior management didn't even know they had a problem until the market cratered."

So full marks to Goldman for smarts. But their strategy wasn't just to short the mortgage market, because sometimes it was better to sell off the riskiest assets instead of paying for insurance on them. Once again, this was accomplished with impressive efficiency, but also with a near-total disregard for ethics, integrity, and their customers' welfare. Whether their behavior meets the standard of criminal fraud may never be entirely known, or provable. But it sure looks like fraud to me, and without question it was really, really greasy.

In reading what follows, you might measure Goldman's conduct against its pretentious corporate declaration that "integrity and honesty are at the heart of our business. We expect our people to maintain high ethical standards in everything they do."[10]

Clearing the Shelves

IT WAS ONE thing to decide to sell off risky assets, but quite another to find people still willing to buy them in late 2006 and 2007. Smart people were already out of the question; only fools would do. In December 2006, Fabrice ("Fabulous Fab") Tourre vetoed a list of sales prospects because it was "skewed towards sophisticated hedge funds... most of the time they will be on the same side of the trade as we will, and...they know exactly how things work."[11]

Luckily there were fools still to be found. The sales team started circulating "axes" (meaning sales priorities) in December 2006. A few months earlier, a trader had mentioned that "sales people view the syndicate 'axe' e-mail we have used in the past as a way to distribute junk that nobody was dumb enough to take first time around."[12]

"The key," according to a March 2007 memo, was "getting new clients/capital into the opportunity quickly." In effect, dumb money, or as another note put it, "non-traditional buyers." A salesman pushing one of Goldman's most toxic offerings to a Korean client thought he could expand the sale, but wanted a better commission "as we are pushing on a personal relationship" [i.e., I only screw my friends if I am paid well for it]. Sparks agreed.[13]

One of the earliest house-cleaning operations was a $2 billion synthetic CDO called Hudson Mezzanine Funding 2006-1. The sales presentation is almost completely misleading. Goldman's intent, it said, "is to develop a long term association with selected partners" by creating "attractive proprietary investments." Goldman, it claimed, had "aligned incentives with those of the investors." The presentation materials stated that "Goldman Sachs CDO desk pre-screens and evaluates assets for portfolio suitability…and reviews individual assets in conjunction with respective mortgage trading desks." True, in a sense— because it was the CDO desk that was choosing the assets they wanted to get rid of.[14] "Assets sourced from the Street. Hudson Mezzanine Funding is not a Balance Sheet CDO." This last statement, however, was a lie. It was made to reassure investors who had already learned to be skeptical of banks unloading bad inventory.[15]

Which was *exactly* what Goldman was doing. When the deal was executed, cheers resounded through the trading group—they had engineered a big reduction of risk and booked $8.5 million in earnings. A few months later, after shedding more risk through another sale, Sparks commended the team for having "structured like mad, and travelled the world, and worked their tails off to make some lemonade out of some big old lemons."[16]

But Goldman had even more tricks to play on the Hudson investors. Virtually all the Hudson securities were severely downgraded in October 2007, which qualified as a liquidation event. As the liquidation agent, Goldman was supposed to sell the securities at the best available price and supervise the settlements with investors. Instead, Goldman told investors that it would delay liquidation until it could find a more experienced agent (!). The price of the securities continued to plummet; instruments worth 60 cents on the dollar in October were worth only

16 cents by January. An asset manager from Morgan Stanley* wrote to Goldman in February, "No good reason to wait other than to devalue our position. It's a shame...one day I hope to get the real reason why you are doing this to me." Well, the real reason they were doing it to him was that Goldman had *shorted* the securities, so every additional drop in price transferred more wealth from the investors to Goldman.[17]

And then there was Timberwolf, another synthetic CDO in the amount of $1 billion—the one that was immortalized by Senate hearings, and that prompted a suggestion for paying "ginormous" sales credits. Here is an e-mail trail prompted by a note from sales saying they had just closed a sale on part of Timberwolf at 65 percent of its original value.

TRADER: This is worth 10. It stinks...I don't want it in our book.

SALES: It is not that bad.

TRADER: Cds mkt thinks that deal is one of the worst of the year... hopefully they r wrong.[18]

Goldman management was happy to get rid of it. A March 28, 2007, e-mail to the sales syndicate reads: "GREAT JOB... TRADING US OUT OF OUR ENTIRE TIMBERWOLF SINGLE-A POSITION."[19]

In June, with $300 million of Timberwolf assets still to be sold, Tom Montag, Dan Sparks's boss, made the comment quoted later at Senate hearings, writing, "boy that timberwolf was one shitty deal."[20] But, of course, Goldman kept on selling it.

Later, in September 2007, Tourre asked for a specific Goldman deal

---

*The puzzle here is why *Morgan Stanley* could have been on the long side in Hudson, since they were also dumping toxic instruments on their own investors. But it merely illustrates how few firms had the internal discipline of Goldman. Both Morgan and Goldman had large asset-management businesses that invested on behalf of their clients; to a naïf at Morgan asset management, a Goldman-sponsored investment-grade security would look pretty reasonable. One can bet that no one at Goldman's asset management group bid for it.

that a potential client could use as an example for a hedging strategy. Two traders exchanged e-mails on the specifics:

TRADER 1: which class, exactly

TRADER 2: Not sure, a class that went from near par in Jan to around 15 now.

TRADER 1: Well [Timberwolf] didn't exist until 3/27/07....Here is the basic history....

3/31/07 94-12

4/30/07 87-25

5/31/07 83-16

6/29/07 75-00

7/31/07 30-00

8/31/07 15-00

Current 15-00

TRADER 2: 3/27—a day that will live in infamy.[21]

But Tourre's question prompts a double take. Why would a customer sales guy want to advertise a product with such dreadful performance?

Why, indeed. Well, we don't know the rest of that particular conversation, but there is a very logical explanation for what Fabulous Fab was doing. He, and Goldman, wanted to do business not only with fools, but also with smart people. People who were looking for things to short. People who even wanted Goldman to help them construct securities specifically tailored to fail. People like John Paulson.

The SEC started investigating the Paulson short in late 2008, but not until 2009, with the publication of Greg Zuckerman's *The Greatest Trade Ever,* was it widely known that Goldman had built a deal just for Paulson to short. ABACUS 2007-AC1, known as AC-1 within Goldman, mostly comprised a menu of bonds chosen by Paulson for being particularly bad, in a market where bad was average.

The Paulson Trade

FUND MANAGERS HAD been shorting the housing market long before John Paulson; we saw that Morgan Stanley started in 2004. But as Morgan Stanley learned to its dismay, market bubbles can outlast bearish investors' resources, and as time passed and the bubble and its inevitable collapse became more obvious to insiders, it became more expensive to short housing.

Paulson ran several hedge funds and had the resources to lose money for a long time. But, convinced as he was of a coming "subprime RMBS wipeout," even he worried about the opacity and complexity of mortgage securities. So Paulson explored whether an investment bank might *custom-design* one, so that he could know and even choose exactly what went inside. Even Bear Stearns, not exactly a paragon of ethics in mortgage dealings, turned Paulson down because his request seemed "improper."[22] As we saw earlier, Bear Stearns behaved in an extraordinarily unethical way, but although they weren't concerned about ethics, they did fear potential prosecution for fraud. Happily for Paulson, Goldman had no such scruples.

Fabulous Fab Tourre designed the deal, communicating with investors and overseeing the preparation of marketing materials. To make the deal easier to sell to the long investors, aka suckers, Tourre needed an independent manager supposedly responsible for selecting the investment assets. In internal correspondence Goldman traders worried that such a manager might not "agree to the type of names Paulson want to use" or would refuse to "put its name at risk…on a weak quality portfolio." ACA Management LLC, which had worked as manager on other Goldman deals, got the assignment.[23]

ACA was never told the real purpose of the transaction. They were aware that Paulson would be involved in the deal, but not that his real goal was to bet on its failure. Paulson provided Goldman with a list of 123 bonds he wanted to short; the list was supplied to ACA, and meetings were held between ACA, Paulson, and Goldman. Although ACA was occasionally puzzled by the names Paulson recommended, or the strong ones he vetoed, an agreement was worked out on a ninety-bond portfolio, which included fifty-five of Paulson's original names. At one point in the discussions, Tourre e-mailed a colleague at Goldman, "I am at this aca paulson meeting, this is surreal."[24]

All the materials strongly emphasized ACA's role; none mentioned Paulson's. The marketing emphasized the deal's attractions for the long investor. The heart of the sales book, for example, is an eighteen-page statement on the credit selection skills of ACA. Sample quotes: "Asset selection...premised on credit fundamentals"..."alignment of economic interest with that of investors"...none of "ACA's CDOs have ever been downgraded." And much more in that vein, including a detailed presentation of the very rigorous ACA credit review process.[25]

The final deal was yet another synthetic CDO, the $2 billion ABACUS 2007-AC1, the majority of whose reference securities had been handpicked for their poor quality. Through the magic of the rating agencies, the majority of the securities were rated AAA. Goldman later said that they lost $90 million on the transaction. This seems unlikely, because Goldman's own internal documents state that they would not be taking any risk on the deal. But perhaps even Goldman was sometimes gamed by its own employees. Maybe Goldman was unable to sell all of it, was pressured to repurchase some of it, or had some form of liability for losses.[26]

The targeted customer was IKB Industrie Deutschebanke AG. It was classic dumb money—a small bank based in Düsseldorf. IKB was an eager buyer in CDO markets, and its sponsored hedge fund, Rhinebridge Capital, was one of the first to collapse in the summer of 2007. IKB bought $150 million of the AAA rate notes in April.

Well before the year end, AC-1 was nearly worthless, and Goldman transferred essentially all of IKB's $150 million to Paulson. Then through complex side deals, some of the long side became a liability of the Royal Bank of Scotland. ACA failed at the end of the year and in early 2008 partial settlements were made, some of which presumably went to Goldman, and from Goldman to Paulson. In August 2008 Royal Bank of Scotland made an $841 million settlement with Goldman on its part of the failed deal, which also would have gone to Paulson.[27]

The SEC quietly opened an investigation into the Paulson trade in August 2008, and in April 2010 filed a civil fraud complaint in federal court—its one and only attempt to pursue Goldman Sachs for its behavior during the bubble and crisis. After declaring that it had done nothing wrong, Goldman settled in July 2010, agreeing to a $550 million fine. In its consent to the judgment, Goldman stipulated that it was "a mistake" to state that ACA had selected the portfolio "without disclosing the role of Paulson & Co.... Goldman regrets that the marketing materials did not contain that disclosure."[28]

Before moving on to Goldman's really serious bets with AIG, we should note briefly that, disgraceful as Goldman's and Paulson's behavior was, they were far from alone. Deutsche Bank and several other major investment banks worked with Paulson, as well as with several other large hedge funds, to construct similar deals with similar results. However, it would be surprising to see the SEC go after Deutsche Bank, because since the Obama administration took office, the SEC's director of enforcement has been Robert Khuzami, who was general counsel to Deutsche Bank for the Americas throughout the bubble. (In a way, though, it could be tidy—he could depose himself, subpoena himself, prosecute himself, and settle with himself.)

As for the other hedge funds that behaved like Paulson, the two best known are Magnetar and Tricadia.

The Magnetar Trade

MAGNETAR IS A Chicago hedge fund that developed a strategy similar to Paulson's. The brief discussion here is based on an excellent investigative series on ProPublica, and a more technical analysis in Yves Smith's book *Econned*.[29]

In the Goldman Sachs ABACUS deal just discussed, Paulson did not make any long investments; he merely bought the short side, which sufficed for him to make gallons of money when the securities defaulted. But Magnetar, and sometimes Paulson too in his deals with Deutsche Bank, did something even more clever. They would find, or help construct, really bad deals, and buy the short side of nearly all of them. But then, seemingly paradoxically, they also bought the *long* side of the so-called equity piece—the lowest-quality part of the whole deal, and the first to fail. Why would they do that?

Because they were handling, in a far smarter way, the same problem that poor Howie Hubler had faced at Morgan Stanley. Until the securities actually fail, the guy holding the short side of a synthetic CDO has to keep making those payments to the long investor. That could get expensive. Magnetar (and sometimes Paulson) covered these payments through the extremely high interest rates (often 20 percent per year, sometimes even more) paid by the equity piece. What Paulson and Magnetar realized, and Morgan Stanley didn't, was that bubbles often last for a long time, but the collapse is usually fast and complete. So the equity piece would keep paying interest, and covering the cost of Paulson's and Magnetar's massive short position, until the collapse came. Then, yes, the equity piece would fail first, but everything else would probably fail soon afterward. This strategy had the additional benefit of disguising their real intentions, at least to naive investors.

Their returns were huge; this was not a small business. An executive from a European bank that managed some of Magnetar's deals said:

> If you told me of a major broker/dealer who had an active CDO under-writing group that *DIDN'T* work with Magnetar...that would surprise me....Rinse and repeat. The credits didn't matter nor really did the managers they contracted....When the math lined up, they would reload the trade.[30]

In a rare error for Jamie Dimon, JPMorgan Chase was heavily involved in structuring one of these deals, called Squared, and lost money as a result. Magnetar's behavior was very similar to Paulson's with ABACUS. Magnetar helped select the assets that went into Squared, with the intent of betting against it. JPMorgan Chase structured the deal, and then sold off pieces of it without telling its customers that the package had been designed to fail, or that Magnetar was involved. But JPMorgan Chase didn't sell off enough of the deal, and lost $880 million as a result.

Magnetar pumped out thirty deals, in the $1 billion to $1.5 billion range *each*. Very rough estimates suggest that this one hedge fund's short payments may have funded a quarter of the 2006 subprime mortgage securities market. Investment bankers (of the Fabulous Fab sort) collected major fees for helping to structure the deals and matching Magnetar with the fools it bet against. Magnetar was a few smart guys who found a way to turn financial muck and the fools owning it into billions for themselves. If they happened to facilitate another $100 billion to $200 billion of stupid lending and investing, well, that was not their problem.* Tricadia's story is very similar.

But now, back to Goldman Sachs, because their best trick was yet to come.

Goldman Sachs and AIG

AFTER GOLDMAN HAD sold off its lumps of coal to various fools, they knowingly put the global financial system at risk. They had played AIG for such a massive sucker while shorting the mortgage market that by 2008 they *knew* that their shorts alone could precipitate AIG's collapse. And what did Goldman do about *that*? Push even harder, *while*

---

*Yves Smith gives a cautious estimate of $128 billion of Magnetar-induced lending. The production of cash subprime CDOs over this period was about $450 billion. Other estimates of the Magnetar impact are as high as $250 billion.

shorting AIG, of course. And while doing this, did they call up their pal and former CEO, Henry Paulson aka the treasury secretary, to warn him that the shit was about to hit the fan? No, it seems that they neglected to do that.

Although no single firm or government agency knew the entire extent of the market's exposures, or even AIG's, Goldman was much better positioned than most, for several reasons. First, Goldman had sold $17 billion of the $62 billion in mortgage CDOs that AIG had insured through its London-based credit default swap (CDS) business, AIG Financial Products.[31] In some cases, Goldman had helpfully referred investors to AIGFP, so that CDS insurance could help reassure potential investors that Goldman's CDOs were essentially riskless. In some cases Goldman even had the right to change the mortgages underlying these securities after their sale, and there have been allegations that Goldman deliberately used this capability to off-load even more of its toxic assets. This capability gave Goldman even more information and control over the performance of its CDOs, and therefore also of AIGFP's CDSs. But second, Goldman was also a huge direct buyer of CDS protection from AIG, in some cases on the very same securities that it had earlier sold. (Some of Goldman's CDOs turned out to be the worst in AIG's CDS portfolio.) Third, Goldman had also created and sold some of the $75 billion in mortgage CDOs that another part of AIG, its securities investment and lending business, had foolishly purchased, and that had started to decline sharply in value. Fourth, as the bubble unraveled, Goldman knew that AIG was being rapidly weakened by cash demands from the holders of the insurer's CDSs. Goldman knew this better than anyone, because as we saw earlier, Goldman was the most aggressive firm on Wall Street in marking down its toxic assets. Because it marked them down earlier than others, it was therefore the earliest and most aggressive in demanding money from AIG based on those markdowns. Goldman knew that its own demands alone could soon reach tens of billions of dollars. And finally, Goldman's equity research organization also covered AIG and regularly provided research reports on AIG's financial condition.

Starting in 2007, when Goldman was implementing its massive short, it quickly purchased over $20 billion in CDS protection on mortgage securities and related indexes from AIGFP. The protection was cheap to buy, because the securities were still highly rated and marked at or near full value, both by the wider market and on Goldman's own books. Soon afterward, however, having locked in the CDS protection, Goldman began aggressive markdowns of the securities' value—and with every markdown, it demanded immediate corresponding cash payments from AIG. In February 2008, partly as a result of Goldman's demands, AIG was forced by its increasingly panicked external auditor to announce losses and also a "material weakness" in its accounting, pertaining to the valuation of its CDS portfolio. Throughout 2008, Goldman radically accelerated its demands, leading to fierce disputes between Goldman and AIG over the securities' value and, therefore, the size of the required payments.

By mid-2008 and perhaps even earlier, Goldman knew that its CDS payment demands alone could easily cause AIG to collapse. Added to this would be further losses from other securities owned by AIG and/or insured via AIG's CDS business. Goldman possessed far more detailed knowledge of many of these securities, and the likelihood of their failure, than AIG did, because Goldman had created and sold them. With this combined knowledge, Goldman unquestionably knew that AIG was in dire straits. Goldman did not warn any regulators, much less its customers or AIG, but it *did* take action. First, it became ever more aggressive in demanding payment on its CDSs, so that it could get its money out ahead of others and before AIG's failure. And second, it spent about $150 million buying $2.5 billion in CDS protection *on AIG,* which it would collect in the event of an AIG default or bankruptcy. At a minimum, this insulated Goldman from risk; and depending upon precise contract terms and events, it could even have given Goldman an affirmative incentive to *cause* AIG's collapse. If, for example, Goldman could get paid fully for its mortgage CDSs just before AIG went bankrupt, it would actually make more money from AIG's actual or feared bankruptcy than from its continued health. And, in the end, this was very close to what happened, although Goldman could not have predicted that in advance.

It was only on August 18, 2008, that a Goldman Sachs research analyst issued the first public comment by Goldman on the catastrophic nature of AIG's condition. The report said that AIG was a major credit risk, likely to be downgraded, and in dire need of raising additional capital. Well, Goldman would have known. By September 12, 2008, shortly before AIG's collapse, AIG had *already* been forced to pay out $18.9 billion on its mortgage CDSs—of which $7.6 billion, over 40 percent, had gone directly to Goldman, which was demanding even more. Then, a few days later, after paying Goldman several hundred million dollars more, AIG ran out of money and collapsed. It was bailed out through $85 billion in "loans" that gave the federal government 79.9 percent ownership of AIG.[32]

Shortly afterward, under directions from the Treasury Department and the New York Federal Reserve, AIG used over $60 billion of the bailout money to pay the holders of its mortgage CDSs in full, via contracts that also barred AIG from later suing anyone for fraud. Goldman received $14 billion. Ever since, the New York Federal Reserve and the Treasury Department, under *both* the Bush and Obama administrations, have fiercely resisted providing information about these payments and their contractual terms. Ironically, it was AIG's new management that pressed for disclosure.

It is not publicly known what Goldman did with its $2.5 billion of CDS protection on AIG, but it almost certainly sold it at a significant profit, probably over $1 billion, sometime in late 2008 or early 2009.

In April 2010, after both the SEC lawsuit and a Senate investigation, Senator Carl Levin's Permanent Subcommittee on Investigations held hearings on Goldman's conduct, focusing on Goldman's shorting strategy of 2006–2007. Here are some excerpts, beginning with testimony by head mortgage trader Dan Sparks. They speak for themselves; as several of the senators noted, the witnesses proved to be stunningly confused and ill-informed, with very poor memories about the business they had been running so well, and about which they had been so focused and ruthlessly clear in their internal communications.

SENATOR LEVIN: Don't you also have a duty to disclose an adverse interest to your client? Do you have that duty?

MR. SPARKS: About?

SENATOR LEVIN: If you have an adverse interest to your client, do you have the duty to disclose that to your client?

MR. SPARKS: The question about how the firm is positioned or our desk is positioned?

SENATOR LEVIN: If you have an adverse interest to your client when you are selling something to them, do you have the responsibility to tell that client of your adverse interest?

MR. SPARKS: Mr. Chairman, I am just trying to understand what the adverse interest means—

SENATOR LEVIN: No, I think you understand it. I do not think you want to answer.

A little later:

SENATOR LEVIN: I am just asking you, look at the bottom paragraph there, the last two lines. "[F]remont [a subprime lender supplying Goldman with loans] refused to make any forward looking statements so we really got nothing from them on the crap pools that are out there now." Do you see that?

MR. SPARKS: Yes, sir.

SENATOR LEVIN: OK. Now, were you aware of Fremont's poor reputation at the time?

MR. SPARKS: This email—

SENATOR LEVIN: Do you remember whether you were aware at the time of their poor reputation? Do you remember?

MR. SPARKS: Whether they had a poor reputation in November?

SENATOR LEVIN: Yes, with high default rates.

MR. SPARKS: Fremont originated subprime loans. People understood that.

SENATOR LEVIN: Yes or no, were you aware of their poor reputation and high default rate.

MR. SPARKS: I do not recall at that time.

And then:

SENATOR LEVIN: Look what your sales team was saying about Timberwolf: "Boy that Timberwolf was one shi**y deal." They sold that shi**y deal.

MR. SPARKS: Mr. Chairman, this e-mail was from the head of the division, not the sales force. This was—

SENATOR LEVIN: Whatever it was, it is an internal Goldman document.

MR. SPARKS: This was an email to me in late June.

SENATOR LEVIN: Right. And you sold—

MR. SPARKS: After the transaction.

SENATOR LEVIN: No. You sold Timberwolf after as well.

MR. SPARKS: We did trades after that.

SENATOR LEVIN: Yes, OK. The trades after—

MR. SPARKS: Some context might be helpful.

SENATOR LEVIN: The context, let me tell you, the context is mighty clear. June 22 is the date of this email: "Boy, that Timberwolf was one shi**y deal." How much of that shi**y deal did you sell to your clients after June 22, 2007?

MR. SPARKS: Mr. Chairman, I do not know the answer to that, but the price would have reflected levels that they wanted to invest at that time.

SENATOR LEVIN: You did not tell them you thought it was a shi**y deal?

MR. SPARKS: Well, I did not say that.

And David Viniar, the CFO:

SENATOR LEVIN: If your employee thinks that it is crap, that it is a shi**y deal, do you think that Goldman Sachs ought to be selling that to customers, and when you were on the short side betting against it? I think it is a very clear conflict of interest and I think we have got to deal with it. Now, you don't, apparently.

MR. VINIAR: I do not necessarily think that is—

SENATOR LEVIN: And when you heard that your employees in these e-mails and looking at these deals said, "God, what a shi**y deal," "God, what a piece of crap," when you hear your own employees or read about those in emails, do you feel anything?

MR. VINIAR: I think that is very unfortunate to have on email. [Laughter].

SENATOR LEVIN: On email?

MR. VINIAR: Please don't take that the wrong way.

SENATOR LEVIN: How about feeling that way?

MR. VINIAR: I think it is very unfortunate for anyone to have said that in any form.

And finally we have Mr. Blankfein, the CEO:

SENATOR LEVIN: Do you think they know that you think something is a piece of crap when you sell it to them and then bet against it? Do you think they know that?

MR. BLANKFEIN: Again, I don't know who the "they" is and—

SENATOR LEVIN: We went through it today.

MR. BLANKFEIN: No, I know. I know, Senator, and there were individual emails that were picked out and some people thought something. But I will tell you—

SENATOR LEVIN: I am just asking you a question. Do you think if your people think something is a piece of crap and go out and sell that, and then your company bets against it, do you think that deserves your trust?

MR. BLANKFEIN: Senator, I want to make one thing clear. When you say we sell something and then our customer bets against it—

SENATOR LEVIN: No. You bet against it.

MR. BLANKFEIN [CONTINUING]: We bet against it, we are principals. The act of selling something is what gives us the opposite position of what the client has. If the client asks us for a bid and we buy it from them, the next minute, we own it. They don't. If they ask to buy it from us, the next minute, they own it and we don't. We could cover that risk. But the nature of the principal business and market making is that we are the other side of what our clients want to do.

SENATOR LEVIN: When you sell something to a client, they think, presumably, you are rid of it. It is no longer in your inventory.

MR. BLANKFEIN: Not necessarily.

SENATOR LEVIN: . . . Is there not a conflict when you sell something to somebody and then are determined to bet against that same security and you don't disclose that to the person you are selling it to? Do you see a problem?

MR. BLANKFEIN: In the context of market making, that is not a conflict.

Later:

SENATOR LEVIN: You don't believe it is relevant to a customer of yours that you are selling a security to that you are betting against that same security. You just don't think it is relevant and needs to be disclosed. Is that the bottom line?

MR. BLANKFEIN: Yes, and the people who are selling it in our firm wouldn't even know what the firm's position is and—

SENATOR LEVIN: Oh, yes, they did.

MR. BLANKFEIN: Senator, we have 35,000 people and thousands of traders making markets throughout our firm. They might have an idea, but they might not have an idea.

SENATOR LEVIN: They have an idea, more than an idea in these cases. But putting that aside, what do you think about selling securities which your own people think are crap? Does that bother you?

MR. BLANKFEIN: I think they would—again, as a hypothetical—

SENATOR LEVIN: No, this is real.

MR. BLANKFEIN: Well, then I don't—

SENATOR LEVIN: We heard it today. This is a shi**y deal. This is crap.

MR. BLANKFEIN: Well, Senator—

SENATOR LEVIN: Four or five examples. What is your reaction to that?

MR. BLANKFEIN: I think there are a lot of opinions about how a security will perform against the market it is in.

A little later:

SENATOR LEVIN: And where you take a short position, do you think that should be disclosed? Where you are betting against that same security you are selling—yes or no, do you think that ought to be disclosed or not?

MR. BLANKFEIN: Senator, you keep using the word "betting against"—

SENATOR LEVIN: Yes. You are taking the short position and you are staying. You intend to keep it. That is a bet against that security—

MR. BLANKFEIN: If somebody bought—

SENATOR LEVIN [CONTINUING]: Succeeding.

MR. BLANKFEIN: As a market maker—

SENATOR LEVIN: No, just try my question.

MR. BLANKFEIN: I have to be able to—

SENATOR LEVIN: No, just try my question. In a deal where you are selling securities and you are intending to keep the short side of that deal, which is what happened here in a lot of these deals, do you think you have an obligation to tell the person that you are selling that security to in that deal that you are keeping the short position in that deal?

MR. BLANKFEIN: That we are not going to cover it in the market?

SENATOR LEVIN: That is—

MR. BLANKFEIN: Well, no—

SENATOR LEVIN: That you intend to keep that short position. Not forever. It is your intention to keep that short position.

MR. BLANKFEIN: No, I don't think we would have to tell them. I don't even know that we would know ourselves what we were going to do. Even if we intended—

SENATOR LEVIN: I said, where you intend to keep a short position.

MR. BLANKFEIN: I don't think we would—I don't think we would disclose that, and I don't know—again, intention for a market maker is a very—

Isn't it wonderful how confused someone can be when testifying before Congress. But enough about Goldman. Let's turn to the government.

Amateur Hour Meets Let Them Eat Cake: Your Tax Dollars at Work

THE BUSH ADMINISTRATION'S handling of the emerging crisis was bizarre and frightening even when it was competent, which was rarely. On the one hand, the year 2008 was marked by unquestionably deep, sincere concern for financial stability on the part of Henry Paulson and Ben Bernanke, who both worked inhumanly hard to forestall global collapse. Yet the administration's response was also marked by a stunning obliviousness to the causes, severity, and consequences of the crisis on the part of the very same Henry Paulson and Ben Bernanke; a totally clueless president who made Jimmy Cayne on the golf course look like an obsessively detail-oriented micromanager; total disregard on the part of the Bush administration for the effects of financial sector and government conduct on the bottom 99.9 percent of the population; and financial sector elites oscillating between fear and greed.

But we must pause for a moment of gratitude that the crisis did not come under the tenure of Alan Greenspan or, worse, that of John Snow, who was treasury secretary from 2003 until mid-2006. Mr. Snow isn't stupid in the narrow academic sense; he has a PhD in economics and a law degree. But he had zero working experience in finance, and seems to have been seriously unethical and/or stunningly out to lunch. After his academic work he became a lawyer, then an assistant secretary of transportation, then CEO of CSX, a railroad company, from which position George W. Bush plucked him to run Treasury.

There is no evidence that Snow had the faintest clue about a bubble. He resigned in 2006 only because it was revealed that he had not paid any taxes on $24 million in income from CSX, which had forgiven Snow's repayment of a gigantic loan that the company had made to him. Upon leaving Treasury, Snow became chairman of Cerberus Capital Management, a huge private equity fund. Cerberus also employs former vice president Dan Quayle, and several of its portfolio companies have benefited from federal contracts dependent upon political influence. But the principal hallmark of Cerberus's first major new investments under Mr. Snow was not corruption; it was breathtaking stupidity. Cerberus purchased half of GMAC, General Motors' financing arm, and 80 percent of Chrysler. Both collapsed immediately after the crisis erupted, wiping out most of Cerberus's investment by mid-2009 and requiring over $20 billion in emergency federal assistance.

But even under Bernanke and Paulson, it still wasn't good. They continued to deny the existence of a bubble or potential crisis until the bitter end, and for two years Bernanke continued Greenspan's refusal to regulate the mortgage industry. Only in late 2007 did the Federal Reserve create draft regulations under the 1994 HOEPA law, and the regulations were not issued until mid-2008, which was just a teeny bit late. By early 2008 warnings of impending crisis were coming from almost everywhere. In addition to Bill Ackman's mid-2007 presentation and Allan Sloan's October 2007 article in *Fortune*, there were warnings by NYU economist Nouriel Roubini; Charles Morris's book *The Trillion Dollar Meltdown,* published in February 2008; verbal warnings by the leadership of the IMF, including its then managing director, Dominique Strauss-Kahn; and warnings by Christine Lagarde (then France's minister of economics and finance, and later Strauss-Kahn's successor at the IMF) at the G8 meetings in February 2008.

In a recent private conversation, a senior financial executive observed to me that Goldman Sachs executives have a decidedly mixed record when operating outside of Goldman Sachs. Referencing Jon Corzine at MF Global, Robert Rubin at Citigroup, and John Thain at Merrill Lynch as well as Mr. Paulson, this executive commented that these men were trained to be traders and managers in a tightly structured universe, but not to think about large-scale structural and conceptual issues, or to deal with organizations far messier than Goldman. Whether this accounts for Paulson's complacency, I do not know. But even in private meetings with his counterparts, and as late as mid-2008, Paulson was stunningly complacent about the oncoming crisis.

Paulson and Bernanke have thus far largely escaped the condemnation they deserve, perhaps out of gratitude for their unquestioned nerve and commitment once the acute crisis period began in September 2008. For the most part, I would not presume to second-guess the majority of their actions during those chaotic, psychotic, terrifying weeks of September and October 2008. But their prior and subsequent conduct is another matter. And even some of the decisions taken during the crisis period reveal an ability to be cool and careful when investment bankers' interests, or their own, were at stake.

Bernanke was a lifelong academic who had never done anything else until appointed to the Federal Reserve Board in 2002. He clearly has excellent diplomatic and political skills, but he had never had any experience either as a banker or as a regulator prior to joining the Fed. He became chairman of the Federal Reserve Board only in early 2006, just as the bubble was peaking. During the crisis, Bernanke appears to have deferred to Paulson, and obeyed his orders, almost without exception.

Paulson certainly had very impressive experience, but also a slightly peculiar and somewhat unsavory career. He had a wholesome, all-American youth in small-town Illinois; he was an Eagle Scout, a football player, and a devout Christian Scientist. (In his frequently selective, dishonest, and self-serving memoir *On the Brink,* Paulson goes out of his way to defend his religion's attitude toward medical care.) But in 1972–73, Paulson served as the personal assistant of White House counsel and domestic affairs assistant John Ehrlichman, another devout Christian Scientist, during the period when Erhlichman was working intensively to cover up his highly criminal activities in the Watergate affair. We don't know what Paulson saw or heard at the office, but by early 1973 there was already clear public evidence that Ehrlichman had done some very nasty things, including running covert burglary and political sabotage operations and assisting in the Watergate coverup. Yet Paulson stayed in Ehrlichman's employ. Under mounting pressure, Nixon forced his aide to resign in April 1973, and Ehrlichman was convicted of conspiracy, obstruction of justice, and perjury in 1975.

Paulson joined Goldman Sachs in 1974, worked very hard, and rose fast, becoming chief operating officer and then CEO in 1999, mounting a coup that forced out his predecessor Jon Corzine. Given Paulson's background, it seems very difficult to believe that he had no sense of the increasingly dishonest, unsound nature of Goldman's mortgage CDOs in 2004–2006, the height of the bubble. By the time Paulson left Goldman in May 2006, it had issued tens of billions of dollars of increasingly toxic mortgage securities, and had extensive dealings with several of the worst originators. It was only seven months after Paulson's departure that Goldman started its Big Short.

Paulson also appears to have fully supported and in several cases championed Goldman's, and his industry's, many deregulatory efforts throughout the 1990s and the 2000s. These included repealing Glass-Steagall, banning the regulation of OTC derivatives, relaxing disclosure requirements for mortgage CDOs (via a joint letter to the SEC signed by Goldman and Morgan Stanley executives in 2004), relaxing the SEC's leverage restrictions on investment banks in 2004, and continuing the Federal Reserve's long-standing refusal to regulate the mortgage industry. As treasury secretary, Paulson also lobbied to reduce the power and funding of the SEC.

As darkness gathered in 2007 and 2008, there was no serious attempt by Paulson or Bernanke to create a systematic monitoring process for the financial system—which, of course, would have been fiercely resisted by Mr. Paulson's former employer and others in the industry. In fairness to Paulson and Bernanke, they inherited a badly outdated and weakened regulatory system. But in significant measure, this was the result of their own deliberate actions to cripple it—Bernanke while on the Federal Reserve Board, then the Bush White House staff, and then finally as chairman of the Fed, and Paulson when he was running Goldman Sachs, which lobbied fiercely and continuously for ever more deregulation.

The combination of the industry's incentives for secrecy or even disinformation, weak disclosure requirements, the progressive crippling of the regulatory system, and Bernanke's and Paulson's own ignorance and/or dishonesty was an extremely destructive cocktail. Indeed, one clear lesson from the crisis is that almost nobody in the financial sector had incentives to be honest or to warn the regulators—not those gaming the system, not most of those betting on its collapse, not even those who were about to collapse themselves. As 2008 progressed Paulson, Bernanke, and the whole world were repeatedly blindsided by developments that could have been predicted, and which in some cases (e.g., the collapse of the CDO market and of AIG) actually *were* predicted—especially by Goldman Sachs, the hedge funds betting against the mortgage market, and various economists. But precise assessment and management of these developments depended upon facts that Paulson and Bernanke never seemed to have. As the various narratives of the crisis make clear, Paulson and Bernanke generally had no more than two to three days' advance notice of the impending collapse of major financial institutions including Bear Stearns, Lehman Brothers, Merrill Lynch, AIG, Washington Mutual, and Citigroup. The same was true of upheavals in the commercial paper market and money market funds. In most cases, these events could have been foreseen substantially earlier.

The further consequence of Paulson and Bernanke's willful information vacuum was that they did virtually no planning for, or analysis of, what would happen if major firms did fail. For example, when Lehman Brothers went bankrupt, neither Paulson nor Bernanke was aware that British and Japanese law required that the assets of Lehman's local subsidiaries be frozen, preventing Lehman's clients from retrieving their money. Nor did they understand that Lehman's bankruptcy would have immediate, major effects on commercial paper markets and money market funds that held large amounts of Lehman's short-term debt.

Their lack of preparedness was worsened by the utter incompetence or inexperience of many senior administration personnel. Christopher Cox, the chairman of the SEC, was a former corporate attorney and Republican congressman with no previous experience either in financial services or as a regulator. He also had significant health problems during the late bubble period, having undergone cancer surgery in January 2006. Cox had gutted the SEC's risk monitoring and enforcement organizations, which did not file a single lawsuit related to the mortgage bubble under his chairmanship. But he was far from alone.

In my film I show selections from my interview with Frederic Mishkin, who was one of the seven members of the Federal Reserve Board from September 2006 through August 2008. (Or rather, one of the few members of the board; during much of the crisis period, two and sometimes three of the Fed Board seats remained vacant.) Mishkin resigned effective August 31, 2008, two weeks before the collapse of Lehman, Merrill Lynch, and AIG, and one doesn't know whether to be outraged or grateful. His record is a stunning litany of stupidity and occasional dishonesty, ranging from his paid boosting of fraudulent Icelandic banks in 2006 to his being unaware of the high credit ratings still enjoyed by major banks on the brink of their collapse in September 2008.

In July 2007 Paulson recruited David McCormick, whom I also interviewed for my film, from the White House staff to become the Treasury Department's undersecretary for international affairs. It was a very odd choice, perhaps designed to ensure that Paulson faced no competition in the international arena. I have known David McCormick, slightly, for a long time, although we haven't talked since the release of my film *Inside Job* (which doubtless made him quite unhappy). David is an intelligent, accomplished man who studied engineering at West Point, served in the first Persian Gulf War, and then had a very successful business career, first in consulting and then in the software industry. In the Bush administration he spent too much energy averting his eyes from everything in front of him, but I think that David is basically a decent, thoughtful guy.

But was David McCormick the right guy to be the Treasury Department's undersecretary for international affairs during the worst financial crisis since the Great Depression? No way. David had no experience with international finance, very little international experience of *any* kind (outside of the Persian Gulf), and had never worked either in a financial institution or at a financial regulator. Here are some excerpts from our exchanges about Lehman and various international issues related to the crisis.

CF: I have to say that I was rather surprised when Christine Lagarde told me that she didn't learn about Lehman's bankruptcy until after the fact.

MCCORMICK: That's probably right. She probably learned about it Monday, or maybe Sunday night. So, typically, it's typically not the case that, when you're debating the pros and cons of different policy options within one government, that you necessarily are going out and sharing the internal thinking with another government.

CF: Were you aware at the time that bankruptcy laws were different in other parts of the world, and that in other parts of the world, in particular in England, Lehman's bankruptcy meant that London accounts would be frozen and people wouldn't be able to trade?

MCCORMICK: You know, there may have been people involved in the specifics of the transaction that were aware of that; I was not aware of that.

It also seems that Paulson kept McCormick out of the loop:

CF: My understanding...is that Barclays was willing to do the trans-action [to purchase Lehman Brothers], but only if it first of all got approval from British regulators, and secondly got a guarantee for something on the order of $30 billion worth of Lehman debt, that was, Lehman assets, which were thought to be very questionable, and in fact proved so, and that the FSA [UK Financial Services Authority] declined to approve the transaction because Secretary Paulson and Chairman Bernanke would not provide the guarantee for the Lehman assets. Correct?

MCCORMICK: I don't know the facts on that.

CF: You were not involved in that.

MCCORMICK: I was not involved in that.

CF: So even though you were the international guy—

MCCORMICK: I was not the intermediary to Barclays.

CF: Or to the FSA?

MCCORMICK: Or to the FSA on that.

CF: Oh, really?

MCCORMICK: No. I'm sorry, I just don't know factually what the answer is.

But whatever their shortcomings, at least Paulson and Bernanke were completely focused on avoiding the collapse of the system once the crisis began. The same cannot be said for everyone else. Consider, for example, John Thain, someone else I have known slightly for many years. Thain had been Goldman Sachs's president and co-COO until 2004, then CEO of the New York Stock Exchange. Thain became CEO of Merrill Lynch in November 2007, replacing Stan O'Neal after O'Neal took his $161 million in severance payments.

While making my film, I spoke frequently and in detail with Thain, who agreed to talk to me on the condition that our conversations remained off the record. Without going into details, I can say that John was not big on accepting personal responsibility—not for Goldman Sachs's behavior in the Internet bubble, not for Goldman's massive lobbying for deregulation, and not for the failure of FINRA (which until 2007 was under contract with the New York Stock Exchange, of which Thain was then CEO) to do anything whatsoever about investment banks' conduct during the bubble. But it was John's behavior at Merrill that was perhaps most revealing, not just about him but about banking culture generally. Before starting at Merrill, Thain obtained a $15 million cash sign-on bonus and a first-year compensation package that would have given him over $80 million if Merrill's stock had recovered. But, of course, Merrill's stock didn't recover, since Merrill proceeded to lose almost $80 billion during the crisis.

John was one of the CEOs summoned by Paulson to meet at the New York Fed over the weekend of September 12–14, 2008—the meetings at which Paulson tried and failed to find a rescuer for Lehman. There were two potential buyers: Barclays and Bank of America. But with Lehman's obvious collapse, and with Paulson telling him directly to look for a buyer, John saw the handwriting on the wall. He excused himself from the meeting to make a phone call—without telling Paulson what he was doing. John's phone call was to the CEO of Bank of America, and pretty soon BofA was no longer interested in Lehman. This may have sealed Lehman's fate, since Barclays was prevented from buying without the approval of British regulators—who refused it.

Less than forty-eight hours later, John had signed a definitive contract for the sale of Merrill Lynch to Bank of America. That contract, even though negotiated and drafted faster than any comparable acquisition in history, was very carefully constructed so that Merrill, and John Thain, retained control over the payment of bonuses until the acquisition closed in January 2009. Then, one month after Merrill's acquisition and Lehman's bankruptcy, on October 13, 2008, Henry Paulson summoned the CEOs of America's nine largest banks, once again including John Thain, to a secret meeting in Washington. Paulson ordered them to accept $250 billion in emergency capital funding, both to strengthen them in reality and to reassure the public. Thain had only one concern, and he asked Paulson about it: would this affect their freedom to award bonuses? The answer was no.

Then, in December, Thain actually awarded those bonuses—two months early, in order to guarantee that they would be paid before Bank of America took control. Despite the fact that Merrill had already lost about $50 billion, the bonuses totaled nearly $4 billion in cash, heavily concentrated at the top. Over seven hundred people received bonuses exceeding $1 million each, and several were in the tens of millions. John had asked for a $10 million bonus for himself, which was refused. The bonuses could not have been paid without the kind assistance of Mr. Paulson, because without federal aid, Merrill (and Bank of America, for that matter) would have been bankrupt. I asked John about the ethics of awarding such bonuses to people who had just caused tens of billions of dollars in losses, not to mention a world-historical financial crisis. His answer did not impress me.

A month later—in January, as usual—the rest of the investment banks announced *their* bonuses, which totaled about $19 billion. Paulson and Bernanke had neglected to attach any conditions or compensation limitations to their assistance to the financial sector, which by that point totaled hundreds of billions of dollars. They also had neglected to take any steps to address the rapidly rising tide of mortgage defaults, foreclosures, and unemployment. Their job was banks, not people.

CHAPTER 6

CRIME AND PUNISHMENT: BANKING AND THE BUBBLE AS CRIMINAL ENTERPRISES

AS ALL BANKERS (INCLUDING crooked ones) will readily tell you, there is nothing more important to the health of the financial system than trust and confidence.

It is therefore all the more disturbing that, since deregulation, no other major industry has broken the law so often and so seriously—behavior, moreover, that is now rarely punished. For the last quarter century even highly criminal behavior has typically resulted at most in civil settlements in which the institution admits nothing, promises not to do it again, pays a fine—and then promptly does it again. Rarely are individual executives even sued, or fined, much less criminally prosecuted. The fines are generally trivial, a minor cost of doing business, paid by the institution, or frequently, by insurance. Thus, while the housing bubble and financial crisis contain the largest and most recent episodes of financial sector criminality, they are far from isolated.

Obviously there are many honest bankers, and even through the bubble and crisis the majority of all banking transactions were performed properly. People still deposited their paychecks, paid their bills, used their credit cards; companies issued stocks and bonds. At the same time, however, there has been a sharp increase in organized, high-level criminal behavior across a wide array of financial markets, ranging from consumer lending to high-end institutional trading. This now occurs on such a large scale, and with such frequency, that it can no longer be dismissed as aberrant or exceptional. It is no exaggeration to say that since the 1980s, much of the American (and global) financial sector has become criminalized, creating an industry culture that tolerates or even encourages systematic fraud. The behavior that caused the mortgage bubble and financial crisis was a natural outcome and continuation of this pattern, rather than some kind of economic accident.

It is also important to understand that this behavior really is seriously criminal. We are not talking about walking out of a store absentmindedly and forgetting to pay, or littering, or neglecting some bureaucratic formality. We are talking about deliberate concealment of financial transactions that aided terrorism, nuclear weapons proliferation, and large-scale tax evasion; assisting in major financial frauds and in concealment of criminal assets; and committing frauds that substantially worsened the worst financial bubbles and crises since the Depression.

This might seem like an exaggeration. It's not. Let us now review 1) the growth of financial criminality and its declining punishment; 2) the nature, severity, and consequences of illegal conduct during the bubble and financial crisis; and 3) actual and potential responses to this conduct.

The Rise of Post-Deregulation Financial Criminality

THE FIRST MAJOR outbreak of deregulation-era financial crime came promptly after the Reagan administration's deregulation of the savings and loan industry. The S&L scandal established a pattern that has intensified ever since. Since the early 1980s, financial sector criminality has sharply increased, particularly in investment banking and asset management, while prosecution and punishment have declined nearly to zero. Criminals employed by major, politically powerful banks are almost never prosecuted, and literally never imprisoned, and there is a striking disparity in treatment of identical crimes as a function of the criminals' institutional affiliations, or lack thereof. The overwhelming majority of financial sector offenses that are criminally prosecuted are committed by asset and hedge fund managers, by individuals who provide confidential information for insider trading, or by individual investors. Thus Bernard Madoff, Raj Rajaratnam, and Martha Stewart are prosecuted; executives of Goldman Sachs, JPMorgan Chase, Citigroup, and even Lehman Brothers are not.

The S&L, leveraged buyout, and insider trading scandals of the 1980s were the only ones for which significant numbers of politically powerful bankers were prosecuted. There were several thousand criminal prosecutions, resulting in prison sentences for prominent and wealthy executives such as Charles Keating and Michael Milken. Even then, few prosecutions were directed at the core of the financial sector, in part because it had not yet become highly criminalized. The worst offenses, and most prosecutions, occurred in the industry's periphery. Keating ran a West Coast S&L that went bankrupt; Milken worked for Drexel, which had been a small, second-tier investment bank until his arrival. Even then, however, there were disturbing signs. For example, the very well-established accounting firm Ernst & Young had deliberately failed to warn about massive accounting frauds by its S&L clients and agreed to pay fines totaling over $300 million, and some prestigious investment banks had worked for greenmailers and fraudulent S&Ls.

But it was in the late 1990s that, for the first time since the 1920s, the largest, oldest, and most important firms in finance became criminalized. The expansion and consolidation of the financial sector in the 1990s, the Internet bubble, the rising power of money in national politics, and further deregulation together created an unprecedented opportunity for bankers to make money improperly, and they seized this new opportunity with astonishing enthusiasm.

On November 7, 2011, the *New York Times* published an article based on its own review of major banks' settlements of SEC lawsuits since 1996. The *Times'* analysis found fifty-one cases in which major banks had settled cases involving securities fraud, after having previously been caught *violating the same law,* and then promising the SEC not to do so again.[1] The *Times'* list, furthermore, covered only SEC securities fraud cases; it did not include any criminal cases, private lawsuits by victims, cases filed by state attorneys general, or any cases of bribery, money laundering, tax evasion, or illegal asset concealment, all areas in which the banks have numerous and major violations. Here is a tour of some major cases.

Enron

ENRON, WHICH SUFFERED the largest bankruptcy in U.S. history, was the stock market's darling in the late 1990s. Enron was also politically well connected, particularly to Republicans. Based in Texas, it was a strong supporter of Governor George W. Bush. As noted earlier, its board of directors (and its audit committee) also included Wendy Gramm, a former chairperson of the Commodity Futures Trading Commission and the wife of Phil Gramm, then the chairman of the Senate Banking Committee.

Previously a staid energy pipeline company, in the 1990s Enron expanded into energy trading, bandwidth trading, and derivatives trading in order to cash in on the deregulation of electricity production, telecommunications, and financial services. Enron's operations were highly fraudulent, both financially and operationally, but the company continued to grow, with twenty-two thousand employees at its peak. Enron faked its bandwidth and energy trading and artificially withheld electricity supplies to raise prices, behavior that played a role in the severe electricity shortages that plagued California in 2000–2001. Enron also committed massive financial frauds to create artificial profits and to hide liabilities and losses.

But what was particularly notable about the Enron affair was that Enron's frauds depended deeply on long-term cooperation from its accounting firm, one of the "Big Five," and also several of America's largest banks.

In its financial frauds, Enron's principal technique was to create off-balance-sheet entities known as SPEs, or special purpose entities, which it used to create fictitious transactions that made streams of borrowed money look like revenues. In the years just before it collapsed in 2001, Enron's earnings may have been overstated by as much as a factor of ten.[2] Some of the world's best-known banks knew exactly what Enron was doing and lined up for the privilege of helping it perpetrate fraud. They all did basically the same thing—namely, create sham transactions to inflate revenues or assets.

Starting in 1997, Chase Bank, now part of JPMorgan Chase, helped Enron create false gas sale revenues. The transactions involved two fictitious offshore entities, both with the same nominal director and shareholders. One of them, Mahonia, borrowed from Chase to "purchase" gas from Enron, for which it paid cash. The second, Stoneville, "sold" the same amount of gas at the same price to Enron, and was paid with long-term interest-bearing Enron notes. Behind the smokescreen, Chase was making a loan to Enron and conspiring to make the loan proceeds look like revenues. Over several years, the scam created $2.2 billion in fake gas revenues and associated profits.

Citigroup started doing the same thing in 1999, when Enron was trying to cover up a huge shortfall in projected revenues and cash flow. Citigroup agreed to help, and presto—Enron had nearly a half billion dollars of new positive operating cash flow. Enron used this trick again and again, and the total fictitious trading cash flows appear to have been on the same scale as the Chase Mahonia scam. Again, the record leaves little doubt that Citigroup knew it was enabling a fraud.[3]

Finally, there was Merrill Lynch. Enron asked Merrill to buy two Nigerian power barges (yes, Nigerian power barges) at an inflated price—

subject to a handshake deal that Enron would buy them back. Merrill clearly understood that it was a sham transaction, but consciences were eased by a 22 percent fee. Enron later tried to weasel out of the deal, which prompted some screaming matches. Merrill eventually got its money back, although Enron had to construct *another* fake transaction to produce the cash. Almost simultaneously, another Merrill team helped Enron with the purely fictitious sale and repurchase of a power plant. Nothing substantive had occurred, but Merrill got a very real $17 million fee for helping Enron create fake revenues and profits.[4]

Enron's accounting firm, Arthur Andersen, was criminally prosecuted and forced out of business. Several Enron executives went to prison; the former president, Jeffrey Skilling, is still serving his twenty-four-year term, while Kenneth Lay, the CEO, died shortly before commencing his sentence. Class-action lawsuits were also filed against Enron, Arthur Andersen, and the banks. A partial list of the financial settlements with the banks from both the private and public actions are shown in Table 2 below.

TABLE 2

ENRON-RELATED SETTLEMENTS

	($ MILLIONS)	
	CLASS ACTION SUITS	SEC SETTLEMENTS
CIBC*	2,400	80
JPMorgan Chase	2,200	135
Citigroup	2,000	120
Merrill Lynch	NA	80
Lehman Brothers	222	NA
Bank of America	69	NA
Goldman Sachs	11	NA

Sources: Class-action settlements at www.enronfraud.com. For SEC settlements, see press releases, March 17, 2003, July 28, 2003, and December 22, 2003.

*Canadian Imperial Bank of Commerce

But not a single one of the banks, or the individual bankers, that helped Enron fake its profits was criminally prosecuted. Aiding and abetting fraud was now permissible.[5]

The Internet Bubble: Eliot Spitzer as a Lonely Man

AT THE SAME time several banks were helping Enron commit accounting fraud, the Internet frenzy was driving the U.S. stock market, particularly the Nasdaq. Nearly the entire investment banking industry, its oldest and most prestigious firms very much included, fraudulently magnified the Internet bubble to gain business. The Internet bubble marked the first appearance of the new culture of dishonesty throughout mainstream finance.

Consider a priceless exchange between a Merrill Lynch broker and Henry Blodget, a youthful Merrill technology analyst, in 1998. In an internal e-mail regarding one of his favorite stock recommendations, Blodget described his private view of the company as "pos." The broker asked Blodget why his view was "positive," since she thought the company's numbers looked pretty weak. Blodget helpfully explained that "pos" didn't mean positive. It meant *piece of shit*.[6]

Morgan Stanley's Mary Meeker, another star technology analyst, was reportedly paid oceans of money for helping Morgan Stanley secure Amazon's investment banking business. (Both she and the bank were later sued on the basis of those conflicts.) Meeker was also deeply involved in pitching the AOL/Time Warner merger to the Time Warner board. Morgan Stanley stood to reap a large fee if the deal closed. And close it did, becoming one of the worst corporate mergers in history.[7]

Even Blodget and Meeker weren't as conflicted as Jack Grubman, the telecommunications analyst at Salomon Brothers (later Salomon Smith Barney). For years, he pushed Global Crossing and WorldCom, both of which turned out to be fraudulent disasters. Grubman was especially close to Bernie Ebbers, then CEO of WorldCom, coaching him on his presentations to other analysts. Ebbers was later convicted of accounting fraud, and is still in prison. An angry broker complained that Grubman maintained his "buy" rating on Global Crossing "from $60 all the way down to $1."

As the bubble peaked, Grubman decided to downgrade a half dozen of the companies he followed but then reversed himself at the request of the investment bankers. After long denigrating AT&T, he switched to a "strong buy" in 1999—allegedly based on the company's new cable strategy, but really because Salomon's new parent, Citigroup, had just won AT&T's investment banking business.[8]

Such behavior was common during the Internet bubble. Particularly for dot-com companies, the divergence between investment banks' public statements and the private views of analysts was frequently vast. Investment banks supposedly maintained "Chinese walls" between their research and investment banking departments, but it was a charade. Favorable analysts' reports were a key marketing tool in selling investment banking services, and analysts' pay was explicitly based on the investment banking revenues they generated. So they danced to their masters' tune, much as the rating agencies did during the mortgage bubble.

The Internet bubble was very profitable—the volume of private placements, IPOs, mergers, and acquisitions was far greater than anything seen before on Wall Street. A very high fraction of it was fraudulent, and it caused an enormous wave of losses, bankruptcies, failed acquisitions, and write-downs in 2000 through 2002. Companies such as Excite, Infospace, pets.com, WorldCom, Covad, Global Crossing, boo.com, startups.com, Webvan, e.digital, and many others received high investment ratings from bankers shortly before collapsing. Frequently the banks also paid barely disguised bribes to individual executives in order to obtain their company's business. But because the major investment banks all wanted IPO business, and also because they syndicated portions of most IPOs to each other, none of them was incented to be honest in their analyst research.

The Clinton administration did nothing—not the SEC, not the Justice Department, nobody. The Bush administration was no better. The

SEC became interested only after the New York State attorney general, Eliot Spitzer, filed a series of highly publicized lawsuits against the leading banks, which public pressure then compelled the SEC to support. In late 2002 there was a mass settlement with ten banks for $1.4 billion for "fraudulent research reports," "supervisory deficiencies," and subjecting analysts to "inappropriate pressures" from investment bankers. The largest single penalty, $400 million, was paid by Citigroup, while Merrill and Credit Suisse First Boston paid $200 million each, and Goldman Sachs paid $110 million. A few mid-level analysts—*very few*—were prosecuted. Blodget and Grubman were barred from the securities industry for life and paid fines of $4 million and $15 million, respectively. Meeker was not fined and went on to lead Morgan Stanley's technology research unit.[9]

Here are some excerpts from my interview with Eliot Spitzer.

SPITZER: Indeed, the defense that was proffered by many of the investment banks was not "You're wrong"; it was "Everybody's doing it, and everybody knows it's going on, and therefore nobody should rely on these analysts anyway."

CF: Did they really say that to you?

SPITZER: Oh yes…this was said to us. This was…And the other piece of it was, "Yes, you're right, but we're not as bad as our competitors, because everybody does it, and you should go after them first." And so there really wasn't an effort to deny that this intersection of analysts and investment bankers had generated a toxic combination. It was really, "Why are you going after us?" Again, it was the jurisdictional issue, and there were what they called Spitzer amendments floated up on Capitol Hill. Morgan Stanley went down to the House Financial Services Committee, this is when it was under Republican control, and they worked very hard with the SEC support to get an amendment through that would've limited and eliminated our jurisdiction and our ability to ask the questions. We beat that back with a fair bit of publicity.

Then I asked him about criminal prosecution:

CF: Did you ever think of prosecuting any of these people criminally?
SPITZER: We thought long and hard about it.
CF: Why didn't you?
SPITZER: I'll tell you why.... The only realistic targets in that criminal case would've been the analysts who are essentially mid-level individuals at the investment houses. And so I said to myself, "Yes, we could probably make a criminal case against a mid-level analyst, but the analyst is doing what he has been asked and told to do by the creation of an entire structure that preordained this outcome." We probably won't be able to make a criminal case against those higher up in the spectrum.
CF: Even though you think they were guilty.
SPITZER: Even though they understood that the system was generating analytical work that was flawed, it was going to be impossible to prove that the CEO knowingly instructed somebody to say something that was untrue, just because the e-mail chatter was down [t]here. As you move up the hierarchy, the CEO would say, "Well, of course we have analysts, of course they're telling the truth. Now, do we compensate them based upon how much investment banking business they bring in? Sure, but I never said to them, 'Lie.'" But the lies flowed almost necessarily from the system that was created.
CF: Was it, and is it, your personal opinion that the senior people were in fact guilty?
SPITZER: My view is that anybody within the investment bank was aware of the fact that the analytical work was tainted by the desire to bring in investment banking business, and that...the entire business model depended upon it....

So if you use the word "guilty" in a generic sense, yes, they were guilty of knowing that something was wrong. Guilty in a sense that they were provably guilty of a criminal case is a very different matter.

CF: Not provably. My question was not about…I understand your point about proof. But there's a difference between proof and what your opinion is about their real culpability.

SPITZER: Were they guilty of knowing that the analytical work was being tainted and damaged by the desire to get investment banking business? Yes.

Part of Spitzer's reluctance to prosecute may have come from the realities of his situation. He had fewer than twenty attorneys dealing with the investment banks, who outspent him at least ten to one; the Bush administration and the SEC were, to put it mildly, unenthusiastic; and although the offenses and their damage were serious by the standards of the time, they were utterly trivial compared to those committed since. The question of proof is, of course, an important one, and we will return to it in considering the mortgage bubble and the financial crisis.

JPMorgan Chase Pillages a County

MUNICIPAL BOND ISSUANCE is one of the murkier backwaters of finance, as subprime mortgages used to be. It is also notoriously corrupt, and left a wake of extraordinary destruction in Alabama's Jefferson County, which includes the city of Birmingham.[10]

In the late 1990s, Jefferson County settled a long-running dispute with the EPA by undertaking a major sewer project, financed with $2.9 billion in long-term fixed-rate bonds with an interest rate of 5.25 percent. As rates fell in the early 2000s, bankers descended on the county offering to restructure the debt and save millions in interest payments. JPMorgan Chase led a group of thirteen banks in structuring the deal and allocating its components. Instead of simply refinancing with straightforward fixed-rate bonds at a lower rate, the banks created an artificially complex deal to increase their fees. They issued $3 billion in various floating-rate instruments, while supposedly offsetting the risk of rate increases with interest-rate swaps. JPMorgan Chase used instruments called auction-rate securities, which caused billions in losses for many cities in 2008, along with other variable-rate bonds.

According to Bloomberg, the banks earned $55 million in fees for selling the auction-rate securities. The interest-rate swap contracts generated another $120 million in fees, which, according to an analyst later engaged by the county, was about six times the market norm. JPMorgan Chase was able to make this deal because it *also* made under-the-table payments of $8.2 million to local officials and brokerage firms. The largest payments, however, were made to other banks, including $3 million to Goldman Sachs and $1.4 million to Rice Financial Products, a New York municipal bond specialist, for agreeing to withdraw from the competition. All of the illicit payments were charged as fees deducted from the funds raised for the county. Naturally, there was no disclosure of the payments in the bond prospectuses.

At first the overall deal, leaving aside the inflated banking fees and bribes, appeared to work. The county commissioners bragged about their financial prowess, and Morgan helped them set up seminars for other counties. But when the exotic bonds that JPMorgan Chase had recommended collapsed during the financial crisis of 2008, the transaction turned into a disaster. When the county announced that it would exit the deal, JPMorgan Chase billed the county $647 million, and threatened to sue.*

As this is written, the county has defaulted on most of its debt and declared bankruptcy. The sewage improvements may never be completed, and sewage and water rates have risen to the point where poorer residents must choose between heat and water. The SEC forced JPMorgan Chase to drop its breakup fee and to pay the county $50 mil-

---

*Swap agreements almost always include breakup fees calculated as the present value of the net stream of income due to the aggrieved party over the remaining life of the deal.

lion in damages on top of a $10 million fine. The local prosecutor has won prison sentences for the corrupt county commissioners.

But what of JPMorgan Chase? Bribe paying is unambiguously criminal, and it is particularly obnoxious for wealthy men in elegant clothes to extract $175 million in fees from county ratepayers, most of whom are poor—and then wreak utter havoc on their government. But JPMorgan Chase has not been prosecuted. The two JPMorgan Chase executives primarily involved were fined and barred from the securities industry, but they were not prosecuted either, even though one of them had a prior criminal record for a similar offense.

Jefferson County was not alone, although its story was worse than average. By 2008 there was between $300 billion and $350 billion in auction-rate securities (ARS) outstanding, issued by thousands of state and local government entities. Investors were institutions and high-end retail investors, attracted by the money-market-like liquidity, at slightly higher yields. The minimum retail investment was usually $25,000.

The Wonders of Auction-Rate Securities

AUCTION-RATE SECURITIES ARE the kind of complex product Wall Street loves to create. They make it look like bond sellers are getting a better deal, so they will cough up higher fees, without understanding the risks that lie in ambush down the road. They offer bondholders a long-term debt deal at apparently low floating interest rates. But the "long-term" part of the deal is a fake. What really happens is that the banks reauction the notes every three weeks or so to reset the rates and allow the investors to depart. But what happens if nobody bids at the reauction? Rarely but occasionally, ARS auctions had failed before the crisis. In those cases, the investment bank that had underwritten them stepped in as a short-term buyer until markets settled. But *thousands* of auctions failed during 2008, because investors pulled their money out of everything except Treasury bonds in a massive flight to safety. And as the banks' balance sheets started filling up with billions in failed auction securities, they collectively stepped aside and let the market collapse.[11]

As a result, issuers were suddenly faced with the need to pay prohibitively high rates, and many defaulted. The resulting collapse of the ARS market wiped out the nest eggs of investors all over the country, as they found themselves with defaulted and illiquid securities. State attorneys general initiated lawsuits, as did class-action plaintiffs, and eventually the SEC. Nearly always, the banks' sales brochures and presentations had represented ARS as "completely liquid," "as good as cash," or as "money market instruments"; and the banks' sales forces continued to make such representations long after the industry was aware of the looming collapse of the entire ARS market.[12]

Settlements with twenty-one banks and investment banks were reached in 2008 and 2009. UBS agreed to buy back $22 billion worth of ARS; Merrill Lynch, $19.5 billion; Wachovia, $9 billion; Morgan Stanley, $4 billion; and JPMorgan Chase, $3 billion.[13]

But the ARS fiasco is just one example of the high levels of predation and corruption found in municipal bond markets. A consortium of state attorneys general, the Justice Department, and the SEC has been pursuing a long-running bribery and bid-rigging case involving more than a hundred municipalities and several large banks. Bribery and fraud settlements have so far been reached with JPMorgan Chase, Bank of America, Wachovia, and UBS for multiple conspiracies with each other, with municipal officials, and with corrupt bid managers who steered municipal bond contracts to banks.[14] The cases were settled with fines, and no bank or senior bank executive has been prosecuted, although several lower-level individuals have been. There have also been similar "pay to play" scandals in the market for managing local and state government pension funds. One such scandal in New York involved Steven Rattner, a prominent hedge fund manager and Democratic fundraiser who was once a strong candidate to become treasury secretary in the Obama administration. Rattner reached settlements with the SEC and the New York attorney general, agreeing to pay $16 million in fines. Obama appointed him to run the administration's rescue of the automobile industry following the bankruptcies of GM and Chrysler.

Barclays Helps Private Equity Firms to Fleece a Client (and Shareholders)

In 2010 Barclays Capital (which contains the remnants of Lehman Brothers's investment banking arm) began working with Del Monte Foods to arrange the sale of the company to one or more private equity firms. However, instead of solely representing Del Monte's interests, Barclays secretly began to work with KKR and Vestar, helping them to coordinate a joint bid rather than generating a competitive auction. This violated the terms of Barclays's contract with Del Monte and allowed KKR and Vestar to buy the company far less expensively. Barclays's motivation was that it wanted the private equity firms' business in arranging the financing of the acquisition, which would bring Barclays lucrative fees. Indeed, once the deal was arranged, Barclays switched sides and began working with the consortium of private equity firms that eventually won the deal—KKR, Vestar, and Centerview. A Delaware judge found that Barclays had "indisputably crossed the line" in its conduct.[15]

There have long been suspicions that similar behavior is widespread— that investment banks steer business to the private equity firms that they work with repeatedly, to the disadvantage of real-economy corporations seeking financing, mergers, acquisitions, or divestitures. There have been no criminal prosecutions for this conduct, in either the Del Monte case or any others.

Tax Evasion and Criminal Asset Concealment

NOT ALL CRIMINAL banking is American. In the domain of large-scale tax evasion, Swiss banks are way ahead, as is natural given Switzerland's long-standing economic dependence on bank secrecy to attract flight capital and criminal assets. Switzerland and more than a dozen other countries including Liechtenstein, the Channel Islands, and several Caribbean nations facilitate tax evasion and asset concealment through their national banking laws. Frequently, major banks have actively assisted wealthy individuals and corporations in using these nations for those purposes. Annual tax revenue losses, just for the United States, are estimated at $100 billion.[16]

The following discussion of tax evasion concentrates on UBS, but investigations have uncovered similar behavior at Credit Suisse, HSBC, Julius Baer, and other European banks. Very unusually, there have been a few criminal prosecutions, although both corporate and individual defendants have been treated *very* leniently.

Bradley Birkenfeld, an American, worked for a UBS business unit that specialized in helping wealthy Americans evade taxes. For more than a decade, in a systematic effort authorized by the highest levels of UBS, bankers created secret numbered accounts, arranged for offshore funds transfers through shell companies, and provided offshore-sourced credit cards (to pay for expensive foreign vacations, say). UBS bankers traveling to the United States carried specially encrypted laptops to hide their files; money was transferred by hand-carried paper checks instead of wire services; sometimes bankers smuggled diamonds or other valuables. They were instructed not to stay in the same hotel on consecutive nights, and never, ever communicate with their clients on UBS letterhead.

Then Bradley Birkenfeld became a whistle-blower in 2007. Birkenfeld explained to Justice Department and IRS officials that UBS had "$20 billion" in American tax evasion accounts, with estimated profits of $200 million a year. The IRS later estimated that the accounts totaled $18 billion; and Birkenfeld's profit estimate is probably low.

A series of Senate hearings in 2008 publicized UBS's behavior and yielded highly embarrassing televised testimony by UBS executives, who refused to provide the names of their U.S. tax evasion clients. Shortly after the hearings, the Justice Department indicted UBS and a number of its executives, including Raoul Weil, CEO of UBS Global Wealth Management and a member of the UBS Executive Board. Weil failed to surrender after his indictment and became a fugitive. Another senior executive pled guilty and received five years' probation. In 2009 the Justice Department and UBS reached a deferred prosecution agreement that required UBS to cooperate in identifying at least ten thousand tax evasion cases, and to pay a $780 million fine, but allowed the bank to avoid criminal prosecution. Shortly afterward, nearly fifteen thousand Americans responded to a reduced-penalty offer for voluntary disclosure.

Although Birkenfeld voluntarily came forward to unveil the entire UBS tax evasion apparatus, *he* was prosecuted and is now in prison. Thus far he is the only person sent to jail.

Phil Gramm, the former senator from Texas who was chairman of the Senate Banking Committee when Republicans controlled the Senate, is now vice chairman of UBS, which he joined immediately upon retiring from the Senate in 2002. As a senator, Gramm had strenuously opposed efforts to control money laundering and bank secrecy.

Many other investigations are continuing. The Germans and British have filed actions against UBS. In July 2011 the Justice Department notified Credit Suisse that it was the target of a similar investigation, and in November 2011 Credit Suisse, under threat of prosecution, began the process of disclosing tax evasion clients to the IRS. Other European and American whistle-blowers have already revealed large-scale tax evasion efforts assisted by Julius Baer and by Liechtensteiner Fürsten-Bank. The total value of the concealed assets already under investigation probably exceeds $100 billion.

In the Service of Rogue States and Drug Lords

TAX EVASION IS not the only motive for bank secrecy, money laundering, and asset concealment.[17] Kleptocratic political leaders, organized criminals, drug cartels, and rogue states engaged in nuclear weapons development or terrorism also require bank secrecy to conceal the size and sources of their funds and to give them secret access to payments systems. Many of the world's largest banks, both American and foreign, have been only too happy to help.

Perhaps the most extraordinary case involves Credit Suisse, Barclays, Lloyds, and seven other (as yet unidentified) international banks that laundered billions of dollars for Iran and other nations; all of the nations in question have been placed under international sanctions for developing nuclear weapons and/or supporting terrorism. In violation of UN sanctions and U.S. law, the banks helped Iran launder transfers to the United States, including payments related to Iran's ballistic missile and nuclear programs, as well as funds that apparently were channeled to terrorist groups in the Middle East. Some banks created internal instruction manuals to help employees strip out incriminating data from wire transfers.

The most detailed public records pertain to Credit Suisse, possibly the most aggressive in marketing its program, which started violating U.S. sanctions on Iran in 1995. The bank produced a special pamphlet for its illegal customers, "How to Transfer USD Payments," and set up a special "investigations" office to manually review each illegal transaction, promising, *"It is absolutely impossible that one of your payment instructions will be effected without having it checked in advance by our specially designated payment team at Credit Suisse in Zurich and all team members are most professional and aware of the special attention such payments of yours do require"* [emphasis in original]. The bank also maintained a sub-business of making transfers to "specially designated nationals," like warlords or other large-scale criminals.[18]

A series of settlements reached by the banks with the Justice Department and the Manhattan District Attorney in 2009 and 2010 yielded $1.2 billion in fines. Credit Suisse agreed to pay $536 million, Barclays $298 million, and Lloyds $350 million. For at least a decade, they had systematically engaged in criminal activity by laundering money for Libya, Iran, Sudan, Burma, and North Korea, among others.[19] It is clear that these activities were known and approved by quite senior executives. But since none of the three banks contested the charges, and all disclosed their records, the cases were settled with fines and deferred prosecution agreements. No bank was required to plead guilty, and not a single person was criminally prosecuted or even individually fined.

Let me pause to ask readers the following question. What do you think would happen to *you,* personally, if, *as an individual,* not a senior bank executive, you were caught laundering money for Iran's nuclear weapons program? Do you think that, perhaps, you might be treated just a little bit more harshly? Well, in fact, we have some interesting comparative data on this question. In 2011 an Iranian American, Reza Safarha, was indicted, tried, convicted, and sentenced to ten months in prison for transferring $300,000 to Iran in violation of U.S. sanctions. He was engaged in low-level trafficking in stolen office equipment and had no involvement with the Iranian government, much less its nuclear programs or support for terrorism.

Even more striking is the case of Mahmoud Reza Banki, an Iranian immigrant who earned a PhD in the United States and worked for an American consulting firm. Over several years, he received a total of $3.4 million from his family in Iran. The money was legally earned, and he reported it on his tax returns; there was never any suggestion that he had committed any crime except violating the sanctions. It is even unclear that the transfers were substantive violations, because personal transfers to family members are exempted. Nonetheless in 2010 Banki was arrested, prosecuted, convicted, and sentenced to two and a half years in federal prison. His conviction was overturned upon appeal, and as of this writing he awaits retrial. It does not appear that he was ever offered a deferred prosecution agreement.[20]

The banks' Iranian sanctions violations were particularly egregious, but far from isolated. JPMorgan Chase dipped its toes into money laundering at about the same time. In 2005 and 2006 the company processed $178.5 million in clearly illegal wire transfers from Cuban nationals. Treasury officials also caught the bank processing illegal wire transfers to Sudan. At first the bank denied it, but after being pressed, it produced documents confirming the transactions. Although Treasury officials called JPMorgan Chase's behavior "egregious," the case was settled for an $88.3 million fine.[21]

The single most notorious money-laundering episode related to political corruption was probably Citigroup's assistance in smuggling $100 million out of Mexico, mostly to Switzerland, for Raúl Salinas and his wife in the 1990s. Raúl Salinas was the brother of Carlos Salinas de Gortari, Mexico's president from 1988 to 1994, who was notorious for large-scale corruption. The discovery of the smuggling, together with an enormous scandal in Mexico involving money laundering and political assassinations, resulted in Raúl Salinas's arrest for murder in 1995. Citigroup was never prosecuted. A GAO report prepared for Senator John Glenn made it clear that Citigroup did not follow proper procedures, but left doubt as to whether the smuggling was systematic policy or an arrangement made solely by local executives.[22]

There have been other cases involving corrupt rulers. In 2004 and 2005 Riggs Bank, one of the oldest and most traditional banks in the United States, paid two fines totaling $41 million, and pled guilty to criminal charges related to money laundering for Saudi Arabian diplomats, the astonishingly corrupt dictator of Equatorial Guinea, and former Chilean military dictator Augusto Pinochet, who turned out to have over $10 million in secret personal assets at Riggs. The bank received a suspended sentence and continues to operate; no executives were prosecuted.[23]

But these cases, while striking, were actually small compared to the money-laundering activities that U.S. banks allowed in support of the Latin American drug trade. The biggest recent case—and it was pretty damned big—involved Wachovia. Wachovia was the sixth-largest lender in the United States when it collapsed in 2008, having lost $30 billion as a result of its highly dubious real estate lending during the bubble. Shortly afterward, it was acquired by Wells Fargo. But Wachovia had another problem too.

Over the previous three years, federal grand juries had served Wachovia with 6,700 subpoenas related to its role in transferring a stunning *$378 billion,* most of it in cash, between Mexican currency exchanges and the United States—without reporting any transactions for suspicious behavior, of which there was an awful lot. In fact, since 2004 Wachovia had ignored or suppressed multiple internal warnings about highly suspicious funds transfers and had marginalized the compliance officers issuing the warnings. For example one compliance officer, a former Scotland Yard investigator, had found numerous, supposedly separate, Mexican transfers made at the same location and the same time, involving sequentially numbered traveler's checks totaling enormous sums of money. He was instructed by his management to stop examining American transactions, and Wachovia's managing director for compliance sent him a letter warning him that he was "failing to perform at an acceptable standard." He sued Wachovia, which paid him an undisclosed amount for damages—on the condition that he leave the bank.[24] The currency exchanges were ideal laundering facilities for drug cartels receiving proceeds from their American drug distributors. Funds processed by Wachovia and also by Bank of America between 2004 and 2007 were traced to the purchase, among other things, of a dozen large commercial jets used for smuggling dozens of tons of cocaine.[25]

Wells Fargo, as the successor/owner of Wachovia, cooperated with the investigation and agreed to pay a $160 million fine and implement a robust money-laundering detection system. Similar settlements for similar violations were reached with Bank of America and twice with subsidiaries of American Express. Amex paid a $55 million fine when its Edge Act subsidiary, AEBI, was caught facilitating money laundering for Colombian drug lords in cooperation with the Black Market Peso Exchange from 1999 through 2004.[26]

And then there is Bernie Madoff—or rather, the banks' treatment of him.

Jumping on Board with Bernie

BERNARD L. MADOFF, philanthropist, reliable friend, former chairman of the Nasdaq stock exchange, and creator of one of the first electronic trading platforms, also ran the biggest pure Ponzi scheme in history, operating it for thirty years and causing cash losses of $19.5 billion.[27]

Shortly after the scheme collapsed and Madoff confessed in late 2008, evidence began to surface that for years, major commercial and investment banks had strongly suspected that Madoff was a fraud. None of them reported their suspicions to the authorities, and several banks and bankers decided to make money from him, without, of course, risking any of their own funds. Theories about his fraud varied. Some thought he was "front-running," examining the orders passing through his electronic trading business and then using this information to place his own trades in front of them. Some thought he might have access to insider information. But quite a few thought that he was running a Ponzi scheme.

Madoff claimed to be tracking the S&P 500 stock index, while using options to slightly increase returns while reducing volatility in the value of his portfolio.

But there were just a few little problems. For instance:

- When others tried to replicate Madoff's strategy or apply it retrospectively, they found that his results could only be achieved by always buying at or near the market's low and always selling at or near the market's high—which is impossible. Madoff claimed to have had negative monthly returns only five times in fifteen years of operation. In one period in 2002 in which the S&P 500 lost 30 percent, Madoff claimed that his fund was up 6 percent. Such performance was both inconsistent with his supposed strategy and totally unprecedented in investment fund management.
- Although Madoff's stated strategy entailed massive trading vol-

umes in both shares and options, no one knew who his trading counterparties were, nor was there ever any visible sign of his moves in and out of the market. Actually pursuing his strategy would often have required trading more options than existed in the entire market.

- Madoff simultaneously served as the broker executing the trades, the investment advisor, and the custodian of the assets. Such an arrangement obviously lacks checks and balances and is conducive to fraud. It is unheard of for an operation on the scale of Madoff's, and was repeatedly noted as a danger sign. Madoff also employed his brother, niece, nephew, and both of his sons in his business.

- His auditing firm was a totally unknown three-person firm in a suburban strip mall. One of the three was a secretary, and one was a semiretired CPA who lived in Florida. The firm was not professionally qualified to perform audits and did not hold itself out as an auditor.

- Account statements were typed, not electronically printed, and the firm used only paper trading tickets, both of which were inconsistent with the required volume of trading. Investors were never given real-time or remote electronic access to their account information; they only received paper statements in the mail.

- Despite his enormous purported success, Madoff did not charge any hedge fund management fees. He claimed that he made his money simply by having his own trading platform process all of his trades, a highly implausible claim. The real reason that he did not charge the typical 20 percent of profits was that he needed to attract new money to keep the scheme going as long as possible.

These problems and many others—we'll get to those in a minute—were repeatedly cited as warning signs by banks and hedge funds that either dealt with Madoff or were considering doing so. Goldman Sachs executives paid a visit to Madoff to see if they should recommend him to clients. A partner later recalled, "Madoff refused to let them do any due diligence on the funds and when they asked about the firm's investment strategy they couldn't understand it. Goldman not only blacklisted Madoff in the asset management division but banned its brokerage from trading with the firm too."[28] Risk managers at Merrill Lynch, Citigroup, UBS, JPMorgan Chase's Private Banking, and other firms had done the same. The Merrill parent company, for example, had expressly forbidden dealings with Madoff from the 1990s.[29] They all suspected fraud of some kind.

As a result, most of the major banks declined to invest their own money with Madoff. However, they did sometimes allow *their clients* to invest. A number of banks, including Merrill Lynch, Citigroup, ABN Amro, and Nomura, also created various tracking funds to replicate Madoff's returns,* even though all suspected fraud.

But UBS and JPMorgan Chase were even more deeply involved. UBS created a new family of "feeder funds" to send assets to Madoff. (Madoff generally did not accept direct investments, preferring to receive money via these "feeder funds.") Most feeder funds acted as little more than drop boxes and made few, if any, investments except into Madoff's fund. There is strong evidence that several of them knew Madoff was a fraud. But Madoff paid them about 4 percent per year for doing virtually nothing, so they were happy to look the other way.

UBS created or worked with several Madoff feeder funds, even though UBS headquarters forbade investing any bank or client money in Madoff accounts. The feeder funds were required by law to conduct due diligence, and one of them hired a due diligence specialist named

---

*Merrill, for example, offered investors the opportunity to recover four times the return on referenced Madoff funds. An investor would put up, say, $1 million, and receive a Merrill note in exchange, plus a top-up loan of $3 million. In return, Merrill received an investment fee, plus a hefty lending fee. To cover its liability, Merrill then would typically invest the $4 million into the referenced Madoff fund—although it was not required to do so. Each month, it paid the amount of dividends the customer would have received if he or she had a $4 million Madoff account, less a 20 percent incentive fee. Note that Merrill itself did not have to take any investment risk, and that customer funds were never directly invested in a Madoff account.

Chris Cutler. After four days, he wrote to the feeder fund: "If this were a new investment product, not only would it simply fail to meet due diligence standards: you would likely shove it out the door. EITHER extremely sloppy errors OR serious omissions in tickets." Cutler found, for example, that Madoff's claimed strategy implied trading a number of options that was far higher than the total number actually traded on the Chicago Board Options Exchange.[30] The fund proceeded with its Madoff investments anyway.[31]

UBS explicitly instructed its employees to avoid Madoff. A memo to one of the feeder funds in 2005 contained a section entitled "Not To Do." In this section was the following, in large boldface type: "ever enter into a direct contact with Bernard Madoff!!!" One of the UBS executives involved in creating the new funds received a headquarters inquiry on what he was doing. He replied, "Business is business. We cannot permit ourselves to lose 300 million," referring to anticipated fund management revenues.[32] UBS proceeded to issue fund prospectuses in which it represented that it would act as custodian, manager, and administrator of the feeder funds, when in fact they had already agreed with Madoff to play no such role. Like all Madoff sponsors, UBS received no information except paper summaries of monthly results.

JPMorgan Chase was, if anything, even more dishonest. Like Merrill Lynch and Citigroup, they set up Madoff tracking funds despite explicit warnings from an executive in JPMorgan Chase's Private Bank unit that he "never had been able to reverse engineer how [Madoff] made money."[33] But JPMorgan Chase had even more evidence, because they served as Madoff's primary banker for more than twenty years.* Anyone with access to those accounts would know that something was seriously wrong. For example:

---

*The original account was opened in 1986 with Chemical Bank, which later merged with Chase. The Chase/JPMorgan merger was in 2001, when Madoff was on the verge of spectacular growth.

- An investment company with thousands of individual customers should have credited incoming funds to segregated customer accounts or directed them into multiple other subaccounts. Instead whatever came in was more or less tossed into a single pot.

- Know Your Customer (KYC) rules for business accounts were greatly strengthened after 9/11, and JPMorgan Chase allegedly takes its KYC obligations very seriously. There is a KYC department attached to every line of business. But the identified KYC "sponsor" on the Madoff account, when interviewed by the Madoff bankruptcy trustee, was unaware that he had been so designated and did not know what the job entailed.

- JPMorgan Chase received copies of the mandatory financial filings that Madoff made with the SEC. They were usually wrong, often wildly so. One statement listed $5 million in bank cash accounts, when the actual amount at JPMorgan Chase was $295 million. Another listed no outstanding bank loans, when there was a $95 million loan outstanding. For years, the statements showed no trading commission revenue, even though they were supposed to be the primary source of Madoff's income (he did not charge management or incentive fees). Then one year, the statements suddenly showed more than $100 million in commissions, although none were in the product categories that were supposed to dominate his strategy. Madoff's prospectuses represented that idle cash was always invested in Treasury bills, when JPMorgan Chase knew it was almost all in overnight deposits.

- Money-laundering regulations are quite strict and impose obligations on banks to report suspicious activity. JPMorgan Chase has an automated alert system that is supposed to trigger a review and report whenever a "red flag" event occurs. How about a customer who received 318 transfers of exactly $986,310 each in a single year, often several per day? No problem, no alert.

- Several of Madoff's biggest customers were also JPMorgan Chase Private Banking customers, so the bank could see both sides of the transactions. And indeed they often saw hundreds of millions of dollars washing back and forth between client accounts and Madoff, sometimes billed as loans but often with no explanation at all. In the entire history of the Madoff accounts, the automated money-laundering system generated only a single alert, which was not followed up.

With all that, they must have suspected something—and indeed they did. The lawsuit filed by the Madoff bankruptcy trustee against JPMorgan Chase makes for astonishing reading. More than a dozen senior JPMorgan Chase bankers had discussed in e-mails and memoranda, as well as in person with each other, a long list of suspicions. On June 15, 2007, one employee said to another: "I am sitting at lunch with [redacted] who just told me that there is a well-known cloud over the head of Madoff and that his returns are speculated to be part of a Ponzi scheme." At the same time—June 2007—three members of JPMorgan Chase's executive committee openly discussed this possibility at a meeting. They were John J. Hogan, chief risk officer for investment banking; Matthew E. Zames, a senior trading executive; and Carlos M. Hernandez, head of equities for the investment banking unit. After Madoff's arrest, Hogan's deputy, Brian Sankey, suggested that it would be preferable if the meeting agenda "never sees the light of day again."[34] But Madoff produced a half billion dollars in fee revenue for JPMorgan over the years, so the bank clearly had no interest in rocking that boat.

The SEC has been deservedly criticized for not following up on years of complaints about Madoff, many of which came from a Boston investigator, Harry Markopolos, whom they treated as a crank. The SEC also bungled its own investigations of Madoff. But suppose a senior executive at Goldman Sachs, UBS, or JPMorgan Chase had called the SEC director of enforcement and said, "You really need to take a close look at Bernard Madoff. He must be working a scam. No proof, but here are five very suspicious facts, and here's what you should look for." If it came from them, the SEC would have had to pay attention, even in the pitiful, toothless state to which it had been reduced in the Clinton and

Bush administrations. But not a single bank that had suspicions about Madoff made such a call. Instead, they assumed he was a crook, but either just left him alone or were happy to make money from him.

The Financial Crisis as the Logical Culmination of Financial Criminalization

TAKEN TOGETHER, THE foregoing suggests a major cultural change in American and global banking, and in its treatment by regulators and law enforcement authorities. Since the 1980s finance has become more arrogant, more unethical, and increasingly criminal. Tolerance of overtly criminal behavior has now become broadly, structurally embedded in the financial sector, and has played a major role in financial sector profitability and incomes since the late 1990s. In some cases, financial criminality has supported truly grave offenses (nuclear weapons proliferation), while in other cases it has been a major contributor to financial instability and recession (the S&L crisis, the Internet bubble).

And yet none of this conduct was punished in any significant way. Total fines for all these cases combined appear to be far less than 1 percent of financial sector profits and bonuses during the same period. There have been very few prosecutions and no criminal convictions of large U.S. financial institutions or their senior executives. Where individuals not linked to major banks have committed similar offenses, they have been treated far more harshly.

Given this background, it is difficult to avoid the conclusion that the mortgage bubble and financial crisis were facilitated not only by deregulation but also by the prior twenty years' tolerance of large-scale financial crime. First, the absence of prosecution gradually led to a deeply embedded cultural acceptance of unethical and criminal behavior in finance. And second, it generated a sense of personal impunity; bankers contemplating criminal actions were no longer deterred by threat of prosecution.

My own conclusion after having examined this subject is that if the

Internet bubble, the abetting of frauds at Enron and elsewhere, and the money-laundering scandals had resulted in prison sentences for senior financial executives, the financial crisis probably would have been far less serious, even if financial deregulation had occurred just as it did at the policy level. The law still leaves considerable scope for dangerous and unethical behavior, but many of the abuses of the bubble depended upon criminality.

And just as the last twenty years of unpunished crime constituted a green light for the bubble, so, too, America's nonresponse to the bubble and crisis is setting the tone for financial conduct over the next decade. Beyond an interest in justice for its own sake, it is therefore important to consider whether the behavior that generated the bubble was criminal, whether successful prosecutions are feasible, and whether putting senior financial executives in prison on a large scale would be ethically justified and economically beneficial.

The Obama administration has rationalized its failure to prosecute anyone (literally, anyone at all) for bubble-related crimes by saying that while much of Wall Street's behavior was unwise or unethical, it wasn't illegal. Here is President Obama at a White House press conference on October 6, 2011:

> Well, first on the issue of prosecutions on Wall Street, one of the biggest problems about the collapse of Lehmans [*sic*] and the subsequent financial crisis and the whole subprime lending fiasco is that a lot of that stuff wasn't necessarily illegal, it was just immoral or inappropriate or reckless. That's exactly why we needed to pass Dodd-Frank, to prohibit some of these practices. The financial sector is very creative and they are always looking for ways to make money. That's their job. And if there are loopholes and rules that can be bent and arbitrage to be had, they will take advantage of it. So without commenting on particular prosecutions—obviously that's not my job; that's the Attorney General's job—I think part of people's frustrations, part of my frustration, was a lot of practices that should not have been allowed weren't necessarily against the law.[35]

In these and many other statements, the president and senior administration officials have portrayed themselves as frustrated and hamstrung—desirous of punishing those responsible for the crisis, but unable to do so because their conduct wasn't illegal, and/or the federal government lacks sufficient power to sanction them. With apologies for my vulgarity, this is complete horseshit.

When the federal government is really serious about something—preventing another 9/11, or pursuing major organized crime figures—it has many tools at its disposal and often uses them. There are wiretaps and electronic eavesdropping. There are undercover agents who pretend to be criminals in order to entrap their targets. There are National Security Letters, an aggressive form of administrative subpoena that allows federal authorities to secretly obtain almost any electronic record—complete with a gag order making it illegal for the target of the subpoena to tell anyone about it. There are special prosecutors, task forces, and grand juries. When Patty Hearst was kidnapped by the radical Symbionese Liberation Army in 1974, the FBI assigned hundreds of agents to the case.

In organized crime investigations, the FBI and federal prosecutors often start at the bottom in order to get to the top. They use the well-established technique of nailing lower-level people and then offering them a deal if they inform on and/or testify about their superiors—whereupon the FBI nails their superiors, and does the same thing to them, until climbing to the top of the tree. There is also the technique of nailing people for what can be proven against them, even if it's not the main offense. Al Capone was never convicted of bootlegging, large-scale corruption, or murder; he was convicted of tax evasion.

In this spirit, here are a few observations about the ethics, legalities, and practicalities of prosecution related to the bubble:

First, much of the bubble *was* directly, massively criminal. One can debate exactly what fraction, where the gray areas are, how much of it can be proven, and so forth. But it sure as hell wasn't zero. And we'll take another little tour of the industry shortly, with this question in mind.

Second, if you really wanted to get these people, you could. Maybe not all of them, but certainly many. Some bubble-related violations are very clear, with strong written evidence. If you flipped enough people, some of them would undoubtedly have interesting things to say about what their senior management knew. And many of the people responsible for the bubble are the same people responsible for the other crimes we just examined that have not been seriously pursued or punished. Many of these people have also committed various personal offenses—drug use, use of prostitution, tax evasion, insider trading, fraudulent billing of personal spending as business expenses. Many of them still have their original jobs and are therefore subject to regulatory oversight and pressure, as are their firms. In fact, there are many techniques, venues, organizations, regulations, and statutes, both civil and criminal, available to investigate these people, punish them, and recover the money they took—if you really wanted to. The federal government has used almost none of them.

Third, the moral argument for punishment is very strong, providing ample justification for erring on the side of aggressive legal pursuit. Whatever portion of banking conduct during the bubble was criminal, it was certainly substantial, and there is no doubt whatsoever that it was utterly, pervasively unethical, designed to defraud in reality if not in law. Since the crisis, the people who caused it have been anything but honest or contrite. They have been evasive, dishonest, and self-justifying, returning as quickly as possible to their unerringly selfish behavior. Their behavior caused enormous damage, both human and economic; the consequences of their wrongdoing are so large as to justify almost any action that could help to prevent another such crisis by creating real deterrence. There would also be intangible but large benefits to raising the general ethical standard of a vital industry, and one whose executives often become high-level government officials.

Given this background, let's now consider the question of criminal liability, as well as the feasibility of prosecution.

J'accuse

A REASONABLE LIST of prosecutable crimes committed during the bubble, the crisis, and the aftermath period by financial services firms includes:

- Securities fraud (many forms)
- Accounting fraud (many forms)
- Honest services violations (mail fraud statute)
- Bribery
- Perjury and making false statements to federal investigators
- Sarbanes-Oxley violations (certifying false accounting statements)
- RICO offenses and criminal antitrust violations
- Federal aid disclosure regulations (related to Federal Reserve loans)
- Personal conduct offenses (many forms: drug use, tax evasion, etc.)

In addition, financial sector firms and executives committed many civil offenses for which they could be pursued in civil actions, which have a lower burden of proof (preponderance of evidence, as opposed to beyond a reasonable doubt). These offenses include civil Sarbanes-Oxley violations, civil fraud, and violations of multiple SEC regulations, particularly regulations related to disclosure requirements.

Let's consider some examples.

Securities Fraud

Here, we face an embarrassment of riches. The primary applicable authority is Rule 10b-5, promulgated by the SEC under the authority of the 1934 Securities Exchange Act. It reads:

It shall be unlawful for any person, directly or indirectly, by the use of any means or instrumentality of interstate commerce, or of the mails or of any facility of any national securities exchange,

(a) To employ any device, scheme, or artifice to defraud,

(b) To make any untrue statement of a material fact or to omit to state a material fact necessary in order to make the statements made, in the light of the circumstances under which they were made, not misleading, or

(c) To engage in any act, practice, or course of business which operates or would operate as a fraud or deceit upon any person, in connection with the purchase or sale of any security.

There are several essential elements to a 10b-5 offense: it must be a *misstatement or omission* that is sufficiently *material* to affect an investor's opinion; that is made *intentionally;* that the investor *relied upon* in making his decision; and that directly caused *actual losses.* The rule can be used by the SEC for bringing civil cases, by the Justice Department for both civil and criminal actions, and also by private parties bringing civil suits. Even if the securities in question are being sold to sophisticated, professional investors, you can't lie to them.

Where to begin?

As we have already seen, almost all the prospectuses and sales material on mortgage-backed bonds sold from 2005 through 2007 were a compound of falsehoods. But it starts even earlier in the food chain. We have *also* already seen that mortgage originators committed securities fraud when they misrepresented the characteristics of loan pools, and the nature and extent of their due diligence with regard to them, when they sold pools to securitizers (and accepted financing from them). Most or all of the securitizers (meaning nearly all the investment banks and major banking conglomerates) then committed securities fraud when they misrepresented the characteristics of loans backing their CDOs, the characteristics of the resulting mortgage-backed securities, and the nature and results of their due diligence in the process of creating those CDOs. The securitizers also committed securities fraud when they made similar misrepresentations to the insurers of, and sellers of CDS protection on, those CDOs.

The executives of both originators and securitizers then committed a separate form of securities fraud in their statements to investors and the public about their companies' financial condition. They knew that they were engaging in fraud that would eventually need to end, and as the bubble peaked and started to collapse, they repeatedly lied about their companies' financial condition. In some cases they also concealed other material information, such as the extent to which executives were selling or hedging their own stock holdings because they knew that their firms were about to collapse.

Next, several investment banks committed securities fraud when they failed to disclose that they were selling securities that they had designed to rid themselves of their worst loans and CDOs, or that were designed to fail so that the investment banks and their hedge fund clients could profit by betting on their failure. The Hudson and Timberwolf synthetic CDOs sold by Goldman Sachs, and which were the focus of the Levin Senate subcommittee hearings, provide a very strong basis for prosecution. Goldman's trading arm had been dragooned into finding and dumping their most dangerous assets to naive institutional investors—midsized German banks, South Korean banks, minor public pension funds, and the like. Important representations in the Hudson sales material—that assets were not sourced from Goldman's own inventory—were lies, and they were material lies, since investors had learned to be wary of banks clearing out their own bad inventory. E-mail trails show that top executives closely tracked the garbage disposals and were gleeful at the unloading of the Timberwolf assets—as they should have been, for the assets were nearly worthless within months. There have been no prosecutions.

Many large U.S. financial institutions, including the banks but also accounting firms, rating agencies, and insurers, were involved in other securities frauds during the bubble. We have already noted the banks' misrepresentations as to the safety and liquidity of auction-rate securities, for example, for which nobody has been prosecuted criminally. Similarly, Citigroup failed to disclose in its investor presentations that it was contractually obligated to repurchase, or pay for the losses on, huge quantities of securities that it had placed in off-balance-sheet structured investment vehicles (SIVs). (In this case, Citigroup may have a legal defense—while its investor presentations were misleading, Citigroup *did* disclose the existence of SIV-related liabilities in the footnotes of the 10-K reports it filed with the SEC.) Similarly, AIG and the other mortgage securities insurers were also highly dishonest in their representations to the investing public when, as the bubble peaked and started to collapse, they faced imminent financial disaster.

In some cases, we already have clear evidence of senior executive knowledge of and involvement in these frauds. For example, quarterly presentations to investors are nearly always made by the CEO or CFO of the firm; if lies were told in those presentations, or if material facts were omitted, the responsibility lies with senior management. In some other cases, such as Bear Stearns, we already have evidence from civil lawsuits that very senior executives were directly involved in constructing and selling securities whose prospectuses contained lies and omissions. In other cases, we do not yet have direct evidence of senior executive involvement, but such involvement is likely. If prosecutors forced the people directly responsible to talk, there is no question whatsoever in my mind that many of them would implicate senior management. There are several reasons for believing this. First, the amounts of money involved were so large. Second, most firms required senior management to approve issuance of major securities. And third, the senior management of several securitizers was dominated by people who, earlier in their careers, had been deeply involved in similar activities, and who would be expected to monitor them closely and understand them.

Accounting Fraud

Here we also have a number of known opportunities for prosecution, as well as many other likely ones. We already know, of course, that both Fannie Mae and Freddie Mac engaged in massive accounting frauds for years until their discovery in 2003–2004. Those frauds resulted in no criminal prosecutions, and only mild civil penalties; some of the individual beneficiaries were able to keep their illicit proceeds, and none were fined more than their illicit gains. The statute of limitations on those offenses has now expired.

However, we also know of other major probable violations. The best known is the "Repo 105" trick by which Lehman Brothers, with the knowledge of its U.S. accounting firm, fraudulently concealed its real level of leverage during the bubble. Lehman's American accountants, Ernst & Young, shielded themselves by insisting that Repo 105 deals be nominally run through an international subsidiary, so they could pretend not to notice when they produced the consolidated numbers. Despite the fact that this was clearly a sham transaction, nobody has been prosecuted or even fined.

Lehman and many other securitizers also inflated the value of their assets. In Lehman's case, the most egregious overvaluation was in its commercial real estate portfolio, whose overvaluation by billions of dollars was discussed explicitly by Lehman senior management in the year prior to the firm's collapse. Other firms such as Merrill Lynch and Citigroup inflated the value of their mortgage-related assets—loans waiting to be securitized, CDOs waiting to be sold, pieces of CDOs that they could not sell or had decided to retain. We have already seen, for example, that Merrill Lynch traders paid traders in another Merrill Lynch group to "purchase" mortgage securities at inflated prices when they could not be sold on the open market. In a number of cases, these overvaluations were known and discussed within the firm; and again, some degree of senior management involvement is likely. Again, nobody has been prosecuted.

Joseph Cassano and AIG's senior financial management aggressively prevented Joseph St. Denis from properly evaluating the CDS portfolio of AIG Financial Products after AIG's auditor had declared a material weakness in AIG's financial statements. Both Cassano and AIG senior management also made a number of extremely inaccurate, misleading public statements to investors and investment analysts in 2007 and 2008. AIG continued to maintain inflated values of its CDS and mortgage securities positions in late 2007 and the first half of 2008, even though Goldman Sachs was sharply reducing its own valuations of mortgage securities and was demanding and obtaining large amounts of CDS collateral from AIG. There have been no prosecutions related to this situation.

It seems inconceivable that the banks' accounting firms were never aware of these frauds. In several cases, such as the Repo 105 fraud and AIG's accounting for its CDS portfolio, there already exists public evidence that accounting firms realized at the time that fraud was being committed. However, there has not been a single criminal prosecution of a U.S. accounting firm related to the bubble.

Honest Services Violations and Bribery

The 1988 amendments to the federal mail fraud statute include the following: "*scheme or artifice to defraud* includes a scheme or artifice to deprive another of the intangible right of honest services." This statute has been used to prosecute many corruption and financial fraud cases. A recent Supreme Court decision found that the statute was unconstitutionally vague, and limited its application to cases involving bribes or kickbacks.

However, several cases would still seem to fit. Yield spread premiums, authorized and even ordered by the senior management of originators, certainly led to massive violations of any right to honest services. Some of those lenders were owned by the banks, and others were undoubtedly pressured or incented by the banks to provide larger quantities of higher-yielding loans. There have been zero bubble-related honest services prosecutions of lenders or senior executives of lenders. In addition, the Jefferson County case involves, first, bribes paid by JPMorgan Chase to county officials but, even more interestingly, bribes paid to Goldman Sachs to induce Goldman not to bid on the project. Nobody at JPMorgan Chase or Goldman Sachs has been prosecuted.

Finally, the rating agencies would seem to be ripe for honest services prosecutions, even within the recently narrowed scope of the statute. While their first amendment free speech defense might protect the rating agencies from many forms of civil liability, it does not protect them from criminal liability. With varying degrees of nakedness, all three of the major rating agencies provided corrupt services to investors. They slanted their ratings to favor issuers who paid them; they failed to disclose the extent to which they were paid consulting fees by those issuers; they failed to disclose that senior management was pressuring employees to rate unreasonably large numbers of securities, precluding any effective due diligence; they failed to disclose that when offered information (for example by Clayton Holdings) that would have improved the accuracy of ratings, they deliberately refused the information; and they represented that they were actually providing unbiased ratings services when, often, they were simply providing assembly-line high ratings for fraudulent securities. There has not been a single criminal prosecution, either for honest services violations or any other offense, of any of the major rating agencies or their executives.

Perjury and Making False Statements to Federal Investigators

It is felony perjury to lie under oath, whether in a civil deposition, in a civil trial, or when testifying before Congress. It is also a felony to lie to federal investigators.

Here, there are many opportunities. Many cases might be difficult to prove, but the blunt reality is that many financial executives lied while testifying before Congress. Angelo Mozilo testified that it was not in his or his executives' interest to make fraudulent loans, when in fact we have seen, and Mr. Mozilo clearly knew, that it *was* in his financial interest to do this, even if it destroyed his firm.

Then there was Lloyd Blankfein. Lloyd Blankfein testified, for example, that he was unaware of the importance that ratings played in the purchasing decisions of institutional investors. Blankfein had spent his entire career at Goldman Sachs (since 1981) in commodities and securities trading. For most of the decade before he became CEO, he was a senior executive in the Goldman Sachs division that included its fixed-income (bond) business. The idea that he was unaware of the importance that ratings played in institutional purchases of CDOs is, to put it bluntly, beyond absurd. When Mr. Blankfein so testified, he was, in my opinion, perjuring himself. Now, could they prove it? I'm willing to bet that if you go through his e-mail carefully and depose everyone around him, there would be plenty of evidence that he knew perfectly well how important ratings are. His testimony before Senator Levin's committee was also highly suspect in maintaining that Goldman was "market making" when in fact it was knowingly selling off its junk and betting against the resultant securities that it constructed and sold for this purpose. His colleagues' testimony was, if anything, worse—Dan Sparks saying that he sold Timberwolf *before* it was described as a "shitty deal" and then admitting literally ten seconds later, when nailed by Senator Levin, that, yes, they had sold it afterward too.

To take another example, this time from the hearings of the Financial Crisis Inquiry Commission (and yes, that was sworn testimony), here is former Citigroup CEO Chuck Prince in an exchange with a commission member questioning him and Robert Rubin:[36]

EXAMINATION BY COMMISSIONER MURREN

COMMISSIONER MURREN: You mentioned capital requirements are very important. Did Citigroup ever create products that were specifically designed to avoid capital requirements?

MR. RUBIN: I don't know the answer to that.

COMMISSIONER MURREN: And you, Mr. Prince, would you create a product simply to—or at least one of the principal reasons for designing the product was to avoid capital requirements?

MR. PRINCE: I—I think the answer is no because the product would have to be designed as something that a client would want. In other words, you wouldn't create a product that was internally focused. If your question is, would the—would the team create products—and in the course of creating the products, try to minimize capital burdens, my guess is the answer is yes, but I don't know for sure.

COMMISSIONER MURREN: So then it wouldn't surprise you to know that in the minutes of one of your meetings that specifically relate to the creation of new products, in this instance, it would be liquidity puts, that there was a notation that specifically referenced the fact that this type of structure would avoid capital requirements?

MR. PRINCE: I have no way of responding without seeing the document and understanding the context of it.

"Liquidity puts" were the mechanism by which Citigroup guaranteed that it would absorb losses on mortgage securities placed in off-balance sheet SIVs. The SIV–liquidity put mechanism had no legitimate economic purpose; it existed solely for the purpose of allowing Citigroup to misrepresent its balance sheet, and to conceal the fact that Citigroup retained the real risks associated with the potential failure of the securities.

One could provide many further examples of this kind.

The congressional hearings produced not only widespread revulsion but a clear, widely shared sense that there was an awful lot of lying going on. There have been no prosecutions for perjury.

Sarbanes-Oxley Violations (Civil and Criminal)

The Sarbanes-Oxley Act establishes a variety of requirements for CEO and senior management conduct and also establishes criminal penalties for certain violations. CEOs and CFOs of public companies are required to certify their companies' financial statements and tax returns, and also to certify the adequacy of the firms' internal controls for accurate financial reporting. The SEC is responsible for establishing regulations in these areas and can pursue civil cases for violating them. But the law also provides for criminal penalties, including up to ten years in federal prison, for knowingly certifying inaccurate financial statements, destroying records, or retaliating against a whistle-blower for contacting law enforcement authorities.

We have already seen the level of misrepresentation in loan portfolios, prospectuses, investor presentations, and so forth. We have seen the inadequacy of internal due diligence and frequently the deliberate suppression of such due diligence, with regard to loan quality, and also with regard to how nonconforming loans were handled—many were securitized in conscious violation of internal guidelines. Does this bespeak adequate internal financial controls? We also know, of course, that both lenders and securitizers were wildly inaccurate in their valuations of loans, of CDOs, and of their own financial positions. How much of this was known to their CEOs? The answer cannot be none. Indeed, we already have considerable public evidence that suggests the contrary.

Consider Citigroup. One day after Richard Bowen sent his e-mail to four senior Citigroup executives including its CFO and vice-chairman Robert Rubin, Citigroup's then-CEO Chuck Prince signed the firm's Sarbanes-Oxley certification. Three months later, after Prince was replaced by Vikram Pandit, the Office of the Comptroller of the Currency sent a letter, addressed to Pandit personally, explicitly warning him of major deficiencies in Citigroup's financial reporting and controls. Eight days later, Pandit signed *his* first Sarbanes-Oxley certification for Citigroup. Over the subsequent two years, Citigroup lost billions of dollars more as its earlier securities valuations proved inaccurate.

Or consider AIG. What do we think of AIG's financial controls in late 2007 and 2008, particularly after AIGFP's internal auditor resigned in protest after warning AIG's chief auditor that he was being blocked from doing his job? And what do we think of Richard Fuld and his CFO, Erin Callan, signing off on Lehman Brothers' accounting statements in 2008?

Indeed, Lehman provides particularly direct evidence, not only through disclosure of the Repo 105 accounting trick, but also through the actions of an internal whistle-blower. Matthew Lee was Lehman's senior vice president with responsibility for overseeing the firm's global balance sheet. On May 16, 2008, Mr. Lee delivered a letter by hand to four Lehman executives: Martin Kelley, Lehman's controller; Gerald Reilly, head of capital markets product control; Christopher O'Meara, chief risk officer; and Erin Callan, the CFO.[37] Lee begins his letter by noting that he had worked for Lehman since 1994, and had been a "loyal and dedicated employee." He then continues:

> I have become aware of certain conduct and practices, however, that I feel compelled to bring to your attention . . .
>
> I have reason to believe that certain conduct on the part of senior management of the firm may be in violation of the [Lehman] Code [of Ethics]. The following is a summary . . .
>
> 1. On the last day of each month, the books and records of the firm contain approximately five (5) billion dollars in assets in excess of what is managed . . . I believe this pattern indicates that the Firm's senior management is not in sufficient control of its assets to be able to establish that its financial statements are presented to the public and governmental agencies in a "fair, accurate, and timely manner." . . . I believe . . there could be approximately five (5) billion dollars of assets subject to a potential write-off . . . at the minimum, I believe the manner in which the firm is reporting these assets is potentially misleading to the public and various governmental agencies. . . .

2. The Firm has an established practice of substantiating each balance sheet account . . . The Firm has tens of billions of dollars of unsubstantiated balances, which may or may not be "bad" or non-performing assets or real liabilities. In any event, the Firm's senior management may not be in a position to know whether all of these accounts are, in fact, described in a "fair, accurate, and timely" manner, as required by the Code . . .

3. The Firm has tens of billions of dollar [*sic*] of inventory that it probably cannot buy or sell in any recognized market, at the currently recorded market values . . .

4. I do not believe the Firm has invested sufficiently in the required and reasonably necessary financial systems and personnel to cope with this increased balance sheet . . .

5. I do not believe there is sufficient knowledgeable management in place in the Mumbai, India finance functions and department. There is a very real possibility of a potential misstatement of material facts . . .

6. Finally, . . . certain senior level internal audit personnel do not have the professional expertise to properly exercise the audit functions they are entrusted to manage . . .

I would be happy to discuss regarding the foregoing with senior management but I felt compelled, both morally and legally, to bring these issues to your attention . . .

For the most part, Lee turned out to be right. About a month later, Lee also warned Lehman's auditors, Ernst & Young, about the Repo 105 trick. (But that wasn't necessary; they had already known about it, and done nothing to stop it, for over a year.[38] They haven't been prosecuted either.) So, what do we think of Erin Callan and Richard Fuld certifying Lehman's financial statements for that quarter?

Or how about Angelo Mozilo's certifications of Countrywide's statements and the adequacy of its internal financial controls? Or Stan O'Neal's signing off on Merrill Lynch's statements, while his employees were bribing each other, and the firm's profits turned to $80 billion in losses in the two years after he departed? Et cetera. Yet there have been no civil or criminal cases filed based on Sarbanes-Oxley violations.

RICO Offenses and Criminal Antitrust Violations

Both RICO and federal antitrust laws provide tools for prosecuting criminal conspiracies. The Racketeer Influenced and Corrupt Organizations Act (RICO) provides for severe criminal (and civil) penalties for operating a criminal organization. It specifically enables prosecution of the leaders of a criminal organization for having ordered or assisted others to commit crimes. It also provides that racketeers must forfeit all ill-gotten gains obtained through a pattern of criminal activity, and allows federal prosecutors to obtain pre-trial restraining orders to seize defendants' assets. And finally, it provides for criminal prosecution of corporations that employ RICO offenders.

RICO was explicitly intended to cover organized financial crime as well as violent criminal organizations such as the Mafia and drug cartels. Indeed, the law professor who drafted much of the legislation, G. Robert Blakey, once told *Time* magazine that "we don't want one set of rules for people whose collars are blue or whose names end in vowels, and another set for those whose collars are white and have Ivy League diplomas." The RICO statute has been used in cases ranging from the sex-abuse scandals of the Catholic Church to Michael Milken. Indeed the criminal cases brought against both Milken and his firm, Drexel Burnham Lambert, were based on the RICO statute. A great deal of the behavior that occurred during the bubble, covered in this and previous chapters, would appear to fall under RICO statutes. Moreover, pre-trial asset seizure is a widely and successfully used technique in combating organized crime, and federal asset seizures now generate over $1 billion per year. However, there has not been a single RICO prosecution related to the financial crisis, nor has a single RICO restraining order been issued to seize the assets of either any individual banker or any firm.

It is important to note here that federal asset seizures would not merely represent justice for offenders, but for victims as well. Federal law allows seized assets to be used to compensate victims. In this case, the potential economic impact of seizures could be enormous. Seizing the personal assets of just seven people bearing enormous responsibility for the bubble and crisis (Angelo Mozilo, Richard Fuld, Jimmy Cayne, Joseph Cassano, Stan O'Neal, Henry Paulson, and Lloyd Blankfein) could provide over $2 billion to compensate victims. If the federal government were to seize assets from, say, five thousand people representing a substantial fraction of total investment banking bonuses (and criminal behavior) related to the bubble, this would potentially generate tens of billions of dollars in victim compensation. Such actions would probably provide more victim compensation than the entire $26 billion settlement of the foreclosure fraud lawsuits brought by 49 state attorneys general.

Antitrust law provides another tool for both criminal prosecution and extraction of financial restitution. Since 1975, federal antitrust law has provided for severe criminal penalties for antitrust violations. Antitrust law also provides for treble damages in civil judgments, which can be based upon evidence from criminal convictions.

There is ample reason to suspect that collusion and antitrust violations are common within the financial industry. Several prominent observers of the industry—including Simon Johnson, Eliot Spitzer, and financial journalist William Cohan—have suggested that American banking deserves serious examination for antitrust problems. One major antitrust investigation, under way as of this writing and being conducted by U.S., European, and Japanese regulators and prosecutors, is focused on price-fixing of interest rates, particularly the London Interbank Offered Rate (LIBOR), the interbank lending rate used to set many short-term interest rates. There have also been a series of civil settlements, described above, related to price-fixing and bid-rigging in the municipal bond market.

More generally the industry has become extremely concentrated, and all the major firms do business with each other, even in markets in which they supposedly compete. The overwhelming majority of all U.S. securities underwriting, private equity financing, merger and acquisition transactions, and derivatives trading is now controlled by Goldman Sachs, JPMorgan Chase, Morgan Stanley, Citigroup, Bank of America, and Wells Fargo. The largest private equity firms (such as KKR, Blackstone, and the Texas Pacific Group) often cooperatively bid for companies, and work not only with each other but with major banks in constructing financing packages for leveraged buyouts.

All the major banks charge the same fees for major services such as underwriting initial public offerings (7 percent), junk bonds (3 percent), or loan syndications (1 percent).[39] Moreover, both stock and bond offerings are often "syndicated." In this case, whichever bank wins the business of underwriting a given offering subcontracts portions of the offering to its supposed competitors. The banks also have created and operate a number of joint ventures, including two, MERS and Markit, that were heavily involved in the financial bubble and crisis.

By sheerest coincidence, the client agreements used for brokerage accounts by the major banks all contain identical provisions, by which all clients give up the right to use the courts to sue their brokerage for fraud. Rather, clients must use arbitration proceedings controlled by FINRA, the industry's generally spineless self-regulatory body. This arbitration provision is not intended to improve efficiency; on the contrary, FINRA arbitrations are protracted and extremely expensive, requiring high legal fees and payments to arbitrators. Rather, the industry's motivation is that FINRA arbitrations tend to favor the industry, and, importantly, they are secret, as opposed to court cases in which embarrassing information could be made public. How all the banks spontaneously decided to use the same brokerage contract terms has not been explained.

The banks, together with Visa and Mastercard, also seem to have arrived at identical conclusions in setting "interchange fees" for processing credit card transactions. Interchange fees in Europe and Australia are generally 0.6 percent of transaction value or less; U.S. interchange fees are uniformly 2 percent. In September 2005, a large coalition of retail industry associations filed a class-action antitrust lawsuit against Visa, Mastercard, and America's thirteen largest banks.[40] As of early 2012, the case is still pending. Potential damages estimates have ranged from several billion to tens of billions of dollars. However, the federal antitrust authorities have taken no action.

Indeed, despite this pattern of widespread industry collusion, there has not been a significant criminal antitrust conviction of any major bank, or any individual banker, in the United States in the last thirty years.

Federal Aid Disclosure Regulations

On November 27, 2011, Bloomberg News reported that as a result of its Freedom of Information Act filings, it had learned that during the crisis, Federal Reserve Board loan assistance to the largest banks had been far larger than previously believed. The Fed had kept the information secret; previous estimates based on then-available documents had set the total amount of assistance at $2 trillion to $3 trillion. Upon obtaining the documents, Bloomberg found that the actual amount, including loans, loan guarantees, securities purchases, and other commitments, was a rather amazing *$7.8 trillion,* with several hundred billion dollars in loans outstanding at any given time during the height of the crisis.[41] Bloomberg estimated that these low-interest loans generated $13 billion in additional profits for the banks; one of my colleagues believes that the banks' profits were probably far larger.

Since 1989, SEC regulations have required public companies to disclose material federal assistance. None of the banks disclosed the size of these loans or their impact on profits.[42] This is a civil, not a criminal, offense. But at the same time that the banks were so heavily dependent upon massive government support, several of them claimed that their financial positions were secure. This could be interpreted as a securities fraud violation. There have been no related SEC civil cases filed or criminal prosecutions.

Personal Conduct Offenses

Personal conduct subject to criminal prosecution might range from possession and use of drugs, such as marijuana and cocaine, to hiring of prostitutes, employment of prostitutes for business purposes, fraudulent billing of personal or illegal services as business expenses (sexual services, strip club patronage, and nightclub patronage), fraudulent use or misappropriation of corporate assets or services for personal use (e.g., use of corporate jets), personal tax evasion, and a variety of other offenses.

I should perhaps make clear here that I'm not enthusiastic about prosecuting people for possession or use of marijuana, which I think should be legal. In general, I tend to think that anything done by two healthy consenting adults, including sex for pay, should be legal too. I'm ambivalent about cocaine, which does seem to be destructive, although its criminalization is hugely destructive too. My general point is simply that, in ordinary circumstances, I would not advocate expending law enforcement resources in this area.

But the circumstances here are not ordinary. First, there is once again a vast disparity between the treatment of ordinary people and investment bankers. Every year, about fifty thousand people are arrested in New York City for possession of marijuana—most of them ordinary people, not criminals, whose only offense was to accidentally end up within the orbit of a police officer. Not a single one of them is ever named Jimmy Cayne, despite the fact that his marijuana habit has been discussed multiple times in the national media. Everyone in New York knows that investment banking is probably the largest cocaine market on the planet, not to mention a pillar of the strip club and escort industries. Who did the Feds bag for hiring escorts? Eliot Spitzer.

There is also a second, even more serious, point about this. If the supposed reason for failure to prosecute is the difficulty of making cases, then there is an awfully easy way to get a lot of bankers to talk. It is a technique used routinely in organized crime cases. What is this, if not organized crime?

As time passes, criminal prosecution of bubble-era frauds will become even more difficult, even impossible, because the statute of limitations for many of these crimes is short—three to five years. So an immense opportunity for both justice and public education will soon be lost. In some circumstances, cases can be opened or reopened after the statute of limitations has expired, if new evidence appears; but finding new evidence will grow more difficult with time as well. And there is no sign whatsoever that the Obama administration is interested.

But enough about criminality. Let's turn to large-scale economic waste and destabilization—because deregulated modern banking is good at that, too.

CHAPTER 7

AGENTS OF PAIN:
UNREGULATED FINANCE AS A
SUBTRACTIVE INDUSTRY

WE NOW TURN TO the large-scale implications of financial sector conduct. The first is that a rogue financial sector is not merely unethical, even criminal; it is seriously dangerous to the economic health of a country.

In the United States (and sometimes elsewhere), financial deregulation is defended by arguing that it is critical to retain "competitive advantage" in financial services, because the financial sector is a major employer, wealth creator, and engine of economic growth. Actually, however, the reverse is true: unregulated finance imposes huge net costs on the American and global economy. Far from enhancing finance's proper role of channeling money to productive uses, the transformation and deregulation of finance has been economically destructive—hugely so.

These costs come in two forms. The first is that the industry is now inherently destabilizing, not just to the financial system but to the entire economy. This is essentially the problem described by Raghuram

Rajan in the paper he delivered at the Jackson Hole conference in 2005, now grown even larger and more threatening. Financial leverage, volatility, structural concentration, toxic incentives, and (often deliberate) information failures have caused the reemergence of increasingly destructive financial bubbles and crises, often intensified by widespread fraud. Since the 1980s, these crises have grown in severity and have increasingly spilled over into "Main Street," causing enormous economic and human damage. Indeed, rather than speaking of systemic risk *within* the financial sector, we must now speak of the systemic risk *of* the financial sector.

The second form of economic destruction caused by the industry is that even when markets are temporarily stable, finance has become increasingly parasitic. A high fraction of financial sector revenues and profits—when there are profits—now come from sophisticated forms of skimming, looting, or corruption, unethical activities with no economic value. The profitability of these activities (and even sometimes their existence) depends upon legal and tax loopholes, concealment of information, artificial legal barriers to market entry, the absence of protection and recourse for victims, cartel-like collusion, and political corruption—circumstances permitted only by the industry's wealth and power. Yet because these activities are enormously lucrative, they attract many of America's most educated people, as well as massive amounts of capital and investments in information systems. The result is an enormous diversion and waste of potentially productive assets and human effort, as well as worsening inequality.

Unregulated Finance and U.S. Economic Performance: An Overview

MODERN ECONOMIES UNQUESTIONABLY need a sophisticated financial services industry. Globalization requires currency exchange, hedging, and payment systems. Wealthier citizens need greater varieties of savings, investment, borrowing, and retirement products. Venture capital has funded enormously productive high-technology firms including Google, Apple, Cisco, Intel, eBay, and Amazon. Some financial innovations are hugely beneficial—examples include debit cards, ATMs, microlending, index funds, Internet banking, and America's venture capital system.

But the uncontrolled hyperfinancialization of an economy is a serious problem. Over the last thirty years, the U.S. financial sector has grown like a malignancy. Many of its recent "innovations" are no more than tricks to evade regulation, taxes, or law enforcement, and some of them have proven profoundly destructive. The extraordinary spikes and declines in financial sector debt and profits—in stark contrast to its modest contribution to GDP—suggest that it has become a bloated, destabilizing force.

Nor has the hypergrowth of American finance been accompanied by improved real economic performance—quite the contrary. The next two charts show that the recent ballooning of the financial industry has been accompanied by a steady decline in GDP growth and a shocking spike in income inequality, to a level not seen since 1929. Most of the *real* growth in U.S. productivity and GNP over the last two decades has been due to information technology, particularly the Internet revolution. If one removes IT, U.S. growth has been poor indeed during this

Finance Share: GDP, Debt, Profits

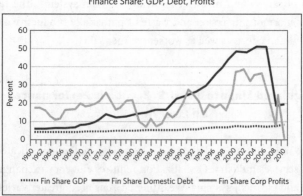

Source: Bureau of Economic Analysis

Growth in Finance, GDP, and Inequality

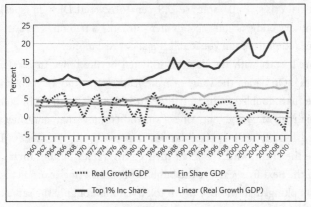

Facundo Alvaredo, Tony Atkinson, Thomas Piketty, and Emmanuel Saez, *World Top Incomes Database*, http://g-mond.parisschoolofeconomics.eu/topincomes/

period. Moreover, the financial sector's contribution to economy-wide wage and income growth has been modest, even if we ignore the damage it has caused.

If we subtract the financial sector, American real wages have been declining. And if we look *inside* the financial sector, we find that its income gains have been heavily concentrated in the top 1 percent of the industry. Its contribution to the welfare of the other 99 percent, even *within the financial sector,* has been minor at best. Moreover, as we shall see, the profitability of some financial sector activities—especially investment banking, asset management, and private equity—frequently comes at the expense of average Americans' incomes and investments.

But can we measure the total economy-wide effects of deregulation of financial services since the 1980s? Yes, in some ways we can, and it's not a pretty picture. To be sure, there have been some benefits—lower commissions for purchasing stocks and bonds, nationwide banking for those who need it, slightly lower interest rates for *some* consumer borrowing (certainly not for credit cards!). But most of those benefits could have been obtained with very limited regulatory changes. In contrast, the *costs* of deregulation have been truly staggering.

Consider, for example, the costs of the recent housing bubble and financial crisis. To paraphrase U.S. senator Everett Dirksen (speaking of military budgets, long ago, in mere billions): a trillion here, a trillion there, and pretty soon you're talking about real money.

We'll start with the damage inflicted by the binge in residential lending. On paper, the value of Americans' net equity in their homes more than doubled from $6 trillion in 2001 to $13 trillion in 2005. It wasn't real, of course, but Americans didn't know that, and they borrowed heavily against their homes' supposedly higher values. Then came the crash, which lowered their equity values but not their debt. Over the next five years, as the bubble collapsed, Americans' net home equity plunged all the way down to $6 trillion, roughly the same as at the decade's start, and less than half its 2005 peak.[1] As of early 2012, approximately 20 percent of all U.S. mortgages are still "underwater," meaning that owners owe more than their homes are worth. The economic whiplash from that will take years to heal.

The effect was all the worse because the lenders were pushing second-lien home equity loans—of the "Unlocking Your Home's Value" variety. From 2000 through 2007, U.S. consumers withdrew $4.2 trillion in cash from their homes—four times as much as in the 1990s. Since much of the money went into imported consumer goods, it fed the worsening U.S. trade deficit, which ballooned by over $4 trillion in those same years (see the chart on page 213). The total trade deficit in the 2000s was five times bigger than that of the 1990s.[2]

By 2005, housing and related industries, such as new furniture and appliances, accounted for half of American economic growth. Much of this activity was pure waste, leaving America with excess and badly located housing, much of it very energy-inefficient. Large-lot construction requires expensive extensions of water and sewer services; big interior spaces and poor insulation are inherently energy-inefficient; and sprawl necessitates multiple-car households. Millions of these homes are now foreclosed upon or vacant, or have been sold for less than their construction costs.[3] Even if they are once again inhabited, they will cause excessive costs for energy and public services.

Net Home Equity Withdrawal and Trade Deficit: 2000–2007

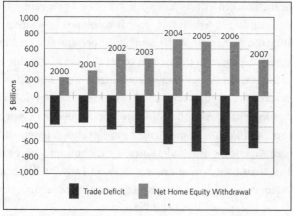

Source: Bureau of Economic Analysis; Federal Reserve

But the costs don't end there, and the crash didn't just hurt home-owners and real estate developers. The federal government spent huge amounts of money saving the financial system from itself, and then saving the economy from finance. Estimates vary widely (do you count the $2 trillion in Federal Reserve securities purchases, or not?), but the cost to taxpayers of the financial sector rescue was certainly in the hundreds of billions of dollars. (Fannie, Freddie, and AIG alone have cost well over $200 billion.) And anyone who owned stock in AIG, Lehman Brothers, Merrill Lynch, and Bear Stearns, of course, lost nearly all of it. Then the entire economy went into recession, hammered by the collapse of housing and lending. One year after the financial crisis began, GM and Chrysler were bankrupt, and American unemployment was officially at 10 percent (in reality probably 15 percent), the worst rate since the Depression. Yet even as Americans contended with unemployment and sharply lower home values, they had a household debt load 80 percent higher than at the start of the decade. Only the country's fabulously wealthy new elite were immune.

So then the federal government spent $800 billion in emergency stimulus at a time when tax receipts were sharply contracting, while Republicans blocked efforts to return taxes for the wealthy back to their pre-Bush levels. As a result, deficits continued to widen and the U.S. national debt has grown by roughly 50 percent as a result of the crisis (again, depending on how you count it).[4] Then, with the end of federal stimulus spending, many state budgets went into crisis, leading to severe cuts in education, child care, and other services critical to economic welfare. And the pain continues. America's poverty rate has soared, millions of homes have been foreclosed upon, and millions more Americans are "underwater"—they now owe more on their mortgages than their homes are worth. As of early 2012, official unemployment remains at more than 8 percent, U.S. economic growth is anemic, and Europe is slipping into recession.

European nations were forced into massive stimulus spending too, which increased their debt loads and contributed significantly to European sovereign debt problems. Indeed, the effects of the U.S. housing bubble and financial crisis deserve far greater attention in the debate over the European sovereign debt crisis. It is true that the EU system and many Eurozone nations have various structural rigidities that have reduced growth and increased borrowing. It is also true that some of these nations, particularly Ireland and Spain, experienced real estate bubbles of their own. However, it is also true that with the exception of Greece most of them (including those whose indebtedness is now so extreme) had perfectly manageable debt levels until the financial crisis.

At the beginning of 2008, Greece had the highest ratio of debt to GDP in the Eurozone—and its ratio was less than 110 percent. Italy's was slightly lower, just over 100 percent. Ireland's debt to GDP ratio was under 70 percent; Spain's was about 40 percent; and Portugal's was only about 25 percent—far lower and more conservative than the United States, Germany, or most other developed nations. But by the start of 2012, Greece's debt level was 170 percent of GDP, Ireland's was over 100 percent, Spain's was over 60 percent, and, stunningly, Portugal's debt to GDP ratio had more than quadrupled to 110 percent. These catastrophic increases were not caused by sudden, simultaneous outbreaks of lavish spending—nothing like, say, the borrowing and spending binge that characterized the United States during the bubble. Rather, this huge, sudden increase in Eurozone debt to GDP ratios was caused by the Great Recession, combined with the need for emergency stimulus (deficit) spending to avert total economic collapse. In other words, it was caused by the U.S. financial sector.

As of this writing, we do not yet know how the European sovereign debt crisis will play out. But its effects have already been horrific. Much of the Greek population now lives in misery, with rioting increasingly frequent. Youth unemployment in Greece, Spain, and Portugal now exceeds 50 percent. Several nations in Eastern Europe, including Hungary and Latvia, were economically devastated, and the crisis pushed Hungary into an extremist government that is threatening its status as a democracy. Extremist political movements have gained surprising strength in other European nations including France and even Scandinavia, especially Finland.

Asia was less affected. Even so, ten million migrant workers in China lost their jobs virtually overnight in 2008–2009. But China recovered more quickly than other nations, in part due to a $500 billion emergency stimulus program initiated by the Chinese central government.

It's impossible to come up with a single, reliable number for the cost of all this, but it is certainly trillions of dollars, probably tens of trillions. Beyond the economic costs, there has been a great deal of human suffering, and America's financial and economic institutions and reputation have been discredited in the eyes of the world.

And what did Americans get in return? Who benefited from the predatory bloating of American finance? Mainly a relatively small number of people in the financial sector—maybe fifty thousand, a hundred thousand at the very most—became very wealthy on the backs of your pain. At the peak of the bubble, the *average* annual income of a Goldman Sachs employee was $600,000; and even within investment banking, incomes are heavily skewed toward the very top. (Recall Mr. Thain's bonus decisions at Merrill Lynch, where about half of total bonus payments went to the top thousand people.) Over the course of the bubble a larger group of people, perhaps half a million in total, made *some* money, perhaps averaging $500,000 each, by accident, petty dishonesty, and speculation—lower-level bankers, dishonest appraisers, mortgage brokers, house flippers, subprime mortgage loan officers, real estate brokers in bubble regions. But this was not an industry or an endeavor that benefited millions of honest, average Americans. Only the suffering was widely distributed.

If nothing else, the experience of the 2000s should squelch the fantasy that an unregulated financial industry inevitably channels capital to its best uses, or that bankers' concern for their sacred reputations would prevent them from putting their institutions or customers at risk for mere money.

But perhaps the housing bubble and financial crisis were just a once-in-a-thousand-years tsunami, one of those random perfect storms that you can't predict or control? Or an epidemic of abuse that won't be repeated now that everyone has learned their lesson?

Not so. First, recall the historical record since deregulation began: the S&L and junk bond bubbles and crises of the 1980s; the 1987 stock market collapse; the derivatives-driven fiasco at Long-Term Capital Management; the Internet/technology stock bubble of 1995–2000. If we include other nations that undertook similar deregulatory experiments, we can add bubbles and crashes in Iceland, Britain, and several other countries. So while the housing bubble and financial crisis were worse than others, they were far from alone.

But second, if you look under the hood, as Rajan started to do in 2005, it turns out that America's new, unconstrained financial services industry is *inherently* dangerous. The instability, dishonesty, bubbles, and crises are not incidental; they are the inevitable result of uncontrolled greed searching for private gain at public expense, intensified by the increased velocity and game playing created by information technology.

But *why*, exactly, is America's financial sector now so inherently dangerous? There are five principal drivers of catastrophic risk in modern unregulated finance. They are volatility, leverage, structural concentration, systemic interdependence, and toxic incentives. When combined, they make for quite a wonderful high explosive. Or perhaps a better metaphor is a cocktail laced with cyanide.

We will start with volatility, particularly the industry's recent shift to much greater reliance on short-term financing.

Rollover Roulette

Since deregulation began, banks—especially investment banks—have increasingly depended upon short-term borrowing from financial markets. In contrast, traditional commercial banks obtain money by taking deposits from consumers. This is borrowing, too, and in principle savers can request their money back at any time. But in reality, consumer savings are generally very stable (unless there is a panic leading to a bank run).

All financial institutions, including investment banks, also traditionally borrowed by issuing long-term bonds. But one of the striking features of the buildup to the financial crisis was the very marked shortening of the average maturity of financial sector debt. Instead of issuing long-term bonds, investment banks began borrowing ever larger sums from short-term lenders such as money market funds. The primary reason for this radical restructuring was simple: it was far more profitable, because short-term interest rates are lower than long-term rates.

But it was also risky and destabilizing. These short-term borrowings have to be constantly rolled over, or renewed, and if the financial system ever ran into problems, the renewals would stop, driving the system into crisis in a matter of weeks, or even days. The graph on page 218 shows the sharp increase in this short-term borrowing.

The big American investment banks accounted for a large share of this surge in short-term borrowing. They used it to take risks—to purchase assets, some intended for eventual resale, others that they gambled would be profitable to keep. Table 3 on page 219 shows the "trading books"—that is, the asset holdings—and short-term borrowing levels at the six U.S. financial firms with the largest investment banking and trading operations as of year-end 2007, when the crisis began.

Global Financial Institution Borrowings, by Maturity

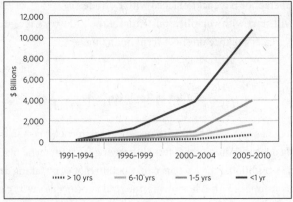

Source: UK Financial Services Authority

The crisis has numbed our ability to absorb large numbers. At the end of their 2007 fiscal years, these six institutions had $2.1 *trillion* in trading assets, a half *trillion* more than at year-end 2006. Their $1.7 trillion in short-term borrowing outstanding was equivalent to 12 percent of 2007 U.S. GDP. But these are instruments that turn over every day, or week, or month. So the sum of their cash calls on the money markets was obviously much higher. Even if the average term was monthly— and it was probably shorter—the total of the annual cash calls would have been in excess of $20 trillion, just for these six banks. Any disruption, even for a short period, would be calamitous.

Moreover, note that astounding $357 billion in *negative* operating cash flow. Most of that reflected the constant growth of assets. But a second reason is that banks can count unrealized gains on their trading assets as profits in the current period, so there was often a big gap between reported profits and actual cash flows. This is another destabilizing force. In normal times, if the banks need some cash, they can sell some of their assets. But what if those assets suddenly plunge in value because they were overvalued during a bubble? What if a crisis forces all the banks to sell assets at the same time, causing a glut, forcing prices down? The banks loved so-called mark-to-market account-

TABLE 3

FINANCIAL POSITION, MAJOR U.S. BANKS, YEAR-END 2007

| | ($BILLIONS) | | |
	TRADING BOOK	YEAR-TO-YEAR INCREASE	SHORT-TERM BORROWING	OPERATING CASH FLOW
Bear Stearns	122.5	13.0	130.3	11.1
Lehman Brothers	313.1	86.5	263.1	(-45.6)
Citigroup	539.0	145.1	450.7	(-71.4)
JPMorgan Chase	491.4	125.7	232.8	(-110.6)
Merrill Lynch	234.7	30.9	316.5	(-72.4)
Goldman Sachs	406.4	118.0	325.1	(-68.2)
Totals	2,107.1	519.2	1,718.5	(-357.1)

Source: Company Annual Reports

ing during the bubble, but then frantically tried to ditch it during the crisis.

As a safety measure, most of the short-term borrowing was collateralized, or secured by the banks' posting supposedly safe securities as a guarantee. If the bank couldn't repay its loan, the collateral could be confiscated and sold. Originally, Treasury bonds were the only acceptable collateral, but during the bubble lenders started to accept mortgage securities. After all, they were rated AAA—as safe as Treasury bonds, right?

This was an accident waiting to happen, and it did. The short-term lending volumes were massive and growing rapidly. The "collateral" was composed of shakier and shakier instruments, some of them fraudulent. Bankers were making enormous amounts of money by keeping the hamster wheel spinning. The wheel spun faster and faster until it flew off into space.

These short-term borrowing markets finally collapsed in the late summer and early fall of 2008, as managers of money market funds and other short-term capital sources became increasingly nervous about the collapse of the bubble. They stopped lending to the banks, thereby creating a massive heart attack throughout global financial markets. It started with Lehman, which was nearly totally dependent on short-term financing. When its lenders stopped accepting even its AAA mortgage paper as collateral, Lehman ran out of money almost instantly. Its bankruptcy filing trapped tens of billions of dollars that had come from money market funds. Unable to get access to their cash, money market fund operators had to dip into their own reserves to maintain their sacred $1-per-share price; the Reserve Fund, one of the largest and oldest, "broke the buck." This was one of the events that Paulson and Bernanke should have predicted but didn't. It caused a huge run on money market funds, as depositors withdrew their funds in panic. The money market funds therefore stopped lending money to banks and industrial corporations. This immediately threatened the solvency of every major investment bank, until the Federal Reserve stepped in and pumped oceans of funding into the banking system.[5] The Treasury Department also announced that for the first time, the federal government would guarantee assets in money market funds.

In other words, excessive dependence upon short-term funding is dangerous. In crisis conditions or even moments of stress, it creates volatility that can rapidly endanger the system. This danger was multiplied exponentially by excessive leverage. The enormous growth in assets during the bubble was permitted only by enormous borrowing.

Extreme Leverage, Overt and Covert

Since deregulation began, total leverage in financial services has increased astronomically, and frequently in ways that are invisible to regulators, customers, and lenders.

Once the Glass-Steagall wall between commercial lending and

broker-dealers was torn down, financial conglomerates such as JPMorgan Chase, Citigroup, and Bank of America started to take advantage. The investment banking and trading side of these institutions now had a vastly larger capital base to support its buying and trading. Then, in 2004, rigid numerical leverage constraints on investment banks were eliminated, replaced by the banks' own estimates. That change alone allowed the five largest investment banks to increase their leverage by about 50 percent, which was deplored even at the time. At the SEC meeting that approved the change unanimously, one commissioner is heard saying, well, we all know that these are the big guys, so if it goes wrong, it will be a really big mess—a comment followed by nervous laughter.[6]

But the leverage that was shown on bank balance sheets was only a portion of the real leverage in the financial system. There were several reasons for this. First, perhaps taking a cue from Enron, which used off-balance-sheet entities to conceal risk, the banks created many new special purpose entities (SPEs), structured investment vehicles (SIVs), and the like, which were used to transfer risky assets off their books. They lobbied heavily for these entities to receive favorable accounting treatment by the Financial Accounting Standards Board (FASB), by auditors, and by regulators, and they won.

Such obfuscations were routine by the mid-2000s. Citigroup wins the honors for the sheer scale of its dishonesty. Citigroup's closing 2007 balance sheet showed total assets of $2.2 trillion, of which $1.5 trillion—in loans, trading assets, and financial investments—were "risky" assets. Deep in the financial footnotes, however, we discover that Citi had *another* $1.1 trillion in risky assets in addition to those on the balance sheet. Its true balance sheet was therefore 50 percent larger than the one shown on its books, and its exposure to risky assets 73 percent larger. Of the $1.1 trillion in undisclosed assets, moreover, many were among the worst produced during the bubble.

The logic of the off-balance-sheet treatment was that Citigroup and the other banks had "sold" the assets to new entities that bore the risks of any defaults. But like so much bank accounting during the bubble, that was a lie. First, in order to reassure investors, Citi had frequently guaranteed these entities against losses. Buried in the footnotes to its financial statements one would see allusions to commitments implemented by "writing a liquidity put or other liquidity facility... [and] guarantees, letters of credit, credit default swaps or total return swaps," which shifted risk from the sham entities back to Citigroup. In other cases, there was no legal guarantee, but there was a complete expectation by investors, completely encouraged by Citigroup, that losses would be covered in a way similar to the federal government's implicit guarantee of Fannie Mae and Freddie Mac.

Merrill Lynch was even worse. To believe the company's accountants, 2005 and 2006, the peak years of the financial bubble, were the best in Merrill's history, with revenues of over $26 billion in 2005 and over $34 billion in 2006. Since Merrill paid out roughly half of all revenues to employees, those were also years of record cash compensation—$12.4 billion and $17 billion respectively.[7]

But over the next two years, Merrill *lost* more money than it had made in all the years since 2003 combined. Merrill held enormous toxic assets whose value collapsed in the crisis. In the end, for the entire period of 2003 through 2008, Merrill Lynch had a total of $100.4 billion in revenues, and paid $80.4 billion in compensation, but lost a cumulative $14.6 billion. Merrill paid 80 percent of its real revenues in compensation because many of its earlier supposed revenues were fake and only on paper, so they evaporated, while the bonus payments based on them were very real and in hard cash.

In October 2007, both Merrill and Citi took very large losses, and both firms "accepted the resignations" of their CEOs. In both cases, losses were primarily related to the forced repatriation of their SPEs and SIVs to on-balance-sheet status. In most cases, they had no choice, for the guarantees they had written required them to do so.

Lehman and several other banks also used garden-variety accounting tricks to conceal the extent of their leverage. Using the Repo 105 trick mentioned earlier, Lehman artificially "sold" and then "repurchased" stuff just before and after each quarter ended, making the firm seem less leveraged than it really was. They found a terribly nice British law firm, Linklaters, that was willing to sign off on this, as long as it was performed in Europe. But it was basically accounting fraud, and Lehman knew it. At the end of the bubble, Lehman admitted to being leveraged over thirty to one; due to its Repo 105 trick, as well as various off-balance-sheet entities, its real leverage was even higher. That's where American investment banking was in 2008.

Structural Concentration: Too Big to Fail, Which Often Equals Too Big to Succeed

As deregulation progressed, the U.S. financial sector became far more concentrated, both within markets and across them. By the time the bubble started, American financial services were dominated by five independent investment banks, four huge financial conglomerates, three insurers, and three ratings agencies. Several firms—certainly Goldman Sachs, AIG, JPMorgan Chase, Bank of America, and Citigroup, even perhaps a number of smaller firms such as Lehman Brothers, Wells Fargo, and Morgan Stanley—were sufficiently large that their collapse would endanger the entire financial system. In other words, they were too big to fail.

This condition was exacerbated by the fact that many individual markets were and remain even more concentrated than the whole industry. Five institutions control over 95 percent of all derivatives trading worldwide, and two—Goldman Sachs and JPMorgan Chase—control nearly half. Three U.S. rating agencies dominate that market globally. A group of about a dozen banks controls the LIBOR—the rate used to set nearly all short-term interest rates—and has been accused of colluding to manipulate this rate. The top five investment banks dominate the market for initial public offerings, frequently share portions of such offerings with each other, and charge exactly the same fees. Joint ventures established collectively by all the major investment banks dominate several markets related to the bubble; for example, the indexes of mortgage securities used as references in constructing many synthetic CDOs. And so on. As a result, many important markets are subject to cartelistic behavior, which can also destabilize them.

Furthermore, some of the biggest banks are also, one fears, too big *to succeed.*[8] They are so large, so complex, with so many disparate activities, that it became impossible even for well-intentioned CEOs to monitor all of them. Citigroup is perhaps the most obvious case; Chuck Prince was hired in large part to clean up Citigroup's legal and regulatory problems dating from the Internet-Enron era. He did that. But he was a lawyer, and he never looked hard enough at what the investment bankers were doing in the mortgage market. He may have trusted Robert Rubin to watch that, but Mr. Rubin was either too lazy or too arrogant. And measured by revenues rather than potential risk, Citigroup's mortgage business was only a small portion of the bank, easy to overlook. Thus, while the failure of Bear Stearns and Merrill Lynch could be attributed to grotesque failures of management and corporate governance, the failure of Citigroup was partially due to sheer size. One wonders how JPMorgan Chase will fare once Jamie Dimon retires, and whether Bank of America can ever be managed effectively now that it has swallowed Countrywide, U.S. Trust, and Merrill Lynch.

Tight Coupling

Information technology and globalization, while enormously beneficial in many ways, have a dark side. They have given rise to a level of cooperation, and therefore interdependence, between many disparate institutions never before seen in economic behavior. And the cost of hyperefficiency is system fragility. We see it in how a tsunami in Japan disrupts the operations of American electronics and car companies, in how twenty terrorists can shut down the United States for a week, and we also see it in finance. In the pre-Internet, pre-deregulation financial system, the failure of any one institution or market did not generally endanger everything else. That is no longer true.

Astonishingly, it was not until the Lehman failure in September 2008 that senior federal officials—Treasury secretary Hank Paulson, Fed chairman Ben Bernanke, New York Federal Reserve president Tim Geithner—apparently realized how interconnected the global financial system had become. Perhaps they had believed their own propaganda. The banks insisted for years that they had off-loaded much of their risk to wealthy investors, hedge funds, pension funds, and the like. Derivatives such as credit default swaps were said to be particularly wonderful for reducing risk. But the risk shedding was a mirage. If you followed the money and the risks all the way through the system, in the end they came right back to the banks. And once a crisis started, it could move through the system much faster and more violently than any human being could understand or manage.

Richard Bookstaber, an engineer and economist with deep experience in finance and risk management, termed this phenomenon "tight coupling." A tightly coupled system is one in which problems propagate faster than managers can react, and where systemic interdependence means that disruptions can rapidly become catastrophic as they progress. In his brilliant book *A Demon of Our Own Design,* written *before* the crisis and published in 2007, Bookstaber warned that modern electronic finance was dangerous in this way. He examined a series of both nonfinancial and financial disasters, seeking their common features. He found that increased velocity and efficiency created a danger that human regulators would be overtaken by events. He also found that measures that supposedly increased the safety of one institution or part of the system could have the opposite effect on the *whole* system, particularly if widely adopted. One example he considered was the role played by "portfolio insurance" in causing the 1987 market crash. More recently, think credit default swaps and AIG; selling mortgage assets when the panic started; or withdrawing money from a money market fund in September 2008.

It is probably pointless to second-guess most of the behavior of the people at Treasury and the Federal Reserve in September 2008, for they were making decisions under great pressure and with poor information. What is to be condemned is the way they behaved before and after the catastrophe. Messrs. Greenspan, Bernanke, Paulson, Geithner et al. could have retained their blissful, oblivious happiness in 2006–2008 only by willfully ignoring masses of contrary evidence. The dangerous financial crises that America had experienced since the early 1980s were both recent and highly visible. And what have these gentlemen advised since? Nothing very impressive.

The chart immediately below, vastly oversimplified as it is, captures some of the relationships that lead to tight coupling within the modern financial system.

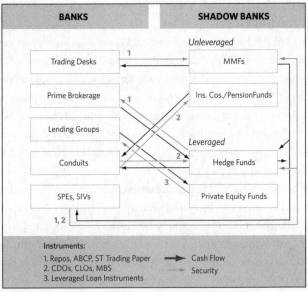

Source: Adapted from Adair Turner/U.K. Financial Services Authority

In effect, during the bubble the banks and the shadow banks were part of a single, highly leveraged organism. But only one side was open to regulatory scrutiny, and even the supposedly regulated sector got precious little of it. As assets were shifted back and forth between the two sides, leverage typically grew sharply, and the interconnections tightened. When one piece of the system cracked, like a flooded safety device in a nuclear plant, a global meltdown was under way almost before officials noticed. In response to the failure of Lehman, the short-term funding market shut down, and the crash was on.[9] And if AIG had failed, all of those credit default swaps that provided "protection" wouldn't have been worth the paper they were written on.

Toxic Incentives Again

In 2008 Paulson and Geithner were certainly correct to save AIG, guarantee money market deposits, and hand out $250 billion to strengthen the banks a month later. Their culpability lies in having allowed the bubble to build and having been unprepared for the crisis, and then in saving the banks without getting anything in return, either then or later, from those who had created the problem. This last issue is perhaps the most dangerous for the future. Letting them get away with it wasn't just morally obscene; it was also destabilizing, because it signaled that they could do it again. One can take comfort from the fact that airline pilots need to be careful because they too would die in a crash—but exactly the reverse holds true in American finance. When the plane had engine trouble, we looked out the window to see the pilots gliding to earth with the only parachutes in sight. But where else can Americans borrow and invest? The American financial sector has a captive audience.

This, in turn, explains much of the risk taking and dishonesty that we have just catalogued. If volatility, leverage, concentration, and systemic interdependence are so incredibly dangerous, why would rational people construct such an industry? There are several reasons, but primary among them is that the architects and contractors don't have to live in the house. There are other reasons for regulation too. There will always be some people willing to do dangerous things, and they need to be kept away from the controls. There are public goods/collective action problems: individuals are powerless to change the system, so they might as well go along for the ride (i.e., if New York prohibits something but California doesn't, then it just moves to California—or London). This means that only broad regulation can be effective. But the single most powerful driver of risk taking and fraud was clearly the fact that all the benefits were appropriated by those running the financial system, while the costs were borne by everyone else.

Recall our earlier dissection of how the toxic incentive structures of financial firms led traders to destroy their own firms. Something similar holds true at the systemic level as well. First, the lesson from 2008 and since is that those who destroy the system will be bailed out and won't be punished. But second, even if you don't bail them out, and even leaving aside little details like criminal prosecution, there is a vast disproportion between the financial sector's financial pain and the pain that it has caused to society at large. Of the trillions of dollars that the financial crisis has cost, only a very small portion, surely less than 5 percent, has been paid for by the financial industry itself.

In the end, then, unregulated finance isn't that different from unregulated medical practice, aircraft maintenance, offshore oil drilling, high explosives, nuclear power (or, perhaps, even *regulated* nuclear power), or military weapons. Do you think that it would be fun to live in a country where absolutely anyone can claim to be a doctor—if you can find such a place? Or perhaps try a country with no real police force, in which everyone has assault weapons and explosives. Try a few years in Iraq, Afghanistan, or Somalia. See if you like it there.

Is Modern Finance a Parasitic Industry?

LORD ADAIR TURNER, chairman of the British Financial Services Authority, is one of a growing number of economists and financial experts who have raised the question of whether the modern financial sector is a burden to society even when it isn't generating crises. Others who have raised the same issue include Burton Malkiel, a professor at Princeton, and John Bogle, the founder and former CEO of the Vanguard Group. Both Malkiel and Bogle have pointed out that the over-whelming majority of investment managers do no better than someone throwing darts at the wall.

The problem, furthermore, is more general than mutual funds. In a series of lectures and papers, Lord Turner asked whether modern finance has become a "rent-extracting" industry, which is economics-speak for "parasite." By "rents," economists mean earnings derived from your position as a bottleneck, or a leech, rather than from any real economic contribution. Surplus cartel earnings, government-sanctioned monopolies, bribes extracted by the powerful, and earnings from inside information are examples of economic "rents."

Large parts of modern finance seem to fit this definition. In some cases, particularly the private equity sector and the tax avoidance industry, financial sector profits depend heavily on tax loopholes and zero-sum exploitation of working people. The following are some examples.

The Portfolio Management Industry

It has long been known that low-cost indexed portfolios nearly always outperform active asset management. While indexing has been making inroads in recent decades, active management still dominates in pension plans and endowments, and in almost all individually directed investment accounts. The high fees paid by many retail investors are a clear case of information failure and/or market power, probably exacerbated by deceptive advertising and the industry's concentration. Even the hedge fund industry, open only to wealthy and institutional investors, has an unimpressive overall record. Net of the high fees that hedge funds charge, the industry has barely outperformed Treasury bonds over the last twenty years. There are, of course, exceptions: Warren Buffett, George Soros, and several others come to mind. But for every Buffett or Soros, there are many who don't deserve their very high incomes.

High-Frequency Trading

Hedge fund billionaire Jim Simons, a former star mathematics professor at Stony Brook, has for years made extraordinary returns by using powerful computers and proprietary trading algorithms to exploit tiny market trends invisible to humans, and which often last only a fraction of a second. The trading is entirely automatic—computers make all the decisions and execute all the trades. The net effect is a small tax, a form of skimming, on the whole market. Normal investors who don't own gigantic computer systems end up paying slightly more for stock trades and have slightly lower investment returns, while Simons and his imitators pile up micro-pennies by the billions.

There is no social benefit at all from high-frequency trading; the positions often last only for milliseconds and have no economic utility. It is a pure drag on the economy, albeit a small one, like spam e-mail. The massive trading volumes the strategy requires impose substantial costs, mainly for computer systems, and on at least two occasions high-frequency trading has caused market disruptions called "flash crashes."

Simons's personal earnings are in the billions, making him one of the highest-paid hedge fund managers in the world. Naturally, all large players now emulate this strategy, and it now accounts for the majority of total trading volume. Indeed, an increasing fraction of hedge fund management is game playing of this kind, exploiting very small, short-lived market imperfections to pile up wealth while providing no social benefit.

Obscuring Debt, National and Otherwise

All readers of the financial pages know that Greece has been mired in a debt crisis. An initial question, naturally, was how much did Greece owe? A team from the European finance authority reported in 2010 on "the difficulties in...[getting] complete and reliable information" on Greek debt. No surprise, because Goldman Sachs had been there first.

Goldman arranged a series of highly favorable currency swaps for Greece, creating an immediate gain of 2.4 billion euros, which was applied against the country's apparent debt. Normally, such a trade should have triggered a cash payment from Greece to Goldman to cover the gain. But Goldman covered that by structuring another swap, but a deferred long-term one that was off the books. The entire transaction served no purpose but to falsify Greece's books and produce fees for Goldman. Several other investment banks have been accused of doing essentially the same thing for a variety of domestic and foreign companies and local governments.

Tax Avoidance

An unknown but clearly significant fraction of American tax attorneys and financial advisors obtain very high incomes from wealthy individuals and corporations for the sole purpose of avoiding taxes. It is greatly to the benefit of these people that the tax code has become extremely complex and that it contains many provisions that can be used to avoid the payment of legitimately owed taxes.

These activities, and their effects, have grown enormously over the last quarter century as a combined result of increasing economic inequality, legal and tax loopholes, and weakened enforcement. In the early 1980s, corporate taxes equaled over 40 percent of corporate profits; in 2010, it was 26 percent. The effect for wealthy individuals has been even more dramatic. The IRS has reported that the effective tax rate of the nation's four hundred wealthiest families, most of them billionaires, declined from 30 percent in 1995 to only 18 percent in 2005, the last year for which data are available (as of early 2012). Some of these declines in tax payments represent changes in tax rates; for example, the Bush tax cuts. But a major fraction of the declines, both corporate and individual, have come from tax avoidance.

On November 27, 2011, the *New York Times* published a long article on the tax avoidance schemes of the billionaire Ronald S. Lauder, who inherited a fortune from his parents, the founders of the Estée Lauder cosmetics firm. Mr. Lauder's own contribution to the American economy has been, let us say... unclear. Although Mr. Lauder has a net worth of over $3 billion, he and his family have used a series of highly aggressive tax shelter strategies implemented by their lawyers and financial advisors. These strategies have included offshore corporate structures in tax havens; trusts that shelter stock tax-free for long periods; forward contracts for the eventual sale of stock, permitting immediate and tax-free access to cash; derivatives strategies such as "shorting against the box"; tax-free borrowing against unsold stock; "fractional donations" of a portion of an artwork whose possession he retained; and others. It was a family affair. The company, its owners, and their heirs have used aggressive tax avoidance since Estée Lauder went public in the 1980s.

Many American corporations now behave similarly. When the transformation of American finance began in the 1980s, very few American corporations used even the tax avoidance methods then available, such as registering subsidiaries in offshore tax havens. It was, quite simply, considered both unseemly and unnecessary. Now, however, most large multinationals do this. Some, such as General Electric, correctly regard tax strategy as a major driver of profits, and maintain large permanent staffs of attorneys and financial planners dedicated purely to tax avoidance. In addition, of course, these companies make extensive use of investment banks and outside law firms.

No matter what you think about tax rates—even if you think that taxes should be lower for billionaires—this is pointless, wasted activity. And if you think that billionaires, and companies with billions of dollars in profits, probably should pay more taxes than construction workers and secretaries, then it isn't simply wasteful; it's highly destructive.

The Private Equity Industry

Private equity companies may be the most efficient money-seeking organisms in the world. Matt Taibbi has immortalized Goldman Sachs as "a great vampire squid wrapped around the face of humanity, relentlessly jamming its blood funnel into anything that smells like money." Maybe. But in 2006, when Goldman's Lloyd Blankfein earned $44 million, which made him Wall Street's highest-paid investment banker, Blackstone's Steve Schwarzman made $398 million, or twice as much as the top five Goldman earners combined. On top of that, due to the "carried interest" tax loophole, most of Schwarzman's income was taxed at a 15 percent rate, equivalent to that paid by ordinary workers in the bottom income tax bracket. Blackstone and all the other major private equity firms use the same fee structure—they charge 2 percent per year of assets under management, plus 20 percent of all profits, with no responsibility for losses.

The best that can be said about private equity companies is that they might not be any worse than many of their publicly owned peers. They are very rough on their rank-and-file employees, but many companies are today—perhaps in part because of the pressures from private equity firms. They do cut costs—at least operational costs. But they often greatly increase the financial costs of the companies they own. They are brutally expert offshorers and outsourcers of jobs. Undoubtedly, there must exist some private equity deals that have produced real economic gains, when incompetent managers are replaced through an acquisition. But there is abundant evidence that this is not the norm.

A great deal of the success of private equity firms comes from exploiting various hidden government subsidies and tax loopholes. A considerable number of companies acquired by private equity firms go bankrupt even though the private equity buyers make money. This is not a marginal matter. Of the ten largest leveraged buyouts made by Bain Capital when Mitt Romney was its CEO, four went bankrupt, *even though Bain made money*. Private equity owners have no liability for a company's debts, so they face relatively little risk. Therefore, they often force the company to borrow huge amounts of money, which the company then pays to the private equity firm as fees and/or dividends. The result is often bankruptcy, as the company runs out of money. But it doesn't stop there. Bankrupt companies are legally prohibited from paying dividends, but they can pay "fees." And, not infrequently, the same private equity firm buys the company again, *out of bankruptcy,* after many of its debts have been reduced or restructured.

Additionally, private equity firms sometimes force employee retirement plans to purchase stock in the company, or even the whole company. This allows the private equity firm to cash out, even (perhaps especially) if the company is failing. This occurred, for example, with Simmons Bedding, a company that I discuss in more detail below. If the company later goes bankrupt, the private equity firm has no liability to pay employee pensions. Either the employees must see their retirement income destroyed, or, if the company is eligible, their pensions are paid not by the private equity firm but by the Pension Benefit Guaranty Corporation, a U.S. government agency. In 2010 the PBGC paid out $5.6 billion to failed pension plans, and had an accumulated deficit of $23 billion. It is not known what fraction of the deficit derives from private equity transactions.

Another recent case of gaming federal subsidies involves for-profit universities, which are nearly entirely dependent upon federal student-loan programs for their tuition revenues. In 2006 a group of private equity firms led by Goldman Sachs bought the Education Management Corporation for $3.4 billion; Goldman owned 41 percent.[10] This acquisition coincided with a change in federal law that had been championed by House leader John Boehner, eliminating the prior requirement that federal loans be restricted to schools where the majority of students attended a physical campus. After the change, schools were eligible for federal student loans even if they barely existed physically, and even if the overwhelming majority of their students were online.

Immediately following its private equity acquisition and the legal change, Education Management started extremely aggressive recruiting efforts, and the number of online students increased sharply. So did dropout rates. From 2006 to 2011, Education Management's revenues increased from less than $1.5 billion to $2.8 billion. Recruiting allegedly became extremely manipulative, even fraudulent; allegedly, for example, students with felony records were told that after obtaining criminal justice degrees, they could work in law enforcement, which is false. Recruiters were paid bonuses very similar to the yield-spread premiums that were paid to mortgage brokers during the housing bubble. But once students received their loans and paid their tuition, Education Management had its money whether the students graduated or not. Education Management had no liability for the loans, even when they defaulted in high numbers.

In 2010 the attorneys general of Florida and Kentucky initiated investigations of Education Management. In 2011 a whistle-blower lawsuit was filed. The Justice Department and four states joined the suit, and accused Education Management of fraudulent recruiting, and of fraudulently obtaining a total of $11 billion in tuition derived from federal student aid. The complaint, however, is only against Education Management; Goldman Sachs has not been sued or charged.[11] As of early 2012, no one has been criminally prosecuted.

More frequently, private equity transactions depend heavily on the favorable tax treatment of dividends and of extreme leverage. Companies owned by private equity firms almost never pay corporate taxes, because they have such huge interest bills. This is because private equity firms force the companies they own to take on enormous levels of debt, often for very nasty reasons (discussed shortly). Interest rates have been extraordinarily low for many years now, so it has been an ideal environment for private equity–owned companies. Falling rates allowed them to continually refinance debt, allowing their private equity owners to extract more and more cash with minimal impact on debt service, in a manner very similar to the refinancing boom during the housing bubble. When a Blackstone-led group bought Freescale Semiconductor in 2005, its debt immediately ballooned elevenfold, from $832 million to $9.4 billion.

Why so much increased debt for the companies they buy? Private equity firms add debt to pay themselves "special dividends," sometimes to the tune of $1 billion or more, distributed among the private equity firm partners and their limited partners in the deal. Firm partners typically have little or none of their own capital in their deals. The equity comes from their limited partner investors, and it is usually completely returned within the first few years from these debt-funded "special dividends." There is an additional benefit to this trick. Often, private equity firms give stock to a small number of senior managers of the companies they buy. These managers therefore receive dividends, too, which are taxed at 15 percent rather than at the far higher rates that apply to "ordinary income."

Moreover, a significant fraction of private equity firms' profits come in a very direct way from screwing the employees of the companies they buy. The United States has very weak protections for most workers, and even those protections have been insufficiently enforced. In addition to wage cuts, private equity firms often attack benefits, especially pensions and retirement health care.

In late 2009 the *New York Times* published a remarkable series of articles on the looting of the Simmons Bedding Company by its private equity owners and the management they installed.[12] After the private equity firm THL (for Thomas H. Lee, its founder) bought Simmons from another private equity firm (Simmons had already been flipped several times by *other* private equity firms), THL ordered the Simmons company to borrow over $1 billion. Simmons then paid huge amounts of this borrowed cash—$375 million—to THL in the form of "special dividends," as well as paying additional, large transaction fees for THL and to the investment banks that arranged the financings. Employees' wages and benefits, including their retirement plans, were cut severely, even for blue-collar workers with over twenty years' seniority. Indeed, the employees' retirement fund had already been victimized by the actions of an earlier private equity owner, William Simon (who was treasury secretary in the Nixon administration). Simon had forced the employees' retirement plan to purchase Simmons stock from him at an inflated price. When the stock price declined, Simmons was purchased by another private equity firm at a far lower price, devastating the employees' retirement savings.

During much of the time that Simmons Bedding was owned by THL, the company's CEO (approved and installed by THL) was a man named Charlie Eitel, who ran Simmons remotely from his homes in Jackson Hole, Wyoming, and Naples, Florida, as well as from his yacht, *Eitel Time*. He also forced Simmons to hire his son. Eitel made more than $40 million, keeping it all even when Simmons was forced into bankruptcy, which caused its employees and bondholders to lose enormous sums. The company laid off a thousand people, over 25 percent of its workforce, including employees with more than twenty years' seniority, giving them little severance pay or retirement benefits. THL was not harmed by the bankruptcy and in fact made a large profit on Simmons, because it had paid itself in cash long before, as well as taking large special dividends and transaction fees from the proceeds of the debt financings that bankrupted the company.

Was this all legal? It is hard to know which answer would be worse—that it was illegal but nothing was done, or that this was all, in fact, perfectly legal in America. As it is also, apparently, perfectly legal to construct and sell a security with the intent of betting on its failure.

There are other ways in which private equity firms may depend upon dubious behavior for their profits. In 2006 the SEC investigated the industry with regard to alleged "club deals," whereby supposedly competing private equity firms would secretly collude in order to reduce the prices they needed to pay for companies. The SEC closed the investigation without filing charges, but several investors filed a major private antitrust suit, which was still proceeding as of 2012. In early 2012 the SEC opened another investigation centered on the possibility that private equity firms inflated the value of their assets when trying to attract new investors.[13]

And without question, private equity firms are superb at avoiding taxes. Mitt Romney's ability to pay a 14 percent tax rate on income of over $20 million per year, much of it coming from Bain Capital *a decade after he left the firm*, is no accident; nor is it unusual. So whatever limited economic contribution might be made by private equity firms, it is outweighed by their practice of redirecting managers' attention to skimming off the maximum financial rewards for themselves.

IT IS EASY TO multiply such examples, and data on the growth of financial transactions volume fills in the rest of the picture. Over recent decades, securitized transactions have increased from nearly zero to trillions of dollars annually. Foreign exchange trading has grown thirty times faster than global GDP. Daily oil futures trading, which used to run at about the same value as the underlying physical supply, is now ten times the underlying supply, while market volatility seems to have increased.[14]

In other words, we seem to have reached an unhappy position in which a substantial fraction of our most intelligent and articulate citizens either sit at Bloomberg terminals or jet around the world in very expensive tailor-made suits "doing deals" that, judging by the recent record, have no purpose except to put more money in their own pockets, and that on a net basis are economically detrimental to the rest of the population.

The drain on America's talents is substantial. In 2008, Harvard reported that 28 percent of its "gainfully employed" new graduates chose jobs in finance; for Yale, it was 26 percent. Even in 2011, the percentages remained strikingly high—17 percent for Harvard, 14 percent for Yale. Princeton had the highest percentage in the Ivy League—40 percent. Whatever cynical thoughts one might have about the value (and ethics) produced by an Ivy League education, there is no doubt that finance has diverted enormous human capacity away from more productive work.

Reflection and self-questioning, however, are not the financial sector's greatest strength. Self-reform is accordingly unlikely. In his January 2011 speech at the World Economic Forum in Davos, Jamie Dimon complained of "this constant refrain [of] 'bankers, bankers, bankers'—it's just a really unproductive and unfair way of treating people."[15] Lloyd Blankfein told a different audience that he was doing God's work.

Can we turn Mr. Hyde back into Dr. Jekyll, *shrink* the financial sector, restore safe banking, and rid the world of the winner-take-all casino controlled by the likes of Goldman Sachs and THL? The truthful answer is that maybe we can't yet; the industry's power is greater than ever, despite the crisis. So it may take another crisis before enough people get angry enough; we consider that question in the final chapter.

Next, however, we examine another important sector of society, one that has long been considered immune to the corrupting influence of corporate money and "revolving door" hiring. Academia, along with the media, has generally been regarded as an important bastion of independent, and if necessary critical, analysis of economic and political behavior. Unfortunately, this is less and less true. As with politicians, the financial sector and other wealthy interest groups have figured out that professors make an excellent investment. They have proven stunningly easy to buy; for very small sums, considering the stakes involved, the financial sector has hired the best propagandists in the world.

CHAPTER 8

THE IVORY TOWER

MANY PEOPLE WHO SAW *Inside Job* found that the most surprising, and disturbing, portion of the film was its revelation of widespread conflicts of interest in universities, think tanks, and among prominent academic experts on finance, economics, business, and government regulation. Viewers who watched my interviews with eminent professors were stunned at what came out of their mouths. It was indeed very disturbing, and sometimes I was stunned myself.

And yet, we should not be entirely surprised. Over the past couple of decades medical professionals, professors very much included, have amply demonstrated the influence that money can have in a supposedly objective, scientific field.

Randomized clinical trials of pharmaceuticals, including those conducted in academic centers, are, according to one large study, 3.6 times as likely to produce a favorable result if they are financed by a pharmaceutical company. Physicians who own interests in diagnostic imaging centers are four and a half times more likely to refer patients for such services. A recent Senate investigation showed how the pharmaceutical manufacturer Sanofi enlisted medical groups and individuals it had financed to help block generic equivalents to one of its drugs. In the course of just a few years in the 2000s, the Justice Department won settlements of more than $1.5 billion against three drug companies for paying kickbacks to doctors or otherwise engaging in illegal marketing of their drugs. It became a common practice even at top medical schools for physician-professors to sign their names to papers drafted by drug company staff. Indeed, Stanford University Medical School banned this practice in 2006; but not all medical schools have done so. In general, medical schools and leading medical journals are responding fairly well to the rise of this problem, with many of them adopting stringent disclosure requirements and even, in some cases such as Stanford, absolute limits on outside compensation from sources that could pose a conflict of interest.[1]

But the economics discipline, business schools, law schools, and political science and public policy schools have reacted very differently. Over the last thirty years, in parallel with deregulation and the rising power of money in American politics, significant portions of American academia have deteriorated into "pay to play" activities. These days, if you see a famous economics professor testify in Congress, appear on television news, testify in an antitrust case or regulatory proceeding, give a speech, or write an opinion article in the *New York Times* (or the *Financial Times,* the *Wall Street Journal,* or anywhere else), there is a high probability that he or she is being paid by someone with a big stake in what's being debated. Most of the time, these professors do *not* disclose these conflicts of interest in their public or media appearances, and most of the time their universities look the other way. Increasingly, professors are also paid to testify for defendants in financial fraud trials, both civil and criminal. The pay is high—sometimes a quarter of a million dollars for an hour of congressional testimony. But for banks and other highly regulated industries, it's a trivial expense, a billion or two a year that they barely notice; and just as with politicians, it's a very good investment, with very high benefits.

I watched the growth of this problem when I was in academia myself, and must confess that I once participated in it. When I was a twenty-four-year-old graduate student, I was hired for a summer by MIT professor Peter Temin, a prominent economist, to help him defend AT&T, which was still a nationwide monopoly and had been sued for antitrust violations by the Justice Department. I was very young and naive, and was stunned at what I saw. Within a month, I realized that AT&T had literally hired the majority of the most prominent telecommunications and regulatory economists in America. Everywhere I went—MIT, Harvard, Stanford, Berkeley, Yale—the main guys were working for AT&T, whose spending dwarfed the Justice Department's, probably by fifty or a hundred to one. I concluded that AT&T was guilty; wrote something very unfavorable to AT&T, which of course never saw the light of day; and returned to graduate school. Peter Temin is actually a very nice guy, and was very kind to me and the six other graduate students he hired that summer. But the experience left me with a bad taste in my mouth.

And, having been sensitized, I noticed over the intervening years that the problem was growing—fast. Vast amounts of money (by academic standards) started arriving from powerful industries, mainly in the form of direct consulting payments to professors. This problem is now so pervasive that the academic disciplines of economics, business, public policy, and law have been severely distorted by the conflicts of interest now endemic to them. The areas most severely affected have been finance, the economics of regulation, industrial organization, corporate governance, antitrust analysis, the economic analysis of law, and the analysis of specific industries affected by government policy. The principal industries involved are energy, telecommunications, health care, agribusiness—and, most definitely, financial services. There are also serious problems in medical research and, disturbingly, even national security policy (we will shortly consider some interesting facts about Libya).

Academics on industry payrolls, and the interest groups that pay them, are now so numerous and powerful that they can prevent universities, professional associations, and academic journals from adopting or enforcing strong conflict-of-interest policies. They also have a chilling, even dominant, effect on several areas of academic research and policy analysis. Most of America's best universities do not limit financial conflicts of interest, do not require their disclosure, and aggressively resist inquiries into the issue. There are several reasons for this, including fear of public embarrassment; the existence of personal conflicts of interest among university presidents and deans; dependence on donations from companies and executives; and the internal power (within the university) of large numbers of professors who wish to preserve their incomes and reputations, and who know that disclosure and reform would endanger them.

The sale of academic "expertise" for the purpose of influencing government policy, the courts, and public opinion is now a multibillion-dollar business. Academic, legal, regulatory, and policy consulting in economics, finance, and regulation is dominated by a half dozen consulting firms, several speakers' bureaus, and various industry lobbying groups that maintain large networks of academics for hire specifically for the purpose of advocating industry interests in policy and regulatory debates.

These consulting firms are not like McKinsey or the Boston Consulting Group. They do not exist to help companies make better products or lower their costs or forecast demand. Their principal focus is on helping companies avoid or influence legislation, public debate, regulation, prosecution, class-action lawsuits, antitrust judgments, and taxes.

The largest academic regulatory consulting firms are the Berkeley Research Group, the Analysis Group, the Brattle Group, Criterion, Compass Lexecon, and Charles River Associates. All have relationships with many prominent academics. Their combined academic roster is around one thousand, and their combined revenues are certainly well over $1 billion per year. (Most are private and don't release revenue information.) In some cases, they include a majority of the prominent academics in important policy-related fields, such as antitrust policy.

The Berkeley Research Group, for example, lists 148 "experts," most of them identified as "principals" or "directors," and most of them high-profile academics—Laura Tyson is one, for example.[2] With eighteen offices in the United States and one in London, it organizes its work around "high-stakes, complex commercial disputes and regulatory and legislative issues." BRG lists nineteen specialties, including antitrust, energy, environmental research, and intellectual property, as well as litigation support services—damages analysis, forensic financial analysis, and class-action certification.[3]

The Analysis Group, headquartered in Boston with offices throughout the United States, has a staff of five hundred and a star-studded list of academic experts, including John Campbell, chairman of the Harvard economics department, Jonathan Gruber, a leading health care economist at MIT, and Glenn Hubbard, the dean of Columbia Business School.[4] Compass Lexecon has three hundred on its staff, which now includes six former chief economists of the Department of Justice's antitrust division.[5] It recently signed several new experts, including a Nobel laureate at NYU.

Charles River Associates was founded by MIT economist and antitrust expert Franklin Fisher in 1965 and is now a publicly traded international consulting firm with seven hundred employees. It also maintains exclusive relationships with forty-four prestigious academics for occasional advisory assignments.[6] And business is good. The Charles River financials show revenues averaging over $300 million annually between 2008 and 2010. Revenues per employee were nearly $450,000 a year, and revenue per consultant exceeded $600,000 per year. Those are investment-banking-type numbers.

Speakers' bureaus are another significant channel, and are sometimes used to launder or disguise payments to academics for lobbying and policy advocacy. Speaking fees (for corporate events and industry conventions, for example) sometimes exceed $100,000 for prominent academics, particularly if they have also served in government. Prominent academics often make half a million dollars a year that way, particularly if they study and write about a highly regulated industry.

But how important and influential are these people and their relationships? What follows is a sample of the academic world's relationships to the financial services industry and their impact on public debate and policy. I think that most readers will find it all too…convincing. The financial sector is, yet again, *very* well connected.

The Money People

THE MOST EMINENT academics in the United States, particularly those who have studied, written about, and/or worked on financial regulation and deregulation, have made fortunes from Wall Street while advocating its interests in Congress, regulatory proceedings, the courts, and the media. Here we will consider some examples in detail, all of them very prominent:

- Glenn Hubbard
- Larry Summers
- Frederic Mishkin
- Richard Portes
- Laura D'Andrea Tyson
- Martin Feldstein
- Hal Scott
- John Campbell

Glenn Hubbard. R. Glenn Hubbard became dean of Columbia Business School in 2004, shortly after leaving the George W. Bush administration, where he was chairman of the White House Council of Economic Advisers from 2001 through 2003. Hubbard has a PhD from Harvard and has taught at Columbia since 1988. He also served in the Treasury

Department in the George H. W. Bush administration. Hubbard is cochairman of the Committee on Capital Markets Regulation, a nonprofit organization that serves as a de facto public policy lobbying organization for Wall Street.

Much of Hubbard's academic work has been focused on tax policy. A fair summary is that he has never seen a tax he would like, particularly one on corporations or the wealthy. He was deeply involved in designing the Bush administration's tax cuts in 2003, which heavily favored the wealthy; half of their benefits went to the wealthiest 1 percent of the population.

Hubbard also coauthored an astonishing article (with William C. Dudley) in November 2004. The article, entitled "How Capital Markets Enhance Economic Performance and Facilitate Job Creation," was published by the Goldman Sachs Global Markets Institute.[7] Dudley, his coauthor, was the chief economist at Goldman Sachs at the time. In 2009, when Tim Geithner became Obama's treasury secretary, Dudley succeeded Geithner as president of the Federal Reserve Bank of New York. This should not reassure you. But neither should the fact that Glenn Hubbard remains dean of Columbia Business School.

Their article warrants quotation at some length. It would be kind of funny, if it weren't deadly serious. Remember, this is November 2004, with the bubble well under way.

- "The ascendancy of the US capital markets…has improved the allocation of capital and risk throughout the US economy.… [The benefits include] enhanced stability of the US banking system… more jobs and higher wages…less frequent and milder [recessions]…a revolution in housing finance."
- "The development of the capital markets has helped distribute risk more efficiently.… This ability to transfer risk facilitates greater risk-taking, but this increased risk-taking does not destabilize the economy.… Thus the capital markets ensure that capital flows to its best uses and that riskier activities with higher payoffs are funded."

- "The capital markets have helped make the housing market less volatile.... 'Credit crunches' of the sort that periodically shut off the supply of funds to home buyers, and crushed the homebuilding industry...are a thing of the past.... The closing costs associated with obtaining a residential mortgage have fallen, and the terms...have become less stringent. At times homeowners can obtain 100 percent financing to purchase a home."

- "The revolution in housing finance has also led to another radical transformation that has been important in making the economy less cyclical."

- "We believe that the economic performance of the United States over the past decade provides strong evidence of the benefits of well-developed capital markets. That is because the US economic performance has improved over time, both absolutely and relative to other G-7 countries in which capital markets are much less well-developed."

Hubbard refused to say whether he was paid to write the article. He also refused to provide me with his most recent federal financial disclosure form (from 2001, when he entered the George W. Bush administration), which we could not obtain otherwise, because the White House had already destroyed it. Hubbard also refused to identify most of his private consulting clients. He is currently on the boards of MetLife, ADP, Inc., KKR Financial Corporation, and BlackRock Closed End Funds. In 2010, the first three paid him $707,000 in cash and stock.[8] Consulting/advisory relationships listed on Hubbard's CV include Nomura Holdings, Bank of America, Capital Research, Citigroup, Fidelity, Franklin Resources, JPMorgan Chase, Visa, Laurus Funds, Chart Venture Partners, and Ripplewood Holdings. Until January 2009, he was also on the board of Capmark, a major player in commercial real estate during the bubble that went bankrupt after the crisis.

Hubbard was paid $100,000 to testify for the criminal defense of two Bear Stearns hedge fund managers prosecuted in connection with the bubble, who were acquitted. That assignment came through the

Analysis Group, one of the large economic consulting firms mentioned earlier. Hubbard lists the Analysis Group as a consulting client but has not divulged the identities of the ultimate, real clients for whom he has worked via his relationship with the Analysis Group. Nor did his Columbia web page (as of February 2012) list his paid speaking engagements. Both of these omissions represent apparent violations of the new disclosure requirements established by Columbia Business School after the release of my film.[9] However, his speaker's bureau, the Harry Walker Agency, is one of the very few such agencies that lists the names of some speakers' clients by name, in its "ovations" testimonials. Clients giving testimonials to Hubbard's speaking abilities include the Alternative Investment Group, BNP Paribas, the Massachusetts Bankers' Association, and Barclays Bank.[10]

My filmed interview with Hubbard in 2009 contained the following exchange:

> **CF:** How does your personal income compare, your private income as opposed to your university salary?
>
> **GLENN HUBBARD:** Vastly times more, because I write textbooks, so that's much more remunerative than being a professor.

Textbooks? Not quite.

In 2011, Hubbard became a senior economic advisor to Mitt Romney's presidential campaign.

Larry Summers. Summers, who is undeniably brilliant, is the son of two economists and a relative of Paul Samuelson and Kenneth Arrow, two of the greatest economists of the last century. Summers became a full professor at Harvard at a very young age and by now has held almost every important government position in economics. After being chief economist of the World Bank, he became, successively, undersecretary of the treasury for international affairs, deputy treasury secretary, and finally treasury secretary in the Clinton administration. He then became president of Harvard, his candidacy championed by Robert

Rubin, until Summers was forced out in 2006. In 2009 he became director of the National Economic Council in the Obama administration; he returned to Harvard in 2011 as a professor at the John F. Kennedy School of Government.

I don't think that Summers is corrupt in any crude, literal way. His thinking has been poisoned by enormous arrogance and a desperate need to be regarded as important by the wealthy and powerful. Although sensible about many issues, Summers has made a succession of progressively more serious mistakes and ethical compromises. And his views on the financial sector would be hard to distinguish from those of, say, Lloyd Blankfein or Jamie Dimon.

Periodically, Summers has gotten himself into trouble. At the World Bank, he authorized a memo suggesting that wealthy nations should export pollution to the poor; when president of Harvard, he suggested that women might be innately inferior to men in scientific reasoning. Then there were his policy choices: remaining entirely silent about the abuses within investment banking that furthered the Internet bubble; working with Robert Rubin and Alan Greenspan to repeal the Glass-Steagall separation between commercial and investment banking; joining with Alan Greenspan to ban regulation of privately traded derivatives. He testified in Congress that "the parties to these kinds of contracts are largely sophisticated financial institutions that would appear to be eminently capable of protecting themselves from fraud and counterparty [in]solvencies."[11]

That statement was made even as Long-Term Capital Management was being rescued from catastrophic defaults triggered by the very class of derivatives Summers was opposed to regulating. His opposition to Brooksley Born, the head of the Commodity Futures Trading Commission at the time, may also have been tinged with the sexism that later contributed to his removal from the presidency of Harvard. In 2005, when Raghuram Rajan presented his prescient paper at Jackson Hole, Summers shouted that Rajan was a "Luddite" and that his paper was misguided.

When Summers became president of Harvard, he also started consulting to, and making speeches for financial services firms. Because Harvard, along with most other major universities, does not require its faculty (or its presidents) to disclose outside income, we do not know how much Summers made. Even now, his Harvard Web page lists none of his consulting clients or speaking engagements. But even while he was president of Harvard, his income from the financial sector was probably already substantial.

Shortly after he was forced to resign as president and returned to being a professor, Summers agreed to work one day a week at D. E. Shaw, a large hedge fund, which paid him over $5 million in the year before Summers entered the Obama administration in 2009.

His government service was, indeed, helpful in one regard. Most of our information about his outside activities at Harvard comes from his mandatory federal disclosure form, not from any disclosures made to or by Harvard. (Harvard's president and provost declined to be interviewed for my film and also declined to respond to written questions.) Summers's 2009 federal disclosure form stated his net worth to be $17 million to $39 million. His total earnings in the year prior to joining the administration were $7,813,000. He made $1,729,000 from thirty-one speaking engagements, nearly all for financial services companies; Goldman Sachs paid him $135,000 for one speech. He was also paid $45,000 by Merrill Lynch for a speech on November 12, 2008— after Merrill had completely collapsed financially, and one week after Obama's election. After questions were raised, Summers donated the Merrill Lynch fee to charity.

A report in an *Asia Times* blog suggests that in the summer of 2007, right after AAA-rated mortgage CDOs blew up a Bear Stearns hedge fund, Summers was marketing Shaw-owned CDOs to Asian sovereign wealth funds. If true, that raises an interesting question: was Summers helping Shaw execute a Goldman-like strategy of dumping toxic assets on naive institutions? Or did he not understand, even in 2007, that these things were so dangerous?[12] But it doesn't really matter. Summers is a deeply compromised man who owes most of his fortune and much of his political success to the financial services industry, and who was instrumental in some of the most disastrous economic policy decisions of the last half century.

In the Obama administration, Summers opposed strong measures to sanction bankers or curtail their income. He has never apologized for any of the decisions or statements he made between 1995 and 2006. He declined to be interviewed for my film, as did all members of the Obama administration.

In 2011 two Harvard professors decided to show my film in their class. When Summers learned of this, he contacted the professors and demanded the right to come to the class and comment on the film. They agreed, on the condition that they invite me to comment as well. When I agreed to come, Professor Summers decided that he didn't need to appear after all. To a remarkable extent, Summers has been able to avoid direct questioning about both his policy record and his financial involvements.

In early 2012, however, Summers was finally forced to address both my film and his earlier policy decisions, albeit briefly, in a televised interview in Britain that was then posted by Reuters financial blogger Felix Salmon.[13] In the interview, Summers defends his role in banning all regulation of OTC derivatives by saying that the credit default swap market "essentially didn't exist" when he advocated the legislation. There are two important points to make about this. The first is that the explicit goal of the legislation, and of Summers's public arguments in favor of it at the time, was to prohibit *any* regulation of *any* OTC derivatives, whether past, present, or not yet invented. The legislation accomplished this, and thereby crippled the ability of the federal government to deal with toxic instruments, and indeed gave the financial sector a green light to develop them. But second, as Salmon points out in his blog post, Summers is flat wrong about CDSs. Not only did CDSs already exist when the legislation was enacted, they had been invented years before and by 2000, the year in which the legislation was passed, they were in fact already a $900 billion market. They were even used at the time to insure against, and to bet on, Enron's imminent failure.[14]

Later in the interview, Summers is then asked about my film. He replies, "*Inside Job* had essentially all its facts wrong," and then goes on to explain that he did not have any financial conflicts of interest. I will now quote him verbatim from the interview, without any editing:

> Whatever I did or did not do right or wrong in the Clinton Administration, I had earned no significant sum of money prior to working in the Clinton Administration, or in association with the financial sector for more than five years after I left the Clinton Administration, and so any suggestion that what I did in the Clinton Administration had to do with loyalty to the financial sector, I think is a bit absurd. You can argue about whether it was right or whether it was wrong, but it didn't come out of any proximity to the financial sector, because I didn't have any before, and I didn't have any afterwards.

However, in at least one further regard, Summers has *his* facts wrong. Contrary to his statement in the interview, he did *not* let five years elapse after leaving the Clinton administration before he started making money from the financial sector. It is true Summers did not begin his most lucrative consulting arrangement (with D.E. Shaw) until he resigned from the presidency of Harvard in 2006. But we know that he had already begun consulting to a major hedge fund, Taconic Capital Advisors, by 2004 (while serving as president of Harvard), a fact only revealed in April 2009 by an article in the *New York Times*.[15] In fact, the same *Times* article also reports, Summers later recommended one of his hedge fund clients for a major job in the Obama administration.

Summers may have had other financial sector involvements as well. However we do not know anything further about Summers's outside activities between 2001 and 2008, because Harvard did not (and still does not) require Summers to disclose them publicly, and Summers himself has never done so. Both Harvard and Summers declined my requests for the information.

Summers continues to speak and consult for financial groups. His Harvard web page still does not list any of his paid outside activities, and little is known about them.[16] But in June 2011, Summers announced that he was becoming an advisor to the venture capital firm Andreessen Horowitz. And as of early 2012, Summers's web page on his speaking agent's website included testimonials from seven clients. All but one (Regent University) were financial; they included the Texas Pacific Group, the Chinese Finance Association, Charles River Ventures, and *Institutional Investor* magazine.[17] Summers has not disclosed the identities of his other speaking or consulting clients.

Frederic Mishkin. Mishkin received his PhD in economics from MIT in 1976 and is now a professor of banking and finance at Columbia Business School. Mishkin also spent two years as director of research at the New York Federal Reserve, and from September 2006 through August 2008, he was on the board of governors of the Federal Reserve system.

When I interviewed Mishkin for my film, he was both evasive and embarrassed about his 2006 paper "Financial Stability in Iceland." And well he should be, because it's awfully embarrassing. The Icelandic Chamber of Commerce paid him over $120,000 to write it, a payment he disclosed only when he was required to, on the federal financial disclosure form required by the Federal Reserve Board.

Mishkin's paper gave legitimacy, and renewed energy, to one of the world's worst financial frauds, one that devastated an entire nation. Iceland, whose population is only 320,000, was until recently a prosperous democracy with very low unemployment and little debt. But then a new conservative government privatized and deregulated Iceland's three major banks in 2001.

The new owners of these banks promptly embarked on a borrowing and spending spree that was as insane as it was criminal. In seven years they borrowed over $125 billion, about $1 million for every adult in the country. Most of it was lent to "investment funds" and various shell companies, often owned by the bankers' families and friends. Suddenly there were yachts, pin-striped private jets, New York penthouses, boutique hotels, private concerts, huge parties. By 2006 bank "assets"— loans the banks had made with the money they had borrowed—were already equal to 350 percent of Iceland's GDP. The nation's financial regulator did nothing; it had a total of fewer than forty employees, including clerical staff, and a third of them left to work for the banks. The stock market, dominated by bank stocks, zoomed upward—because the banks were using borrowed money to purchase their own stock. Much of it was a Ponzi scheme, with new borrowed money used to prop up the banks' untenable positions. In March 2006 analysts at a Danish bank wrote that "Iceland looks worse on all measures than Thailand did before its crisis of 1997."[18]

This was the environment in mid-2006, when Professor Mishkin wrote, "Iceland is not an emerging economy... [and] comparisons of Iceland with emerging market countries, like Thailand and Turkey, are not only facile, but completely misguided." He went on:

> Iceland, however, has excellent institutions: indeed, as we have seen, the quality of its bureaucracy and low levels of corruption, rank it among the best-run countries in the world as we saw in the overview chapter. In contrast to the inadequate prudential supervision in countries that have experienced financial instability, Iceland's prudential supervisors are seen as honest and competent. Their statements that the banking system in Iceland is safe and sound should be taken at face value.[19]

Mishkin and his report were paraded through the media and the financial industries of both Iceland and the United States, and his report played a role in helping the Icelandic banks to continue to borrow. Icelandic bank bonds were even incorporated into a number of CDOs issued during the bubble by U.S. banks. The bankers were able to continue their Ponzi scheme until 2008; when the global financial crisis started, it revealed that Iceland was insolvent, with bank losses of $100 billion. Unemployment tripled in six months, and Iceland now faces decades of economic hardship, as well as chronic disputes with foreign nations and banks that lost money from the fraud. Post-crisis investigations revealed that the "excellent" prudential supervisors of Mishkin's imagination had failed to spot gross embezzlement and other crimes by bankers and their co-conspirators in the investment funds.

After the crash, Mishkin falsified the title of his report on his CV, changing it from "Financial Stability in Iceland" to "Financial *In*stability in Iceland." In a *Financial Times* article written in response to my film, he claimed that this was a temporary typographical error that had been corrected long before. This is a lie; I had downloaded his CV from his Columbia website the morning of our interview.

Mishkin's other writings display a similar kindness toward the financial sector. In 2003 he wrote a paper entitled "Policy Remedies for Conflicts of Interest in the Financial System." In this paper, Mishkin basically says there's nothing to worry about. For example, while rating agencies may *appear* to have conflicts of interest—granting high ratings to securities sold by powerful customers will increase their business—Mishkin concludes that "there is little evidence that ratings agencies engage in such conflicts of interest," because exploiting their position "would result in decreased credibility of the ratings...and a costly decline in [their] reputation."[20]

The year before Mishkin joined the Federal Reserve board, his salary at Columbia (for a half year) was $232,000, and he had textbook royalties and advances of $522,000. His total consulting revenue, including Iceland, was $274,000, and he earned $30,000 in speaking fees, for a total income of $1,058,000. He also listed securities valued between $6,740,103 and $21,356,000. When I asked him whether he consulted for any financial institutions after leaving the Federal Reserve, he replied that he did, but that he did not want to discuss them.[21]

Like Summers and others we shall encounter shortly, Mishkin is on the speaking circuit, too. And here, I am grateful to one effect of my film. As mentioned earlier, after *Inside Job* was released, Columbia Business School (and several other academic organizations) finally adopted disclosure policies. Columbia still doesn't require disclosure of dollar amounts of outside income, but professors are now required to disclose the identities of their clients. Here is Mishkin's disclosure of all of his speaking engagements between 2005 and February 2012:

ACLI	International Monetary Fund
Bank America	Kairos Investments
Barclays Capital	Lexington Partners
Bidvest	Miura Global
BNP Paribas	National Business Travel Association
Brevan Howard	NRUCF
BTG Asset Management	Penn State University
CME Group	Pension Real Estate Association
Deloitte	Premiere, Inc.
Deutsche Bank	Shroeder's Investment Management
Fidelity Investments	Treasury Management Association
Freeman and Co.	Tudor Investment
Futures Industry Association	UBS
Goldman Sachs	Urban Land Institute
Goodwin Proctor	Villanova University
Handelsbanken	

Richard Portes. Although he is an American, Richard Portes is one of the most prominent economists in Europe. He is a professor of economics at London Business School, and founder and director of the Centre for Economic Policy Research, as well as holding several other positions.

And in 2007, Professor Portes, like Frederic Mishkin, became another happy consultant for the Icelandic Chamber of Commerce, which in November 2007 published his opus "The Internationalization of Iceland's Financial Sector," coauthored with a professor of economics at Reykjavik University. Just a year later, Iceland totally collapsed. But Portes was, if anything, more confident than Mishkin, and apparently oblivious to the fact that Icelandic bank "assets" had risen to 800 percent of GNP. His paper and accompanying PowerPoint presentation are full of phrases like "Internationalization of Icelandic Financial Sector Is a Major Success" and "Financial Volatility Not a Threat." Even well into 2008, Portes continued to make media appearances on behalf of the Icelandic banks. In July 2008, three months before the implosion, Portes wrote an opinion piece in the *Financial Times*. It did not disclose that he had ever received payments from the Icelandic Chamber of Commerce. In the article, Portes harshly criticizes another economist, Robert Wade, who had recently written an article entitled "Iceland Pays the Price for Financial Excess." An excerpt from Portes's reply:

"Iceland could not get away with 'as light a regulatory touch as possible.' It has had to apply exactly the same legislation and regulatory framework as European Union member states, and its Financial Services Authority is highly professional. Prof Wade repeats the common claim that Icelandic banks 'operated like hedge funds.'"

And Portes's article concludes:

"The Icelandic banks had virtually no exposure to the toxic securities that almost all other banks did buy.

"The rest of Prof Wade's comments are political, including rumour-mongering. This and his carelessness with the data are regrettable in the fragile conditions of today's international financial markets. He would prefer that the Icelanders adopt 'a more Scandinavian model.' The advice is doubtless well-intentioned, but we should not be surprised if they ignore it."

That was July 4, 2008. In October, the banks collapsed, and many of their executives fled to London. Some of them even had to sell their private jets, yachts, and penthouses. Those who have not been arrested seem to be living very comfortably. Some of them, however, *have* been arrested and are facing trial. Defendants include the former CEOs of two of the three major banks, as well as the former prime minister, Geir Haarde.

Professor Portes's CV states that he is an advisor to two hedge funds. He is also on the speaking circuit. With no apparent irony, his speaking web page introduces him as follows:

Richard Portes is a distinguished economist celebrated for his global outlook and his penetrating analyses of the financial markets. He is known for his expertise in financial engineering and the exotic and—often toxic—derivatives invented by Wall Street.[22]

Laura D'Andrea Tyson. Tyson received her PhD in economics from MIT in 1974, and subsequently taught at Princeton, MIT, Harvard Business School, and UC Berkeley. She served as dean of the UC Berkeley Haas School of Business, and then of the London Business School, before returning to Berkeley as a university professor. During the Clinton administration, she was chairman of the Council of Economic Advisers and then director of the National Economic Council. Shortly after leaving the administration, Tyson joined the board of Morgan Stanley, which pays her $305,000 per year, and also of Ameritech, a regional monopoly telephone company that was later acquired by AT&T; she is now on the AT&T board, as well as several others.

According to SEC statements, as of 2011 she earned approximately $784,000 per year in cash and stock from her four public company directorships.[23] Tyson has also been an advisor to Credit Suisse and to an Asian private equity fund and is a member of the same Committee on Capital Markets Regulation that is cochaired by Glenn Hubbard. She was also a principal of the Law and Economics Consulting Group and works with its successor, the Berkeley Research Group. Tyson also serves on many nonprofit boards and advisory committees, including the Peterson Institute, the Brookings Institution, and the Center for American Progress.

Tyson has made few public statements about the crisis; when she has addressed it, she has made vague references to greed, mania, and bubbles.

She too is on the speaking circuit. Her speakers' bureau (the Harry Walker Agency) names some of her speaking clients. Their web page for Tyson quotes glowing testimonials from past clients including Wescorp, a credit union seized by federal regulators in 2009; the European Petrochemical Association; Northern Telecom; the Commercial Real Estate Women of San Francisco; the Vice President of Government Affairs of Siemens Corporation; Nomura Securities; and Callan Associates, an investment consulting firm.[24] UC Berkeley has no public disclosure requirements for outside activities or income, so we do not know Tyson's speaking income or the identities of any other consulting clients.

Martin Feldstein. Feldstein is one of the most prominent economists in America; a professor at Harvard, he was chairman of the Council of Economic Advisers in the Reagan administration and for nearly thirty years was president of the National Bureau of Economic Research, the economics discipline's largest and most prominent research organization.

Professor Feldstein was also on the board of directors of AIG and AIG Financial Products for over twenty years, a relationship that ended only when AIG collapsed and its board was replaced. And although he has written over three hundred papers on a wide variety of topics, you will look in vain for any writing on the dangers of unregulated credit default swaps, financial sector compensation, or lax corporate governance. He too does a great deal of paid public speaking. His speaker's bureau web page lists him as an expert on the housing crisis, again with no apparent irony; no mention is made of his having been on the AIG board.[25]

An unedited excerpt from my filmed interview with him, portions of which appear in *Inside Job*:

CF: Do you think the financial services industry has had too much influence over government policy?

FELDSTEIN: Every industry tries to affect the policies that Washington sets on it. The airlines, the financial services, whatever it may be. No, I wouldn't say so. I think that the decisions that were made to change, to relax some of the regulations, whether it was the Illinois regulation that you could only have one branch, or it was Glass-Steagall, I think these were things that had widespread intellectual support within the economics profession, so that it wasn't because of some dark of night lobbying efforts that the financial sector managed to bring these changes about.

CF: Maybe not dark of night, but over the last decade the financial services industry has made about $5 billion worth of political contributions in the United States. That's a lot of money. That doesn't bother you?

FELDSTEIN: No.

CF: Do you think the financial services industry has excessive influence over the economics profession?

FELDSTEIN: I would say no. I can't even think of the root that you might have in mind for that one. I think of my colleagues... I can't even think of how they would be influenced. Most of them have nothing to do with the financial services industry.

Hal Scott. Like Laura Tyson and Glenn Hubbard, Scott is involved with the Committee on Capital Markets Regulation. He's also on the board of Lazard, an investment bank whose 2010 revenues, small by current standards, were $1.9 billion. Professor Scott frequently testifies in Congress, usually stressing the dangers of excessive financial regulation. In 2011, for example, he urged narrow application of the "Volcker rule" limiting proprietary trading by banks.[26]

In early 2012 Scott spoke out publicly against the SEC and in favor of the Carlyle Group, when the Carlyle Group had attempted to embed a provision in its public stock offering that would have prohibited shareholders from ever being able to file class-action lawsuits against it. The SEC blocked the attempt, and Carlyle retreated shortly afterward.[27] Scott declined to be interviewed for *Inside Job* and did not respond to written questions about his outside activities and income.

John Campbell. When I interviewed him for my film in 2009, John Campbell had just become chairman of Harvard's economics department. He's a prominent specialist on finance, a former president of the American Finance Association. Campbell is not deeply involved in politics, policy, or power in the fashion of a Larry Summers, Laura Tyson, or Martin Feldstein. He is, rather, an example of the environment produced by pervasive financial sector influence. When I asked him about the causes of the crisis, he gave a long, lucid answer in which the word "deregulation" did not appear even once. Then, when I asked him about the conflict-of-interest issue in economics, he was by turns oblivious and defensive. Here are some excerpts from my interview with him:

> **CF:** So, does Harvard require disclosure of financial conflict of interest in publications?
>
> **CAMPBELL:** Not to my knowledge.
>
> **CF:** Do you think it would be a good idea?
>
> **CAMPBELL:** I'd have to think about that.

And then:

> **CF:** Do you require people to report the compensation they've received and the size of the compensation they've received and the size of the compensation they've received from outside activities?
>
> **CAMPBELL:** No.
>
> **CF:** Don't you think that's a problem?
>
> **CAMPBELL:** I don't see why.

And then:

> **CF:** So, you go to your doctor. Your doctor says to you, "Take this drug." You later learn your doctor receives 80 percent of his personal income from the manufacturer of this drug. This does not bother you at all?
>
> **CAMPBELL:** I think doctors are in a position that's closer to the position of regulators. Doctors are doing clinical work, right? They're in effect making policy on the microscale. I think that's not the analogy.
>
> **CF:** Okay, so let's change it. A medical researcher writes an article saying to treat this disease you should prescribe this drug. Turns out the doctor makes 80 percent of his personal income from the manufacturer of this drug. It does not bother you?
>
> **CAMPBELL:** I think it's certainly important to disclose the...I think

261

that's also a little different from cases that we're talking about here, because…

CF: Would you let me look at the annual outside activities reports of your faculty?

CAMPBELL: Well, I don't see them. The dean sees them. I know mine, but I don't see anybody else's.

CF: Are they public information?

CAMPBELL: No.

Campbell's view is the dominant one in American universities, most of which do not disclose the outside activities of faculty members— or even university officials. Major involvement with financial services firms also, increasingly, includes academic administrators and university presidents.

Until 2009 Ruth Simmons, while president of Brown University, was on the board of directors of Goldman Sachs. Her replacement was Debora Spar, president of Barnard College at Columbia University, who remained on Goldman's board as of 2012. Dr. Spar's earlier academic specialty was the study of international cartels, which must come in useful. Carol Christ, the president of Smith College, was on the board of Merrill Lynch until it was acquired by Bank of America in 2009. Susan Hockfield has been the president of MIT since 2004; in 2012 she announced her intention to resign upon a replacement being found. She has been on the board of General Electric since early 2007. Although General Electric is usually regarded as an industrial company, it relies heavily on finance in two ways. First, its subsidiary GE Capital was heavily involved in the bubble and provided nearly half of GE's corporate profits during the bubble. During the crisis period, GE Capital lost huge sums, largely due to its bubble-related activities. (In 2004, for example, GE acquired WMC Mortgage, the sixth-largest subprime lender in the United States.) Second, GE is one of the most aggressive users of legal and financial engineering to avoid taxes.

Financial services is not, however, the only industry that employs university presidents. Shirley Jackson, the president of Rensselaer Polytechnic Institute, is on seven boards of directors including those of IBM, Federal Express, and Marathon Oil.

These conflicts of interest in academia show up with disturbing directness in later appointments to government office. Indeed, most of what we know about academic conflicts of interest comes from mandatory federal government disclosures—to the SEC for public companies, to regulatory agencies, and to the federal government when professors enter the government. For example, the chief economist of the Justice Department's antitrust division is typically an economics professor. Three people who have held that position are Carl Shapiro, Daniel Rubinfeld, and Richard Gilbert, all economics professors at UC Berkeley. All three have done extensive antitrust defense consulting for telecommunications and/or energy companies, both before and after their government service. Rubinfeld and Gilbert were cofounders of the Law and Economics Consulting Group. When Gilbert was appointed to be the Justice Department's chief economist, he had to sell his large block of LECG stock; but two years later, as soon as he left DOJ, he bought it back. A few years afterward, he and Rubinfeld left LECG to found their own firm, which was acquired by Compass Lexecon, which has become a large and prominent firm, particularly in antitrust consulting. Compass Lexecon also represented Angelo Mozilo when he was sued by the SEC for fraud; the firm's 2010 newsletter proudly states: "After depositions, the Defendants settled with the SEC on the eve of trial on favorable terms that were widely described as a 'slap on the wrist' in the press."[28]

The United States' largest telecommunications firms—particularly AT&T and Verizon, the two incumbents who still have significant monopoly positions—have been extraordinarily thorough in buying economic support. Prominent economists consulting for them, and often writing and testifying in Congress about telecommunications policy, and/or serving in government, have included Jerry Hausman at MIT, Robert Crandall at Brookings, Paul Macavoy of Yale, Gregory Sidak of Tilburg University, Carl Shapiro of UC Berkeley, Peter Temin of MIT, David Teece of UC Berkeley, and many, many others. A number of years ago, I spoke with senior officials in the Justice Department's Antitrust Division about possible antitrust action against AT&T and Verizon. They told me that one significant barrier to any such action was that few if any prominent telecommunications economists would be willing to testify for the government, because nearly all of them worked for the incumbents, at pay rates typically ten to fifty times higher than government consulting rates. As we shall see in the next chapter of this book, the telecommunications issue is important. The United States currently ranks about twentieth in the world in broadband deployment, and continues to fall further behind other nations in Europe and Asia. Since broadband deployment is a major driver of future economic growth, as well as critical to reducing greenhouse emissions and dependence on foreign oil, this lag is a significant problem for the United States. The inefficiency, structural concentration, and political power of the U.S. telecommunications sector all contribute to this state of affairs. However, economists hired by the industry have consistently defended it against antitrust and regulatory actions that might increase competition.

Other industries that make heavy use of the same techniques, and many of the same people and firms, are energy (of course), several industries related to health care, and software. Richard Schmalensee, a professor and former dean of the Sloan School of Management at MIT, was Microsoft's chief economic witness in its antitrust trial; in his testimony, he was caught contradicting his own prior academic work. He had testified that Microsoft's persistently very high profits were not indicative of any monopoly power, when he had previously written precisely the contrary. In 2004 Steven Weber, a professor at UC Berkeley, published a book about the open-source software movement titled *The Success of Open Source*. The book described how noncommercial, bottom-up activism in software produced successful open-source products such as Linux. Nowhere did the book mention that much of the open-source movement has been funded by IBM, Hewlett-Packard, Dell, Google, and other large companies as a way of reducing the power of rivals such as Microsoft and Oracle. Nor did the book mention that Professor Weber was, at the time, consulting for IBM on precisely this issue.

The phenomenon of paying professors for policy advocacy has recently begun to expand beyond economics and law into political science and foreign policy. The most extraordinary recent case, though not the only one, involves Libya. In 2006 Muammar al-Qaddafi, Libya's dictator for more than forty years until his overthrow and execution in 2011, decided that it was time to improve his image. And there was an extraordinary collection of highly prominent British and American academics ready to help him.

Qaddafi's Libya, Such a Wonderful Place

ANTHONY GIDDENS IS famous in the academic world. He is a long-time Cambridge University professor and former director of the London School of Economics (LSE) and was an advisor to Prime Minister Tony Blair and "New Labour." In 2007 Giddens wrote a column for the *Guardian,* "My Chat with the Colonel," describing an interview with Qaddafi. To investigate the genuineness of new policy attitudes on Colonel Qaddafi's part, Giddens says that he "went to Libya with David Frost and Professor Benjamin Barber, a celebrated theorist of democracy, to engage him in debate." Describing Qaddafi as "an imposing figure, clad in a gold-colour robe," Giddens concluded:

As one-party states go, Libya is not especially repressive. Gadafy seems genuinely popular. Our discussion of human rights centred mostly upon freedom of the press. Would he allow greater diversity of expression in the country? There isn't any such thing at the moment. Well, he appeared to confirm that he would. Almost every house in Libya already seems to have a satellite dish. And the internet is poised to sweep the country. Gadafy spoke of supporting a scheme that will make computers with internet access, priced at $100 each, available to all, starting with schoolchildren.

Will real progress be possible only when Gadafy leaves the scene? I tend to think the opposite. If he is sincere in wanting change, as I think he is, he could play a role in muting conflict that might otherwise arise as modernisation takes hold. My ideal future for Libya in two or three decades' time would be a Norway of North Africa: prosperous, egalitarian and forward-looking. Not easy to achieve, but not impossible.[29]

Giddens did not mention the Palestinian medical student and the group of Bulgarian nurses Qaddafi had long been holding under sentence of death on the absurd charge of intentionally infecting hundreds of children with AIDS. But when Qaddafi finally released the nurses later that year, Giddens's companion, Benjamin Barber, a professor at Rutgers, wrote in the *Washington Post:*

> Written off not long ago as an implacable despot, Gaddafi is a complex and adaptive thinker as well as an efficient, if laid-back, autocrat. Unlike almost any other Arab ruler, he has exhibited an extraordinary capacity to rethink his country's role in a changed and changing world.
>
> I say this from experience. In several one-on-one conversations over the past year, Gaddafi repeatedly told me that Libya sought a genuine rapprochement with the United States and that the issues of the [nurses]—along with the still-outstanding final payment from Libya to families of the Lockerbie, Scotland, bombing victims—would be resolved. And behold: The nurses are free.[30]

Later that same year, Joseph S. Nye, former dean of the Harvard Kennedy School of Government and a former assistant secretary of defense, also wrote of visiting Qaddafi, who, amazingly, displayed copies of the professor's latest book, *Soft Power.* Nye wrote in the *New Republic,* "There is no doubt that [Qaddafi] acts differently on the world stage today than he did in decades past. And the fact that he took so much time to discuss ideas—including soft power—with a visiting professor suggests that he is actively seeking a new strategy."[31]

Nye, however, was at least honest—unlike most of the others. He voluntarily disclosed that he had visited Qaddafi because he had been paid to do so, by a consulting firm called the Monitor Group. In 2011 *Mother Jones* magazine revealed that Monitor had been hired by Qaddafi to improve his public image; Monitor was paid $3 million.[32] The "one-on-one conversations" that Barber described in his *Post* article— as if he just happened to be in the area, and Qaddafi naturally invited him to drop in—were arranged as part of a public relations campaign. (Barber also served on the board of the Saif Qaddafi International Charity and Development Foundation, named after Qaddafi's son Saif, until Barber resigned in February 2011 following Qaddafi's violent repression of Libyan demonstrations.) Monitor also arranged for another Harvard professor, Robert Putnam, to visit with the colonel. At the time all of these people, for a fee, were perfectly happy to be used on behalf of Monitor's contract. Putnam voluntarily disclosed that he was paid, although he did not mention that he was part of a Libyan public relations campaign run through Monitor. He later said that he regretted doing it. Giddens and Barber did not even disclose that they were being paid, much less that they had a relationship with Monitor, and have refused to discuss their fees.

The Monitor Group was founded in 1983 by Harvard Business School professor Michael Porter. Its initial focus was on corporate strategy, Porter's primary field, but Monitor later expanded into consulting for foreign governments. In fact Monitor was also working for Jordan, likewise to improve its public image, at the same time it was working for Qaddafi. In both cases, Monitor violated the law by failing to register as a foreign agent. No one may act "within the United States as a public relations counsel, publicity agent, information-service employee or political consultant" for a foreign government without registering. On its website the Justice Department states that the law "facilitates evaluation by the government and the American people of the statements and activities of such persons in light of their function as foreign agents."[33] Precisely. That is the whole point of disclosure.

Giddens, Barber, Putnam, Nye, and Monitor were not alone in helping out Libya. Qaddafi's son and heir apparent, Saif, attended the London School of Economics. Professor David Held, a faculty member, was on the Saif Qaddafi Foundation board at the same time as he was Saif Qaddafi's PhD thesis advisor. LSE awarded Saif Qaddafi his PhD shortly after Qaddafi pledged to donate approximately $2.5 million to the school and the Libyan government awarded LSE an additional contract for training government officials. In March 2011 LSE's director, Howard Davies, resigned, citing "errors of judgment." Monitor later admitted that it had helped Saif Qaddafi with his dissertation, which appears to have contained substantial plagiarism.

The Consequences

THE PROBLEM OF academic corruption is now so deeply entrenched that these disciplines, and America's leading universities, are severely compromised, and anyone thinking of bucking the trend would rationally be very, very scared. Consider this situation: you're a graduate student, or an untenured junior faculty member, considering doing some research anytime in the past decade on the effect of, say, compensation structures on risk taking in financial services, or the potential impact of public disclosure requirements on the market for credit default swaps. The president of your university is...Larry Summers. The president of the National Bureau of Economic Research is...Martin Feldstein. The chairman of your department is...Laura Tyson, or Glenn Hubbard, or Richard Schmalensee, or John Campbell. Or you're at MIT, and you want to examine the decline in corporate tax payments over the last quarter century. The president of MIT is Susan Hockfield, on the board of GE, a company that has managed to avoid paying any corporate taxes for several years despite having billions of dollars per year in profits.

Or, if you're at the think tank run by the Council on Foreign Relations, you might notice that Robert Rubin is cochairman of the council. Other members of the board include Stephen Friedman, who is on the board of Goldman Sachs; Henry Kravis of KKR; and David Rubinstein of the Carlyle Group. The place you work is called the Maurice R. Greenberg Center for Geoeconomic Studies—as in Hank Greenberg, former CEO of AIG. The chairman of the Brookings Institution board of trustees is John Thornton, former president of Goldman Sachs; about half the members of the Brookings board are financial services executives. The Brookings Hamilton Project, focused on improving U.S. economic prosperity, was established by Robert Rubin.

You also know that the committees that review grant proposals and the review panels that decide whether papers get published in academic journals are full of professors who consult for financial services companies. These people will have a major say in whether you get published, get a job, or get tenure.

Here is what Frederic Mishkin—a comparative lightweight relative to, say, Larry Summers or Glenn Hubbard—lists on his CV under "Journals":

> Editorial Board, *American Economic Review,* 1982–85.
> Associate Editor, *Journal of Business and Economic Statistics,* 1986–93.
> Associate Editor, *Journal of Applied Econometrics,* 1985–2000.
> Associate Editor, *Journal of Economic Perspectives,* 1994–2004.
> Editor, Federal Reserve Bank of New York, *Economic Policy Review,* 1994–1997. Editorial Board, 1997–2006.
> Associate Editor, *Journal of Money, Credit and Banking,* 1992–2006.
> Advisory Board, *Macroeconomics and Monetary Economics Abstracts,* 1996–2006.
> Editorial Board, Central Bank of Chile Series, *Central Banking, Analysis, and Economic Policy,* 2001–2009.
> Editorial Board, *Journal of International Money and Finance,* 1992–present.
> Advisory Board, *International Finance,* 1997–present.
> Editorial Board, *Finance India,* 1999–present.

Associate Editor, *Emerging Markets, Finance and Trade,* 2008–present.

Editorial Board, *Review of Development Finance,* 2010–present.

So, as a young economist you've just finished your research on the causes of Iceland's financial bubble. Where are you going to publish it? Or, you've just finished your analysis of Obama administration financial regulatory policy. You are thinking of applying for jobs of various kinds. Any chance you might run into Larry Summers? Well, here's what he lists on his CV under "Professional Activities":

Board of Trustees, The Brookings Institution, 2002–present

Board of Trustees, Committee for Economic Development, 2002–present

Board of Directors, Center on Global Development, 2001–present

General Member, Council on Competitiveness, 2001–present

Member, Trilateral Commission, 2001–present

Member, Bretton Woods Committee, 2001–present

Board of Directors, Institute for International Economics, 2001–present

Member, Inter-American Dialogue, 2001–present

Board of Governors, Partnership for Public Service, 2001–present

Board of Directors, Global Fund for Children's Vaccines, 2001–2005

Member, Group of 30, 1997–present

Permanent Member, Council on Foreign Relations, 1989–present

Editor, *Quarterly Journal of Economics,* 1984–1990

Executive Committee, American Economic Association, 1989–1992

Member, American Economic Association Commission on Graduate Education, 1988–1990

Board of Advisors, Congressional Budget Office, 1986–1990

National Science Foundation Economics Panel, 1986–1988

Consultant, Foreign Governments of Jamaica, Indonesia,
Canada, Mexico, and Japan Program Committee,
Econometric Society Meetings, 1982, 1984
AEA Meetings, 1986, 1987

So you're thinking about what your analysis might say. What are you going to do? Rock the boat? Good luck with that. Or maybe go along to get along?

How much do these forces actually affect academic research and government policy making? It is of course difficult to measure the effect precisely, and very few economists have tried, but my experience and the available evidence suggest that the effect is large. In early 2012 Professor Luigi Zingales of the University of Chicago described his analysis of the 150 most frequently downloaded economics papers on the subject of executive pay. Papers supporting higher executive pay were 55 percent more likely to be published in the most prestigious journals, and far more likely to be cited in other papers.[34]

My own experience suggests that the effect of conflicts of interest in economics is far more severe than that. Two examples deserve mention: the financial crisis and antitrust analysis.

Both before and even since, academic commentary on the financial crisis by economists and finance specialists has been remarkably muted. There are, to be sure, some very notable and impressive exceptions—Raghu Rajan, Nouriel Roubini, Simon Johnson, Lucian Bebchuk, Ken Rogoff, Robert Shiller. But for the most part, the silence has been rather deafening. How can an entire industry come to be structured, and incented, such that employees are systematically encouraged to loot and destroy their own firms? Why did market forces permit this to occur? Why did market forces not give rise to any firm that systematically collected and analyzed information about the total size of risk exposures in the industry? Why did deregulation and economic theory fail so spectacularly and completely? There has been astonishingly little examination and public discussion of these questions by economists, and what little they have said has not, for the most part, been impressive. Conflicts of interest certainly play a major role here. Bloomberg News reported in 2012 that in the case of the Squam Lake Group, a committee of prominent economists formed to issue reports on the crisis, thirteen of the study's fifteen principal economists had ties to the financial sector.[35]

The fields of industrial organization and antitrust analysis have, if anything, been more severely affected by academic conflicts of interest. The overwhelming majority of both academic and federal work in these areas is devoted to examining whether a firm or an industry engages in predatory behavior or charges excessive prices. Over time, even these limited questions have been analyzed in ways increasingly favorable to the interests of dominant firms and highly concentrated industries. My experience is that at least two-thirds of the leading economists in this area routinely work for antitrust defendants, and that very few are willing to consult or testify for the Justice Department in antitrust cases.

Equally important, economists simply avert their eyes, declining to study major issues if they threaten the interests of their consulting clients. There has also been very little examination of how entrenched management groups have used their power and the power of their firms to enrich and perpetuate themselves. Economics has strikingly little to say about how the U.S. economy has produced the decades-long inefficiency of GM and Chrysler, IBM until 1993, the integrated steel industry, or, for that matter, Jimmy Cayne and Stan O'Neal. Nor has the economics profession spent much time assessing the effects of industrial concentration or managerial entrenchment on the long-term performance of the U.S. economy.

The avalanche of money from antitrust defendants and industries seeking relaxed regulation has thus unquestionably warped both economics research and public discussion. And this is an area in which economic analysis truly is important to America's well-being.

The release of *Inside Job* clearly touched a nerve with regard to these questions. I was contacted by a large number of students and faculty at Columbia, Stanford, Harvard, UC Berkeley, the University of Michigan, and other institutions. There has been a great deal of debate, and some forward movement. Stanford has generally excellent disclosure requirements, far superior to those of most other universities, and several departments, including the Wharton School and Columbia Business School, have adopted disclosure requirements for the first time. But most universities still have no public disclosure requirements at all, and few if any have any limitations on the *existence* of conflicts of interest or of income from such sources. The same is true of most academic publications and industry associations. This is in striking contrast, for example, to the policies of most private companies and journalistic organizations. Reporters at the *New York Times, Fortune,* and other major news publications are strictly prohibited from accepting money from any industry or organization they write about. Not so in academia.

There has been one significant positive development. In response to the information presented in *Inside Job,* in early 2011 the American Economics Association formed a committee to consider whether the AEA should adopt a code of ethics—for the first time in its history. Then, in early 2012, the AEA actually adopted a disclosure requirement for the seven journals it publishes, which are among the most important in the discipline. But most institutions and prominent professors continue to oppose further disclosure, and nearly all of them oppose any actual *limits* on financial conflicts of interest. When I was making the film, most institutions and university presidents refused even to discuss the subject. The presidents and provosts of Harvard and Columbia declined to be interviewed for my film, or even to discuss the issue off the record. I did discuss the issue once with President Hockfield of MIT, who clearly grew very uncomfortable and has declined further meetings or conversation about it. Just before the release of my film, her office called to ask whether any MIT faculty were named; the concern was public image, not the reality of the problem. The chancellor of UC Berkeley has also been very reluctant to deal with the issue, and avoided questions about it at one meeting I attended with him.

I'm very sad about this. I feel a great deal of affection for both UC Berkeley, where I was an undergraduate, and for MIT, where I spent nearly a decade as a graduate student and postdoctoral fellow. Both institutions have done great things to further knowledge and educational opportunity. For nearly all of its history, UC Berkeley was the best, and most widely accessible, public university in the world. MIT has recently made its entire curriculum available online, and has begun to provide inexpensive certificates of completion for students who study via the Web. This is wonderful and important. I love the academic world, which was very generous to me, and where I spent an extremely happy decade of my life. And I should perhaps also make clear that I am not against professors making money, consulting to industry, or starting companies to commercialize something that they have invented. I have no problem with that at all; in fact, I think that it is often very beneficial to academia as well as industry. But providing openly disclosed expert advice is very different from acting as a covert, highly paid lobbyist. Just as Monitor is legally required to register as a foreign agent, so academics with conflicts of interest should be required to disclose them whenever they make any public statement about policy issues. I also, frankly, think that it is completely improper for professors to be paid for making public policy statements of any kind—whether testifying in Congress or as "expert witnesses" in antitrust, fraud, or tax cases, or appearing in the media. I truly hope that somehow the progress of this particular disease can be arrested, because it's very important.

However, the gradual subversion of academic independence by finance and other large industries is just one of many symptoms of a wider change in the United States. It is a change that is more general, and even more disturbing, than the financial sector's rising power. As many others have recently noted, over the last thirty years the United States has lost its historical status as a nation of fairness and opportunity. America used to provide broad opportunity, particularly educational and economic opportunity, to its population. It no longer does. The rise of a predatory financial sector is just one component, albeit a very important one, of a bigger issue. America is in decline—economically, politically, and also, in some ways, ethically and culturally. This is the issue to which I now turn, in order to conclude this book.

CHAPTER 9

AMERICA AS A RIGGED GAME

The Harder They Fall

IT'S HARD TO BELIEVE now that in the year 2000 the United States was universally considered to be the first "hyperpower" in world history—a nation so wealthy and powerful that it had achieved global dominance without seeming even to try.

The United States was the richest and fastest growing of the major industrialized nations, with the most advanced technology base and an utterly dominant military. The Internet industry, the source of the most profound technological and industrial revolution of the century, was completely dominated by America. With the former Soviet Union in collapse and China converted to government-led capitalism, there would even be a "peace dividend." Even during the Asian financial crisis of the late 1990s, American growth continued and the unemployment rate stayed below 5 percent. America could do no wrong.

But the fall of the mighty is a classic theme of tragedy. And few nations have fallen as far and as suddenly in the world's eyes as the United States since the beginning of the new millennium. How could this happen? Superficially, it seemed to come from nowhere; but in reality, America's descent has been in the making for decades.

One common interpretation, particularly among progressives and Democrats, is that the Bush administration did it. According to this view, a superbly managed Democratic administration (Clinton's) bequeathed a broad prosperity to George W. Bush, who squandered it on wars and tax cuts while letting the banks run wild. Then the Bush administration left the mess to Obama, who is struggling to pick up the pieces and get the economy back on track, a task made even more difficult by the intransigence of Republicans in Congress.

There is *some* truth to this story. The George W. Bush administration was certainly in a class by itself. First, Bush devastated America's finances with his incompetently managed wars and enormous tax cuts. The tax cuts, which heavily favored the very wealthy, were enacted even as military spending rose in the wake of 9/11 and the invasion of Afghanistan, and even though federal tax revenues had plummeted with the collapse of the dot-com bubble. Then came the almost unbelievably incompetent, unplanned, politicized occupation of Iraq, which turned a three-week war into a $2 trillion, ten-year quagmire, at a time when the United States already had its hands full with Afghanistan. And, of course, the Bush administration's coup de grâce was the outrageous, frequently criminal financial bubble that brought us to the edge of the abyss in 2008 and left the American (and world) economy damaged for years to come.

So, yes, there was unquestionably enormous hubris, greed, stupidity, and dishonesty in the George W. Bush administration. But, tempting as it may be, blaming everything on the Bush administration is deeply wrong, and it misses the main point.

Because the main point is this: over the last thirty years, under Democrats as well as Republicans, the United States' political-economic system has lost its way. There have been occasional episodes of real progress such as the Internet revolution; and in some areas, such as theoretical computer science and entrepreneurial high technology, America remains unmatched. But the dominant underlying trend has been, and remains, severely negative. America has quietly become a profoundly different place, with its economic competitiveness, its basic fairness, the education of its population, and its politics all in sharp decline.

Economic power in America has become far more concentrated, both structurally and individually. Structurally, several of America's largest industries and the American economy as a whole have become far more concentrated since deregulation began. We have already seen this with regard to financial services. But the same thing has happened in energy (the four largest oil companies), telecommunications (AT&T, Verizon, the cable industry), the media (which overlaps with the cable and entertainment industries), retailing (Walmart, Amazon, etc.), agribusiness and food (McDonald's, Yum Brands), and other industries, even information technology.

In part this trend toward consolidation has been caused by the Internet and information technology, which allow the efficient management of much larger organizations covering wider markets and geographical areas. But in large part, this trend has been the result of corruption—corporate money that neutered antitrust policy, the political system, and the economics discipline. In many industries that have sharply consolidated or have been concentrated for a long time—including financial services, automobiles, telecommunications, and the media—there is absolutely no reason to believe that higher concentration brings higher efficiency.

In fact, the evidence points in exactly the opposite direction. Many of the most successful foreign industries that have overtaken America's—cars, telecommunications, and consumer electronics, among others—were less concentrated than America's. If GM had been broken up long ago, forming two or three firms that really had to compete, the American car industry would almost certainly be in better condition. Unquestionably, such concentrated power also contributes to income inequality. Large firms in concentrated industries have much more bargaining power relative to employees and suppliers. Walmart, McDonald's, and other huge firms are famous for being brutally tough on their suppliers, forcing them to cut costs, and also for their opposition to unionization of their enormous, low-wage, retail workforces, who often have very difficult working conditions.

Nonetheless, the structural concentration of American industry has continued over the last thirty years. At the same time, economic power in America also became more concentrated at the individual level, with a small number of households owning the majority of America's financial wealth and providing a high fraction of individual political campaign contributions.

The combined result is that the United States is increasingly controlled by an amoral oligarchy that has progressively corrupted the federal government and the political system, including *both* political parties. This political corruption has in turn further entrenched the wealthy and the financial sector, and has now become a major driver of America's economic and social decline.

The wealthy are safe from the effects of this decline, at least for now; indeed, they have benefited from it, because they have skills, financial assets, mobility, and political power. They are also increasingly insulated by parallel, private systems for education, security, infrastructure, and financial services. The absence of significant political or social protest in response to these changes, Occupy Wall Street notwithstanding, has emboldened them to continue. At the same time, and in part as a result of these changes, the bottom two-thirds of the American population has become less educated, less informed, less prosperous, angrier, and ever more cynical about its political leadership. There is good reason for this cynicism. In their stomachs, most Americans know that their leaders are lying to them and that the system is rigged. America is still a wonderful place for thirty or forty million people. But for the bottom hundred million or more, not so nice.

When America started its economic decline in the 1970s, Americans' first responses were simply to work longer hours and go into debt. But after a confused, failed reform attempt by Jimmy Carter, American politics turned increasingly to demagoguery and corruption. The political system's response, particularly among Republicans, was to pretend that the problem was taxes and excessive government, while hypocritically using deficit spending and financial bubbles to cover up America's long-term problems. Democrats made vaguely progressive noises but did little about them, while giving ever more to the financial sector and the wealthy. But those options are wearing thin and will eventually be exhausted. Unless America reverses course, things will end badly, at least for the bottom 90 percent of the population, and possibly even for the wealthy who consider themselves safe.

For most of American history, the American people have responded well to challenges, including dangerous or corrupt leadership. But this is the first time that America has faced a combination of structural political corruption, rising inequality, and long-term economic decline. And so far, American politics has mostly been producing decisions that make things worse, not better—and are economically and politically unsustainable.

America is entering a dangerous zone. On the one hand, excessive concentration of power tends to produce an echo chamber, in which those at the top only need to deal with each other. There is less pluralism, less competition, a narrower range of options and views, less room for maneuvering. Companies have more power, because there is less choice; it's harder for employees, suppliers, and customers to talk back to them, or threaten to switch. This isn't healthy.

But in addition, America's economic decline will inevitably produce increasing social pressures. Economic and social insecurity can produce activism for reform, but they can also produce anger, desperation, and dangerously simple solutions. They encourage nasty charlatans to distract public opinion from America's real challenges in favor of stupid, extremist, counterproductive measures—or simply doing nothing.

America's deterioration is now systemic and structural, and it is causing the unthinkable to become possible in the United States, just as this is already occurring in Europe. Until the global financial crisis, the "great recession," and the European sovereign debt crisis, nobody would have believed that Europe faced a serious risk of financial crisis, possibly accompanied by major social and political instability. But now it is clear that Europe *does* face these problems. And not so long from now, America could too.

For reasons explored below, the *American national system*—the combination of educational and economic opportunity, farsighted government policy, freedom of debate through an independent press, an academic system that provided critical analysis of self-interested arguments, and two-party political competition that kept America prosperous and dynamic for many decades—has come undone. This has destabilized, and yet paradoxically also frozen, American politics; when you look below the surface, since about 1980 there has been a frightening continuity in political behavior. With each decade, federal policy under both political parties has tilted ever more toward the financial sector, the very wealthy, and the most powerful, most concentrated, and frequently most inefficient or damaging industries in the United States.

There is also, undeniably, a cultural dimension to this. The American people have become increasingly scared, frustrated, angry, cynical. Some demand reform, but many others want a return to a simpler, more secure, more traditional time. They are susceptible to extremist politics and religion, and to fake promises of easy prosperity, whether coming from preachers, politicians, or bankers. Many others have just given up, not bothering to vote or pay attention to politics at all. In this environment it has proven all too easy for politicians, who are so easily hired by America's new oligarchy, to exploit popular anger and fatigue while actually delivering oligarchic policy. Newt Gingrich attacks government after being paid $1.6 million to lobby for Freddie Mac; Mitt Romney pretends that the financial crisis was caused by excessive regulation; and their archenemy, President Obama, promises reform while protecting Wall Street.

On balance, the Republican Party has produced the worst, most flagrant behavior, but this has become a thoroughly bipartisan process. In fact, some of the most destructive policies leading to the financial crisis were initiated by the Clinton administration, not by George W. Bush, and some of Bush's most destructive policies were supported by many congressional Democrats. More recently, Barack Obama has chosen both personnel and policies stunningly close to both the Clinton and Bush administrations, and in some ways even worse. Obama has brushed the mud off the same dishonest and discredited people, kept the financial sector's privileges and incomes intact, avoided prosecution of financial crime, and done almost nothing about the foreclosure crisis and the millions of Americans who owe more on their homes than they are worth. (As of 2012, about 20 percent of American mortgages were still "underwater.")

Perhaps worst of all, the Obama administration has done nothing to address the long-term decline of the United States. It has said little, and done less, about America's growing inequalities of income and wealth, the deterioration of public education and educational opportunity, the predatory criminality of the financial sector, or the many ways that money now corrupts American economic policy. As soon as he took office, Obama quietly dropped his reformist, activist campaign rhetoric in favor of claims that recovery was under way and all would be well. As the 2012 election approached, he started to move back toward the reformist rhetoric, but without actually *doing* anything.

In short, when it comes to the central issues facing the American economy, both parties are moving in the wrong direction. The noisy arguments that dominate the headlines are sideshows. On the critical questions, America's new rulers are calling the tune. What is going on here?

In May 2009 Simon Johnson, an MIT professor and former chief economist of the IMF, published a powerful article in the *Atlantic Monthly* entitled "The Quiet Coup." Johnson catalogued the uncontrolled growth of America's financial sector and its toxic consequences, warning that the United States was starting to look dangerously like an emerging market oligarchy (or to say it less pleasantly, a banana republic, a third-world dictatorship), complete with sovereign debt problems, financial crises, bailouts of the rich whenever they mess up, and caste-like divisions between rich and poor. Johnson pointed out that often this process ends with the oligarchy overreaching itself so severely that financial crisis leads to depression, which in turns leads to political revolution. For America to avoid this fate, Johnson argues, it must break up its largest banks and reassert control over the financial services industry.

My own view is that in one way things are more hopeful than Johnson suggests, while in others he actually underestimated America's problems, because they go beyond the financial services industry.

On the hopeful side, I believe that America *is* still a sufficiently open and democratic society, however imperfectly so, that when the American people finally decide they have had enough, change will be possible. The numbers—at least the numbers of people—are on the side of reform. It isn't even really the financial *industry* that is on the other side; it's the financial sector's *elite,* the fifty thousand people who make the serious money and control the companies. This is not an insurmountable opposition. And, several times in the last half century, America has seen citizens' movements that successfully brought about major political change from below, even when both political parties initially paid no attention. The civil rights, women's rights, and environmental movements come to mind. Popular anger can even remove a president and his entire administration, as we saw with Richard Nixon and his cronies after Watergate. I think the major reason that money-driven politics has succeeded for the past several decades is simply that most of the American people are not yet angry enough, not yet aware of just how badly they have been taken. Many others are too cynical to use the established system but not angry enough to make the system change.

On the other hand, America faces two problems beyond those Johnson mentions, and which complicate reform efforts. First, as I will describe in more detail below, America's political parties and governmental machinery have been hijacked in a very clever, powerful way that defies easy remedies. In 2010 I coined the term "political duopoly" to describe this situation, in which the two political parties agree to disagree violently on social issues while both serving America's economic oligarchy and blocking the rise of third parties and reform efforts.[1] Economic decline and America's new oligarchy are therefore more resistant to popular activism than was (and is) the case with regard to, say, discrimination against women or environmental pollution.

And second, America's problems go beyond any one industry. While the financial sector has unquestionably become America's most powerful and dangerous industry, it isn't alone. For much of its deregulatory agenda, the financial sector has important allies, particularly in the telecommunications, energy, media, health care, and industrial agribusiness/food industries, as well as several thousand ultrawealthy families. These people share the financial sector's desire to translate their wealth and cohesion into political power in order to shelter themselves, their families, their personal assets, and their industries from competition, prosecution, effective regulation, proper corporate governance, and taxes. They can even count on substantial support from people who run honest businesses but who still benefit from lower taxes and less regulation.

But this situation is not merely unfair; it is economically disastrous. The least-discussed but perhaps most important effect of money-based politics is that it has caused government policy to shield incompetent and/or predatory industries from internal reform and competitive discipline. This problem goes far beyond finance, and is critical to understanding not only the financial crisis but also America's broader economic decline.

General Motors and Chrysler didn't go bankrupt just because of the financial crisis in 2008; they went bankrupt because for decades previously, they had been in unchecked managerial decline. They were run by incompetent, lazy, insular, selfish managers, with no interference from their complacent boards of directors or the antitrust authorities—and, indeed, with the frequent *assistance* of U.S. government policy. They should have been broken up or forced to reform their corporate governance long ago. But they weren't, and we all paid for it—literally. The same was true earlier of other American industries, such as steel and consumer electronics, that failed so completely that they have largely disappeared from the American economy. As we shall see shortly, the same is now true of telecommunications. America's telecommunications oligopoly is retarding progress in broadband infrastructure, an extremely dangerous situation given the role that Internet services now play in economic performance. So although the financial sector is the most obviously dangerous part of America's new oligarchy, it is not the only one contributing to American decline.

In the remainder of this book, I shall examine first the causes, and then the implications, of America's political-economic decline. Then I will describe the emergence of America's political duopoly—the system by which both the Democratic and Republican parties are now dominated by America's new oligarchy, and how the parties handle this situation strategically. I will examine the consequences of this situation, including the Obama administration's personnel and policies. I will then consider the current and future determinants of American competitiveness, using broadband communications, Internet services, and information-technology hardware as examples. Finally, I will offer some ideas about what the future holds, what the most critical goals for reform are, and whether America can pull itself out of this morass.

I will begin by examining the beginnings of American industrial decline in the 1970s, and how America's major industries responded to this decline. Faced with growing challenges, America's business elites found a cheap way out—one that has turned into America's biggest problem.

Explaining Decline: The Destabilization of the American National System Since the 1970s

WHY DO WE see, over and over, the cyclical rise and fall of companies, national industries, nations? The British Empire, General Motors, U.S. Steel, Microsoft, the United States—we see the same pattern over and over again. An initially small, powerless company or nation devises a superior way to run itself; it becomes enormously successful, vanquishing all rivals; but then, at the height of its apparent power, it begins to decay from within. It starts to coast. It becomes lazy, politicized, complacent, dysfunctional, corrupt; and eventually, after a period of internal decay, it collapses under its own weight or falls prey to some aggressive new competitor.

The United States has now entered such a systemic decline, and the rise of America's economic oligarchy and money-based political system is both a cause and a symptom of it. As is typical in such situations, the decline of the United States' political and economic systems began at the height of American national power. Money-based politics was not the initial cause of American decline, but it was the way that America's largest industries responded when they were threatened. It turned out to be easier and more effective (more effective for *them*, not for the country) to pay people off than to undertake real, painful, internal reform.

The initial source of American decline was the complacency of American industry, permitted by the concentration and global dominance of what then constituted the core of the U.S. (and world) economy. In part because World War II had devastated most potential competitors, and in part due to the enormous size of the U.S. domestic market, American industry faced no serious competition, either foreign or domestic, for a quarter century after the war. During this time, America's largest and most important industries gradually became complacent, rigid, highly inefficient oligopolies or even in some cases monopolies. They also came to have complacent, low-quality corporate governance and, in some cases, unions that contributed to systemic rigidity. They were not attuned either to innovation or to competitive threats, either domestic or foreign. Many senior managers also deliberately resisted innovations that would have rendered their skills obsolete, and would have reduced their internal power and status.

The industries displaying this pattern in the 1970s and 1980s included automobiles, steel, telecommunications, mainframe computers, minicomputers, photocopiers, cameras and film, semiconductors, and consumer electronics. Together they formed the core of the U.S.

economy. They accounted for a major fraction of GNP, and they were among the wealthiest, most powerful industries in the United States and in the world. They dominated U.S. and often world markets, and were either regulated monopolies, oligopolies, or industries dominated by a single firm whose competitors lived in its shadow.

In the automobile industry, the Big Three (GM, Ford, Chrysler) dominated the U.S. market and held roughly half the total global market. An oligopoly of a half dozen integrated steel companies, led by U.S. Steel, similarly dominated the domestic steel market. IBM held about two-thirds of the total global computer market, with smaller mainframe producers (the so-called "Seven Dwarfs") and a half dozen minicomputer producers holding most of the rest. AT&T was a regulated monopoly that controlled over 90 percent of all U.S. telephone and data services. Kodak dominated the film and camera industries; Xerox held a patent monopoly on photocopying for many years.

The growing inefficiencies of these industries also affected their suppliers and customers. The stagnation of the U.S. automobile industry contributed significantly to the decline of automobile parts suppliers and of the machine tool industry. By the late 1980s, Japan had definitively surpassed the United States not only in the automobile industry but also in machine tools and robotics, as well as in their advanced use in a variety of manufacturing sectors. Similarly, Japanese excellence in producing commodity semiconductors and liquid crystal displays pulled along its semiconductor capital equipment industry.

America's largest industries had always wielded political influence, but for the first quarter century of the postwar period they did not wield it very aggressively, because they did not need to. They were naturally successful and profitable, with an almost leisurely dominance of both their domestic and international markets. Because their industries were mature, entry into their markets by small start-ups was for the most part impossible due to scale, capital requirements, and systems effects. In some cases, such as telecommunications, the media, and parts of financial services, new competition was legally limited or even prohibited. In a few cases (AT&T, IBM), antitrust actions were undertaken to limit the incumbents' power. But for the most part American industry and the federal government left each other to their own devices for the three decades following the Second World War.

Over time, however, oligopoly and lack of competition led to complacency, which in turn led to inefficiency. By the 1980s, these inefficiencies were so severe that the productivity and product price-performance ratio delivered by the dominant firms in major U.S. industries came to lag best practice by enormous margins—factors of two or more in productivity for traditional manufacturing industries, and up to an order of magnitude in the price-performance ratio of high-technology products such as computers.

One of the most striking demonstrations of this occurred in Fremont, California. General Motors opened an assembly plant there in 1962 and then closed it as unprofitable in 1982, in part because the UAW-unionized workforce was regarded as unmanageable. By this time GM's inefficiency was obvious, and it was facing intense competition from the Japanese. Under enormous political pressure from the U.S. government, in 1984 Toyota agreed to form a joint venture with GM and to reopen the Fremont plant under Toyota management. The unstated but clear intent was to force Toyota to save GM from itself by teaching GM how to use Toyota's "just-in-time" or "lean" production system. The result was a stunning indictment of GM. Using the same unionized workforce that GM had written off as hopeless, Toyota rapidly doubled productivity and sharply increased the quality of the cars that Fremont produced. But despite Toyota-organized tours of the plant for GM managers and videotaping of plant activities, the rest of GM learned very, very slowly.

This was not an isolated situation. Careful studies conducted by MIT and Harvard in the 1980s and 1990s demonstrated that Japanese car companies were approximately twice as productive as their American (and some European) competitors in both design *and* manufacturing.[2] Similar results were found when American integrated steel firms were compared with the Japanese industry and American start-up "minimills." Even stronger results were found when comparing American to Japanese manufacturers in their use of robots and computerized flexible manufacturing systems (FMSs).[3]

By the early 1990s, an even more remarkable situation held within the U.S. computer industry. The price-performance ratios of microprocessor-based personal computers, workstations, and servers were twenty to fifty times superior to those of the mainframe computers and minicomputers that constituted the core business of IBM, the Seven Dwarfs, and most of the minicomputer industry. But in the case of the computer industry, the vastly superior challengers were predominantly American. The U.S. venture capital industry and Silicon Valley are superb at creating new start-ups, and entry costs for companies based on new information technologies are generally relatively low. In those cases, the U.S. system largely self-corrected through domestic start-up entry. IBM deteriorated and most of the others went out of business. But in their place we got Intel, Microsoft, Compaq, Dell, and Apple. Alone among the earlier generation of firms, IBM was able to reform itself, after falling into a deep crisis in the early 1990s.

But IBM was an exception; most of America's declining giants failed to reform themselves. And in more mature sectors such as automobiles, steel, machine tools, photographic film, and photocopiers, start-up entry was and is impractical. To create a new competitor would require a gigantic, lengthy commitment. And the U.S. financial and industrial system, unlike those of Japan, South Korea, and China, is not good at creating new companies in mature industries that require large initial capital investments.

In contrast, the Japanese (and later, South Korean and Chinese) *did* finance new entry into these industries. This was because the Japanese business sector was dominated by six diversified, vertically integrated financial-industrial complexes (*keiretsu*) that could create new companies even in mature industries. Japanese industry also engaged in large-scale technology licensing, copying, and intellectual property theft, aided by Japanese industrial policy. South Korea had a similar system (based on the *chaebol*). In China the central government, the People's Liberation Army, provincial governments, and state-owned enterprises are now playing a similar role in technology extraction, financing of new domestic entry, and protection of the domestic market from uncontrolled foreign competition.

The comparative ability of different national economic systems to generate new competition in large, mature industries is a subject that the economics discipline has mostly ignored. But the inability of the U.S. national system to create major new competitors in mature industries is extremely important, because it means that the United States faces a very limited set of options when large companies and concentrated industries go into decline. If start-up entry is feasible, as in most IT and Internet markets, U.S. industry renews itself and remains healthy. But if start-up entry is *not* feasible, then there are only three possibilities. They are:

- The U.S. government acts to restore competition and/or reform corporate governance; for example, through antitrust action that breaks up the largest firms.
- Foreign competitors take over, with some resultant loss of U.S. economic welfare.
- If no foreign competition appears, the U.S. industry goes into uncontested decline, imposing the costs of its inefficiency on the American economy and population.

The result has usually been some combination of the second and third options. Since the 1970s, in case after case—GM, Chrysler, most mainframe and minicomputer companies, major steel companies, nearly the entire consumer electronics industry—the failure to adjust has eventually led to wrenching crises, downsizings, bankruptcies, or acquisitions at fire-sale prices. Whether the challengers were foreign or domestic, the incumbents generally resisted change as long as they could, often through political activities, and consequently suffered even more severely when reality could no longer be denied. In many cases, including automobiles, steel, and telecommunications, incumbents were able to retard both competition and reform sufficiently that they imposed major costs on the American economy. And now, to those costs we must add the impressive damage caused by powerful predatory industries—especially financial services.

Indeed, seen in the context of broader American industrial decline, the financial services industry is not *entirely* exceptional. While much of the damage it caused was rationally, amorally predatory, some of it came from the same kind of managerial decadence that ran GM and Chrysler into the ground. Jimmy Cayne, Stan O'Neal, Chuck Prince, Richard Fuld—these were people way above their rightful pay grade, kept there by oblivious, complacent boards of directors, just the way things worked at GM, Chrysler, U.S. Steel, Kodak, and IBM before 1993. The principal difference was that finance can be *really dangerous*. In contrast to the automobile industry, people in finance were able not only to loot their companies but also to bring the global financial system to its knees.

The rise of China, India, and other Asian nations had another effect on the calculation of American industrial executives, of course. It provided a gigantic new pool of extremely low-cost labor to American firms. This meant that even a very efficiently run American company (in fact, perhaps *especially* a well-run company) no longer needed, or even wanted, high-cost American workers for many low-skill jobs, ranging from manual labor in manufacturing to call center personnel used in routine customer service. Outsourcing and offshoring were much more effective.

This meant that the United States could only remain economically healthy, and provide high-wage employment, if it radically improved the education and skills of its population, as well as its attractiveness as a location for high-technology activities. In fact, the reverse has occurred: America's high school dropout rate is actually increasing, and American infrastructure, particularly broadband deployment, is falling ever further behind world standards. As a result, manufacturing in the United States has all but disappeared; it now accounts for 12 percent of GDP. High-skill custom manufacturing (such as for machine tools) is dominated by Japan and Germany, while labor-intensive mass manufacturing is dominated by China, Vietnam, Bangladesh, and other low-wage nations. This has rendered an enormous number of American workers all but unemployable, except in minimum-wage service occupations.

But how and why was all this permitted to occur? It's complicated, of course. But a very big part of the answer is that an effective response to internal industrial decline and foreign challengers required major changes in American government as well as industry. It required major improvements in the educational system, aggressive pressure to force incompetent industries to reform, deployment of advanced broadband infrastructure, and a variety of regulatory changes.

But those measures had no focused, powerful, well-financed interest group to lobby for them. There is no wealthy, powerful industry that has an urgent, immediate need to improve the education and skill levels of the bottom half of the American population. In contrast, there were many other things that powerful, well-financed groups *did* want, and started to lobby for. When faced with internal decline and foreign competition, the executives in charge of large, concentrated American industries decided to start using money to get what they wanted. But only what *they* wanted, *individually*—not what the country as a whole needed. Indeed, what was good for their company's profits was quite often bad for the nation. If the CEO and senior management were lazy, outdated, and incompetent, then they wanted protection from antitrust policy, proper corporate governance, and competition. If the company and its industry were run by competent but predatory management, then additional lobbying goals might include evisceration of regulatory oversight and white-collar law enforcement.

And once they started down this path, executives in incompetent American companies discovered that corruption was a brilliantly easy, effective way to forestall, or at least delay, their *personal* day of reckoning. Later, their highly predatory friends in financial services realized that the same techniques would enable them to rape the entire country, even the entire world. And the rest of us have been paying for it ever since.

American Economic Decline and
the Rise of Money-Based Politics

LET'S BEGIN WITH a case study: broadband infrastructure.

As noted above, the United States has fallen far behind other nations in broadband deployment. Broadband service in much of Asia, and even parts of Europe, is now vastly superior to U.S. services in speed, cost, and universality. To cite just one example among many, as of early 2012, 60-megabit per second Internet access was available in Taiwan for $30 per month, and by the time this book is published in mid-2012, 100-megabit per second service will be available for the same price.[4] Japan, South Korea, Singapore, and even portions of mainland China now have far better broadband service than most of the United States. America, home of Silicon Valley and inventor of the Internet, does not have universal broadband access, for either landlines or Wi-Fi, and its services are slow, unreliable, and expensive. This situation has now existed for over a decade, and America's lag relative to Asia and Scandinavia is if anything worsening.

Why?

The reason is that both the traditional telecommunications and cable TV industries are tight, powerful oligopolies deeply threatened by high-speed Internet services. They view as particularly dangerous a nationwide infrastructure of universal high-speed Internet service combining both wireline and Wi-Fi access. This would sharply reduce the cost of data services; it would also enable universal, inexpensive Internet telephony and streaming Internet video that would render traditional telephone service, cable TV, and broadcast television totally obsolete. In the case of AT&T and Verizon, this would destroy the majority of their current revenues. In the case of the cable TV companies, advanced Internet infrastructure would also threaten them by allowing new competition in video content production and distribution.

While there exists some real competition between AT&T, Verizon, the cable industry, and smaller competitors such as Sprint and T-Mobile, the competition is very limited. After the breakup of the AT&T monopoly in the 1980s, there were about a dozen major telecommunications companies in the United States. There are now two; instead of competing with each other, they merged. They are still trying to consolidate further. AT&T recently tried to acquire T-Mobile; the acquisition was blocked by the Justice Department, the one and only time in the last decade that DOJ has halted the industry's consolidation, which is still continuing. In late 2011 Verizon signed a major deal with America's three largest cable companies, allowing them to cross-market each other's services.[5]

Despite very rapid progress (50 to 100 percent per year) in underlying digital technologies (routers, fiber-optic cable, software, digital wireless systems), the industry exhibits very low rates of improvement in its price-performance ratios. The United States now lags behind Scandinavia, Japan, and South Korea by a factor of ten or more.

The reason is money and politics. Lobbying is this industry's real core competence. It spends more on lobbying, political contributions, and other political activities than it does on R&D. For example, the incumbents have successfully lobbied for state laws prohibiting municipalities from constructing their own fiber-optic networks, and they are probably the largest industrial users of antitrust "consulting" from academic economists.

A decade ago, my last project while a senior fellow at Brookings was to write a book about this issue. As a condition of publishing the book, Brookings censored my manuscript in exactly one place: the passage in which I had named the academic economists who had consulted for the telecommunications incumbents—including Brookings's own Robert Crandall, as well as Laura Tyson, Peter Temin, Daniel Rubinfeld, Rich Gilbert, Jerry Hausman, Carl Shapiro, and the Law and Economics Consulting Group.

The industry's political connections are superb. Laura Tyson isn't just on the board of Morgan Stanley; she's on the board of AT&T, too. In May 2011 Meredith Baker resigned as one of the five members of the Federal Communications Commission to become the chief lobbyist for NBC-Universal, four months after voting to approve its merger with Comcast. Verizon's board includes a former chief accountant of the SEC, a former secretary of transportation, and a former treasury secretary. And Bill Daley, who replaced Rahm Emanuel as chief of staff in the Obama administration from 2011 to 2012, was formerly the president of SBC, one of the regional Bell companies acquired by AT&T. The political situation is further worsened by the fact that the industry's union, the Communications Workers of America, has consistently sided with the incumbents in opposing antitrust actions and other measures to improve competition and technical progress.

As a result, the total cost of using Internet services, smartphones, tablets, and personal computers in the United States is dominated not by hardware or software costs, but by the high cost of data services. The economic consequences of this situation are enormous. In economic policy debates, nearly all discussion of "infrastructure" concentrates on modernizing highways, airports, bridges, sewage systems, electric power, and the like. Those things are important too. But the future economic welfare of the United States depends more heavily on competitive broadband infrastructure. Education and Internet technology are the two principal drivers of productivity growth in advanced economies. Improved broadband services could also play a major role in reducing U.S. greenhouse emissions and dependence on fossil fuels through telecommuting, videoconferencing, and intelligent energy management systems. Moreover, universal broadband deployment would be an enormous physical construction project, an ideal stimulus for the U.S. economy in its weakened state. And finally, competitive broadband services are important to both the quality and the affordability of distance (online) education.

In other words, the United States is now paying a very high price for the rise of money-based politics. It's not just unethical, it's economically disastrous; and it's not just in financial services.

Money, Politics, and Economic Performance

BEGINNING IN THE late 1970s, America's major industries discovered, and began to exploit, a critical weakness in the American national system, one that enabled them to escape or at least soften competitive discipline. Stated bluntly, they discovered that buying people off was much easier than doing their job properly. It turned out that American politicians, academics, regulators, auditors, and political parties were highly corruptible. Their governance systems had been designed for an earlier age, and were not equipped to withstand serious efforts to corrupt them.

So, beginning in the 1980s, the senior management of America's declining incumbents became ever more aggressive in paying off their boards of directors, placing former government officials on those same boards, hiring former politicians as lobbyists, contributing to political campaigns, hiring academic experts to testify in antitrust cases, and so on. They merged with each other, sent production offshore, and cut the wages and benefits of their employees. They sought and obtained weaker antitrust enforcement, exemptions from environmental regulations, tax breaks, favorable accounting standards, protection from foreign competition via domestic content requirements. For example, despite the fact that U.S. corporate earnings reached a historical record of over 14 percent of GDP in 2011, federal corporate tax receipts were near historical lows, at less than 1.5 percent of GDP.[6] American companies also resisted attempts to strengthen corporate governance. They kept public sector salaries low, thereby increasing their ability to subvert policy through revolving-door hiring. They weakened regulations, enforcement, and penalties for violations, and virtually eliminated any risk of criminal prosecution.

And to accomplish all this, since the beginning of this process several decades ago, America's largest businesses, banks, and wealthy individuals have sent money into American politics in a completely unprecedented way, first in rivers, then floods, and now in *oceans*. The money came in several forms: political contributions; lobbying; employment, through the revolving door; sometimes, outright bribery; and, often, access and connections for many purposes, ranging from private schools to personal loans to great parties to rides on private jets.

And the money is often nonpartisan, bipartisan, or to use a recent term, *post*-partisan. Many wealthy individuals now give simultaneously to *both* parties, and to incumbents regardless of their party. Goldman Sachs has a deliberate policy of maintaining equal numbers of Democrats and Republicans in top management, including one of each at the very top. Companies choose lobbyists and board members from among former government officials of both parties in roughly equal numbers. Democrats now receive nearly as much money from business as Republicans do, although some industries, such as oil, still heavily favor the Republicans.

Here are some numbers.

In 1974 total campaign expenditures by all Senate candidates were $28.4 million. In 2010, they were $568 million. For the House of Representatives, total campaign spending in 1974 was $44 million; in 2010, it was $929 million.[7] The presidency has become even more expensive. Campaign expenditures since 1976 are shown in Table 4 below:

TABLE 4

TOTAL SPENDING BY PRESIDENTIAL CANDIDATES
(NOT ADJUSTED FOR INFLATION)

YEAR	TOTAL ($MILLIONS)
2008	1,324.7
2004	717.9
2000	343.1
1996	239.9
1992	192.2
1988	210.7
1984	103.6
1980	92.3
1976	66.9

Source: OpenSecrets.org, http://www.opensecrets.org/pres08/totals.php?cycle=2008

Furthermore, the sources of the money changed. The rise of money-based politics coincided with rising income inequality, and the two have reinforced each other. Political campaign donations have become highly concentrated. By 2010 approximately 1 percent of 1 percent of the American population—fewer than twenty-seven thousand people—accounted for 24 percent of all campaign donations, totaling $774 million.[8]

The increase in campaign spending is starting to produce another dangerous effect: weakening media oversight of political dishonesty. Thankfully, America still has a very robust and independent free press. But the media industry, especially television and print, has been under increasing financial pressure as a result of the shift of both audiences and advertising to the Internet. In this period, there has been one sector whose advertising in the traditional media has continued to grow very sharply: politics. In presidential election years, the combined advertising expenditures of federal, state, and local campaigns, including PACs and so-called super PACs, probably now exceeds $5 billion. As financial services and other large industries have become more concentrated, the advertising spending of individual firms has also grown larger. The combined effect of higher political advertising and more concentrated corporate advertising has begun to generate pressure on major publications and news programs.

Lobbying has escalated similarly. Here are lobbying expenditures by the finance, insurance, and real estate industries from 1998 through 2010:

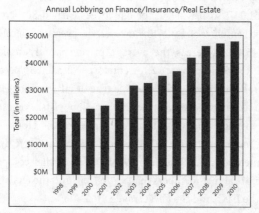

Annual Lobbying on Finance/Insurance/Real Estate

Source: OpenSecrets.org, http://www.opensecrets.org/lobby/indus.php?id=F&year=2011

The personal financial positions of politicians, government officials, and regulators are equally important. Hence the spectacular growth of lobbying expenditures and incomes has a very real utility beyond the job that lobbyists do. Indeed, the lobbying industry's largest effect on policy probably isn't that lobbyists really convince anyone of anything. On the contrary, its principal impact derives from the simple fact of its existence, meaning that all senior public officials—whether elected, appointed, or civil servants—now know that if they behave properly, they can land a lobbying job when they leave government. And if they do, they will immediately quintuple their salary simply by moving to the other side. Here, the growth in income inequality, and in the differential between private and public sector salaries, has further worsened America's political corruption. In some nations, such as Singapore, senior civil servants and regulators earn competitive salaries, sometimes upward of $1 million a year. Not in America.

Here are some statistics on the salaries of public officials and their approximate private counterparts.

The Bureau of Labor Statistics compiles information on average federal government and private sector salaries for "employees in the securities, commodity contracts, and investments sectors in the United States (NIACS 523)." In 1990 the average federal employee in these professions earned $32,437, while the average private sector employee earned $61,047; so private sector employees earned 88 percent more than federal employees. By 2010, however, the average federal employee earned $45,462, whereas the average private sector employee now earned $196,339; so private sector employees made 331 percent more than federal employees. The same was true of other senior federal employees, including those most desirable as lobbyists. For example, in 2010, the average chief of staff for a member of the House of Representatives made less than $140,000; the average legislative director for a House member made less than $90,000. For further comparison, in 2010, federal cabinet members made $199,700, and the chairpersons of the SEC, the FTC, and the CFTC made $165,300.[9]

But these numbers, bad as they are, vastly understate the problem. The private sector numbers include many people in small local financial services companies, and they don't include lobbyists. Average compensation for all Goldman Sachs employees, for example, has fluctuated between a mere pittance of $433,000 in 2010 and its record high of $661,000 in 2007, when it was still selling mortgage-backed junk but had already started to bet against it as well. Senior Goldman executives make vastly more, and you can be sure that Goldman pays its lobbyists very, very well.

Thus, in the end, by industrial standards it proved shockingly inexpensive to purchase federal policy; and keeping public sector salaries low made it even easier to buy influence. Combining campaign contributions, lobbying, revolving-door hiring, and payments to academic experts, the whole process probably costs no more than $20 billion a year, perhaps 1 percent of total U.S. corporate profits. For this trivial sum, America's most incompetent and predatory industries could obtain favorable political and regulatory treatment, reducing their need to be more productive, honest, or competitive.

In this process, the financial sector first became an enthusiastic follower and then, by the 1990s, the *leading user* of money-based political strategy. As the financial sector grew more powerful, more concentrated, and more politically active, it arguably became the first major industry to use lobbying and policy primarily for offensive and predatory, rather than defensive, purposes.

It was under the Clinton administration that the really heavy lifting started for financial services. In fairness, Clinton did some very good things in economic policy. He stopped the deficit spending. He initiated the last major antitrust action in the United States (against Microsoft, although the Bush administration later ended it with a trivial settlement). He also tried to open the telecommunications industry to real competition, including in broadband services, through the attempted grand bargain of the Telecommunications Act of 1996. And Clinton did several very productive things to support the Internet revolution, including legalizing commercial Internet services and privatizing the Internet backbone in 1994–95.

However, the Clinton administration also tilted decisively toward the wealthy and the financial sector, a fateful choice whose full consequences Clinton himself may not have understood at the time. Then George W. Bush finished the job, completely neutering the regulatory and law enforcement systems. And so America got the bubble and then the crisis.

But then, in 2008, with the global financial system on the brink of collapse, Barack Obama presented himself during his presidential campaign as the reformer who would bring the financial sector under control and restore fairness to America. Instead, he screwed us.

Mr. Obama's Wall Street Government

BARACK OBAMA WAS elected with an overwhelming mandate for change, and the best political opportunity since the Depression to achieve it. He won because of reformist and idealistic campaign statements, and the unprecedented popular mobilization efforts they generated. His party obtained overwhelming majorities in both houses of Congress, and he took office with the nation in deep crisis, still on the brink of financial catastrophe and with unemployment increasing by half a percent per *month*. The banks were still in desperate trouble, and the federal government had enormous power over them. The federal government owned major pieces of AIG, Citigroup, and Bank of America; it was supporting all the others through TARP and Federal Reserve loans; Goldman Sachs and Morgan Stanley had agreed to become bank holding companies, which made them subject to Federal Reserve and FDIC regulation. Ben Bernanke's first term as Federal Reserve chairman was ending soon, giving Obama enormous leverage over him, and the ability to replace him if he didn't perform. If ever there was a chance to do something in Washington, DC, this was it. And yet we got just another oligarch's president.

The first troubling sign was his personnel appointments. Not a single critic or voice of reform got a job—not Simon Johnson, Nouriel

Roubini, Paul Krugman, Sheila Bair, Joseph Stiglitz, Jeffrey Sachs, Robert Gnaizda, Brooksley Born, Senator Carl Levin, none of them.

Instead we got Larry Summers, the man behind nearly every disastrous policy that created the crisis, fresh from making $20 million from hedge funds and investment banks, as director of the National Economic Council. (When Summers left office in early 2011, his replacement was Gene Sperling, who had received a $1 million consulting fee from Goldman Sachs for guidance in its nonprofit work.) Tim Geithner, who had been president of the New York Federal Reserve Bank throughout the bubble, was put in charge at Treasury. Geithner chose a former Goldman Sachs lobbyist, Mark Patterson, as his chief of staff. One of his senior advisors was Lewis Sachs, formerly overseer of Tricadia, one of the hedge funds that made billions by helping banks structure mortgage securities for the purpose of Tricadia betting against them. Geithner's choice for undersecretary for domestic finance was Jeffrey Goldstein, a private equity executive. Geithner's deputy assistant secretary for capital markets and housing finance (the person most directly responsible for cleaning up the housing mess) was Matthew Kabaker, an executive at Blackstone, America's largest private equity firm.

The new president of the New York Fed was William C. Dudley, who had been chief economist of Goldman Sachs throughout the bubble, and coauthored with Glenn Hubbard the paper I described earlier, which proclaimed the triumph of financial markets and the role of derivatives in softening recessions. And then, of course, Obama reappointed Ben Bernanke.

Almost all regulatory appointments followed that pattern. Gary Gensler, a former Goldman executive who had previously helped push through the ban on derivatives regulation, became chairman of the Commodity Futures Trading Commission, which regulates derivatives. Mary Shapiro, who had run the Financial Industry Regulatory Authority, the investment banking industry's worthless and timid self-policing body, moved over to run the Securities and Exchange Commission (after receiving a $9 million severance). For the SEC's new director of enforcement, Ms. Shapiro chose Robert Khuzami, who had been (since 2004) general counsel for the Americas for Deutsche Bank.

Mr. Khuzami was a particularly stunning choice, since he must have been deeply involved in the legal approval process for the many unethical actions of Deutsche Bank's U.S. subsidiary during the bubble. Deutsche Bank didn't have Goldman Sachs's laser-focus top-management ruthlessness, but it wasn't a naive boy scout either. It held a large mortgage portfolio, on which it took some losses, but it hedged aggressively, thereby keeping its losses to under $5 billion. Greg Lippmann, head of the Deutsche Bank CDO trading desk, actively shorted the mortgage market, making $1.2 billion for Deutsche. Lippmann also worked with John Paulson and Magnetar to create deals that they could bet against. (As a joke, Lippmann passed out T-shirts to his employees that said "I'm Short Your House.") And like the other banks, Deutsche Bank started unloading its junk on the unsuspecting. Indeed, Lippmann himself occasionally continued to sell CDOs to Deutsche customers, in some cases referring to the products as "crap" and the customers as "dupes." In a June 2007 e-mail message, a Deutsche Bank managing director, Richard Kim, wrote to Lippmann that Deutsche would package unsold pieces of CDOs into a CDO squared, and sell them as a "CDO2 balance sheet dump."[10] The Levin-Coburn report issued in 2011 lists several cases in which risks of CDOs discussed internally were not mentioned in public offering materials. How much did Mr. Khuzami know? We don't know that, but appointing Mr. Khuzami certainly sent a very bad signal about the administration's interest in prosecutions. And, indeed, Mr. Khuzami's record has been a depressing validation of that signal.

The same was true of Obama's choice to run the criminal division of the Justice Department, Lanny Breuer. Breuer had been cochair of the white-collar defense and investigations practice at Covington & Burling, a law firm also heavily involved in corporate lobbying. (Between 2001 and 2007, Attorney General Eric Holder was also at Covington & Burling.) While Breuer and Holder were partners at the firm, its clients included Bank of America, Citigroup, JPMorgan Chase, and Freddie

Mac. The firm was also involved in creating MERS, the banking industry consortium now being sued by the state of New York in connection
with foreclosure abuses.[11] Other Covington clients included Halliburton, Philip Morris, Blackwater, and Enron executives; Breuer personally represented the Moody's rating agency in relation to Enron, and
has also represented Halliburton. Breuer and Holder have declined to
state whether they have been forced to recuse themselves from any financial crime investigations. More recently Covington & Burling has
represented many individuals and firms involved in the financial crisis,
including Indymac, an unidentified Big Four accounting firm, Sterling
Financial/PNC, and others; it has also lobbyied the SEC, on behalf of a
coalition of financial firms, to weaken the Volcker rule.[12]

Eric Holder's deputy chief of staff, John Garland, and Lanny
Breuer's chief of staff, Steve Fagell, both also came from Covington &
Burling, and both have now returned there to work on white-collar defense cases and regulatory issues. At DOJ, Fagell had been in charge of
coordinating DOJ's financial fraud task force. After returning to Covington, he began "representing" (not "lobbying for"—that would be illegal, given how recently Mr. Fagell had left the government) a coalition
of financial firms in their efforts to persuade the SEC to weaken the
whistle-blower provisions of the Dodd-Frank law. Mr. Fagell also "rep-
resents" various other banks and financial executives in regard to various regulatory, legal, and policy disputes.

Even senior Obama administration foreign policy and national
security positions were filled by bankers, including several who had
been deeply involved in, and profited from, the financial bubble. Michael Froman, who was appointed to lead economic policy at the National Security Council, had been an executive in Citigroup Alternative
Investments, a unit that was deeply involved in the financial crisis
and subsequently lost billions of dollars. Froman started working on
Obama's transition team while still employed at Citigroup, and Citigroup awarded him his final bonus after his appointment was announced in January 2009. Under media pressure, Froman gave that
bonus to charity. But Froman still made over $7 million at Citigroup.

Jacob Lew, who had been CFO of the same Citigroup unit, became the deputy secretary of state and then, in 2010, Obama's choice to run the Office of Management and Budget. In 2012 he became Obama's chief of staff when Bill Daley resigned.

The new deputy secretary of state for management and resources was Thomas Nides, brought over from Morgan Stanley, where he had been chief administrative officer. I had met him there once, introduced by Laura Tyson after our final conversation. Ah, yes, he said, he knew Laura from the Clinton administration; he had been in the administration too, "before I sold out." Yes, he really did say that to me.

Obama's—or Hillary Clinton's—undersecretary of state for economic affairs was Robert Hormats, previously vice chairman of Goldman Sachs International. Richard Holbrooke, the State Department's special envoy to Afghanistan and Pakistan until his death in 2010, had been on the board of directors of AIG and AIG Financial Products. Tom Donilon, Fannie Mae's chief lobbyist between 1999 and 2005, became deputy National Security Advisor in 2009 and then, in late 2010, the National Security Advisor. The flow in the reverse direction began soon afterward; Peter Orszag, Obama's first head of the Office of Management and Budget, resigned in 2010 to become vice chairman of Citigroup.

The fears immediately prompted by this pattern of appointments have proved fully justified. From the outset, Obama opposed serious reform of corporate governance, breaking up the largest banks, or closing legal loopholes. It is still not per se illegal, for example, to create and sell a security for the purpose of betting on its failure. Obama also opposed efforts to reform or control financial industry compensation—even for firms dependent upon federal aid, as almost all of them were in the immediate aftermath of the crisis. There was a long period of total inaction, followed by a weak and ridiculously complicated reform bill (Dodd-Frank). There has been almost no significant action on the foreclosure crisis, and the White House played little or no role in the investigations undertaken by the Senate Permanent Subcommittee on Investigations and the Financial Crisis Inquiry Commission. In fact, the administration deliberately kept the FCIC's budget to a mere $6 million, sharply limited its subpoena power, and scheduled its report to appear only after the 2010 midterm elections.

Most tellingly, the new Justice Department's complete lack of interest in prosecuting banks and bankers soon became painfully obvious. White-collar and financial crimes were given low priority, and the administration chose not to appoint a special prosecutor, or create a task force, to investigate and prosecute major crimes related to the bubble and crisis. Investigations against Countrywide, Angelo Mozilo, AIG, Joseph Cassano, and others were dropped. The few financial crime cases brought forward, such as those involving Wachovia's bid rigging and money laundering, were settled with deferred prosecution agreements and fines. As a consequence, as of early 2012 there still had not been a single crisis-related criminal prosecution, of either a firm or an individual senior financial executive, by the Obama administration—literally zero.

The SEC has brought only a handful of civil cases, ending in mostly trivial fines, with neither firms nor individuals required to admit any wrongdoing. In not a single case has an individual executive been required to pay more than a tiny fraction of either his net worth or his gains from the bubble.

In fact, when a few courageous state attorneys general, particularly Eric Schneiderman of New York, tried to get just a little tough with the banks in 2011 (in several civil cases), the Obama administration pressured them to stop. Senior Obama officials and their proxies, including the secretary of housing and urban development, called Schneiderman directly and told him that he should accept the sweetheart deal that the administration favored, whose terms included surrendering all future rights to sue the banks for fraud.

But then came the Occupy Wall Street movement, the *60 Minutes* two-part series in December 2011 on the lack of criminal prosecutions, and, above all, an election year in 2012. So, suddenly, four years after the crisis, in his January 2012 State of the Union address, President Obama decided to announce a federal-state task force focused on financial crime, and that New York state attorney general Eric Schneiderman would co-chair it. The other co-chair, however, is Lanny Breuer, the same head of the same criminal division that hadn't brought any cases for four years. The task force was assigned a total of ten (yes, ten) FBI agents, and when fully staffed will have a grand total of fifty-five employees.

Shortly afterward, we saw the predictable political results. Three Credit Suisse traders were arrested for a trivial fraud allegedly committed in 2007, and which victimized Credit Suisse rather than investors or homeowners. Then the state foreclosure cases were settled for $26 billion. Less than a million people who have lost their homes will receive checks averaging $2,000 each. Another million will receive some degree of mortgage relief. Over twenty million others whose mortgages are underwater, or who have lost their houses to foreclosure, will receive nothing. As of this writing, there have still been no arrests or indictments either of major firms or senior executives related to causing the bubble, the crisis, or subsequent foreclosure abuses.

Obama has been similarly inert with regard to financial compensation, at either the corporate or individual level, even as foreign governments took action. In 2009, Britain enacted a 50 percent tax on banking bonuses. Then in September 2009 Christine Lagarde (then France's finance minister) and six other European finance ministers published a joint letter in the *Financial Times* calling for the G20 nations to enact strong measures to bring financial compensation under control, arguing that "the bonus culture must end." Most of the G20 nations did in fact adopt compensation controls, including mandatory clawbacks of bonuses when losses occur subsequently. The Obama administration had no comment. Later, in 2010, the Federal Reserve and the SEC issued regulations, but they were exceedingly weak and little has changed.

In contrast, in 2012, such clawbacks were in fact implemented in Europe, forcing senior executives of Barclays, Lloyds, and several other European banks to surrender millions of dollars each in prior bonus payments.

Thus far there have been no executive bonus clawbacks by regulators in the United States. At both corporate and industry levels, the same major conflicts of interest remain embedded in the financial system. Accounting firms performing audits are still paid by the firms they are supposed to audit. Rating agencies are still paid by the issuers of securities. Traders, executives, and members of boards of directors still receive large amounts of cash relative to stock.

In short, the Obama administration's policies toward the financial sector are nearly indistinguishable from those of its predecessors, regardless of political party. What happened here?

First, the Democratic Party has changed—not so much its popular base, but its funding sources. For most of the twentieth century, and certainly from the Depression through the 1970s, the Democrats were reliably the party of unions, of working families, and the poor, while the Republicans were reliably the party of business. That divide was dramatized many times during the Great Depression, but it endured for decades afterward. It showed in 1962, in John F. Kennedy's confrontation with the steel industry, whose major firms often behaved like a cartel. The Kennedy administration had brokered a labor agreement with the steel unions and was shocked when the companies immediately increased steel prices together, even though Kennedy's agreement had kept wage costs down. Kennedy held a brief, blistering press conference that forced the companies to back down. The punch line actually drew applause from the reporters:

> A few gigantic corporations have decided to increase steel prices in ruthless disregard of the public interest. Some time ago I asked each American to ask what he could do for his country. Today Big Steel gave its answer.

But that was *your parents'* Democratic Party. In the *new* Democratic Party, when President Obama hosts a White House State Dinner in January 2011 for Hu Jintao, the president of China, he invites Lloyd Blankfein and Jamie Dimon.[13] In fact, Mr. Blankfein had visited the

White House ten times as of early 2011, including several times during the period that his firm had been charged with fraud by the SEC.

The subordination of mainstream Democrats to the financial oligarchy's agenda first became apparent during the Clinton administration, whose policies, as we have seen, were sharply more favorable toward the wealthy and the financial services sector than those of any Democratic administration in the last century. That the control of the oligarchy became even greater during the Bush administration goes without saying.

But what is perhaps most revealing is that Obama continued in Bush's footsteps, even though he had an unprecedented opportunity to change course. How to explain this?

America's Political Duopoly

AMERICA HAS EXPERIENCED a profound realignment of its politics over the last generation, driven by a combination of globalization, American economic decline, and the rising use of money to shape American politics and government policy. The core of this realignment is that the two political parties now compete for money, while colluding to hide this fact. They provide the appearance, and often the reality, of fierce partisan conflict on social and "values" issues, whereas on the issues of critical concern to the financial sector and America's economic oligarchy, their actions are almost identical. We have, in short, a *political duopoly*—a cartel formed by the two parties that, between them, control all of American politics.

At first glance, the suggestion that both parties are colluding and under the influence of a single oligarchy seems absurd. There are red states and blue states; the two parties are viciously polarized. And there is real political conflict in America, especially on social issues that matter to the two parties' bases—abortion, gay marriage, sex education versus religion in schools, creationism and evolution, guaranteed-health-insurance-as-socialism, taxes-and-government-as-evil, gun control, welfare, drug policy, immigration, environmental policy, the reality of global warming. These are very real, very important issues; and on these issues, each political party can credibly tell its base that defeat would mean real, painful losses.

But that is exactly the point. It's a brilliant strategy. These social and "values" conflicts serve excellently to divide and distract people who should, and perhaps otherwise *would,* be dangerously united in feeling that they were being raped by their CEOs, their bankers, their elected leaders, and the political establishment. Thus, each party can continue to command the grudging support of people who fear that if the other side won, they would lose something important, which leaves the two parties free to collude on the most important thing to both of them—money.

Of course, not everyone likes this new arrangement. Even many wealthy people and some major industries are disturbed, and even directly harmed, by America's descent into political corruption, financial instability, and economic decline. Information technology, both in Silicon Valley start-ups and major firms, is one example, and it is hardly alone; many industries suffered as a result of the crisis, and continue to do so. But for the most part, even these people and groups dare not resist, or find it not in their interest to do so. The wealthy, and the businesses they own and run, depend upon access to the increasingly separate, private financial system operated for the wealthy by the big banks, hedge funds, and private equity firms. Functions such as private banking, wealth management, estate and trust planning, tax minimization, mergers and acquisitions, initial public offerings, and securities issuance are now dominated by a small number of large financial firms. Moreover, in some regards, such as individual taxation, the interests of senior executives in all industries are aligned with those who run the financial sector. And successful individuals of conscience are not a concentrated, naturally cohesive industry, whereas finance and the ultrarich *are,* so it's not really a contest.

Consequently the rational decision is to adjust, rather than try to reform the system. This is particularly true of high technology, which is the only other industry whose wealth and power could potentially rival the financial sector's.

Consider, for example, the political and lobbying interests of Apple, a firm correctly regarded as a remarkable testament to American high technology. Apple engages in no manufacturing; its manufacturing contractors are Taiwanese-owned companies whose headquarters are in Taiwan, but most of whose operations and employees are in China. (At least Apple still *designs* its own products; many American electronics companies don't anymore.) These firms, in turn, use Taiwanese and Chinese engineers and managers, predominantly Chinese manual labor (their factories are in China), and a combination of Japanese, German, Taiwanese, and Chinese capital equipment.

For Apple and others like it, this outsourcing decision is entirely rational; but its economic and political implications are enormous. Apple has approximately 70,000 employees worldwide. Just one of Apple's Taiwanese-Chinese manufacturing contractors, Foxconn, has *1.3 million* employees. While perhaps three-quarters of them are relatively unskilled manufacturing workers, several hundred thousand of them are engineers, managers, accountants, and other professional employees. Moreover, the technology level of Foxconn's operations (and of Chinese manufacturing generally) is rising rapidly. In 2011 Foxconn announced that due to labor shortages and increasing demand, it was purchasing 300,000 *robots* for its Chinese factories. The process of selecting, installing, programming, and maintaining those robots will require a large number of highly skilled employees, almost none of them American.

Apple's decisions in this regard are no longer motivated entirely by labor costs. The infrastructure and skills to manufacture its products no longer exist in the United States. American schools no longer produce enough people with enough skill to enable such manufacturing facilities to be designed, constructed, and operated in the United States. But Apple doesn't need its products to be manufactured in the United States; in fact, its use of Chinese manufacturing is critical to obtaining full access to the Chinese market. And Apple, like other U.S.

high-technology companies, is now far less dependent on the U.S. market than previously. In 2011 less than 40 percent of Apple's revenues, and less than 20 percent of its growth, came from North America.

So Apple, Hewlett-Packard, and Dell are not going to declare war on Wall Street over the future of the American labor force. Indeed, some high-technology companies share the financial sector's interest in gutting regulation and antitrust enforcement. Everyone likes lower corporate taxes. Google now holds over 60 percent of the U.S. Internet search market, and its share is growing, so they're not so excited about strong antitrust policy, either. So American high technology may not always like how the financial sector behaves, but it won't wage war against it. Similarly, the technology sector isn't going to go to war over universal high-speed broadband service or public education.

America's new money-driven political system also has strong self-reinforcing characteristics. The more wealthy, concentrated, and powerful America's financial sector and wealthiest families become, the more they affect policy in their favor; the more policy tilts in their favor, the wealthier and more powerful they become. Similarly, the system makes it difficult to mount truly effective third-party challenges or insurgencies within the two major parties. The electoral college system in presidential elections makes it difficult for a third party to become the deciding swing vote for the presidency. Nor does America have a parliamentary system that might give a new third party a critical swing vote in choosing a leader. Similarly, very few American cities or states have ranked-order voting, which would prevent third party votes from being wasted. Over the last quarter century, gerrymandering of election districts (engineering their borders to control voting outcomes) has produced increasing "security" of congressional districts, with incumbents rarely unseated. And, as a major fundraiser for the Democratic Party recently told me, the one thing that both parties can always agree on is the undesirability of third parties.

There is still *some* difference between the two parties. The Democratic Party is still more progressive than the Republicans on matters of *individual* economic opportunity, education, personal taxation, the social safety net, environmental policy, and safety regulation. And for now, disbelief in evolution, vaccines, and climate change remains a uniquely Republican aberration. But the margin of difference between the two parties, at least on economic issues important to business and finance, as opposed to individuals, has narrowed sharply. As the power of the financial sector and the wealthy has increased, the entire political spectrum has shifted toward the wealthy on economic issues, and the Democrats have shifted along with it.

And thus, Americans are stuck. There is now little difference on where the parties stand toward regulation of Wall Street or other concentrated and regulated industries (telecommunications, energy, the media), or the role of money in politics, including the revolving door. America is increasingly in the hands of a cynical political duopoly whose policies are antithetical to economic progress and fairness.

Obama's failure to act has been blamed on his inexperience, his unfamiliarity with finance and business, and a personal tendency to avoid conflict (or, to be blunt, on his being a coward). Some, including my colleague Charles Morris, also feel that the political system is now so gridlocked and dysfunctional that transformative policy changes are simply no longer feasible by anyone, so that Obama really couldn't have done anything even if he had tried. If so, then we're *really* screwed. But if anyone had a shot, it was Barack Obama in 2009, and he *didn't* try. Admittedly, it would have taken real personal courage, and it would have been a hard fight—Wall Street would not have just rolled over. The logic and incentive structures of America's political duopoly are such that in taking the path of least resistance, Obama was surely acting in his, and his party's, rational self-interest. But whatever Obama's personal motivations, America (and indeed the whole world) will pay dearly for his failure for a long time.

Let us now turn to the pain that America suffers under this regime.

Inequality, Stagnation, and
the Decline of American Opportunity

BOTH IN PERSONAL conversations and in the statistics, I sense a change among America's young, who increasingly display both a pervasive cynicism about politics (particularly after Obama turned out to be business as usual) and also, unless they are in the upper 5 percent or so, a fatalism about their personal career prospects. Their general view is: if you have rich parents, a computer science background, or an MBA, you're okay; otherwise, you're not okay, and if you want to change that and make some money, you had better concentrate really hard on pleasing the boss. Outside of Silicon Valley and Wall Street, the America of possibility, openness, progress, and opportunity seems increasingly distant. Most older Americans, in contrast, still do not seem to realize how unfair their society has become over the last generation unless they have become victims of it themselves.

First, the numbers. Since 1980, there has been a pronounced shift of taxable income toward the top tenth. As the top chart on the next page illustrates, their share of all reported income, including capital gains, grew from a bit over a third in 1980 to virtually half (49.7 percent), in 2007. The top tenth's share of income in 2007 is the highest on record, just above the 49.3 percent share garnered by the top tenth in 1928, the year before America entered the Great Depression.

Even more remarkable, however, is the growth of inequality *within* the top tenth, as the bottom chart shows. Since 1980, the top tenth has increased its share of income by about half. But the share of the top 1 percent of taxpayers more than doubled, from 10 percent of total income in 1980 to over 20 percent in 2010. And what is truly stunning is that by 2007, the top one-hundredth of the *top 1 percent,* less than twenty-five thousand households, earned more than 6 percent of all national income—nearly $1 trillion. This percentage was considerably higher than the previous record, also set in 1928. This striking divergence of share gains within the top tenth is shown in the second chart on the next page, taking the respective shares in 1980 as 100.

Income Share of the Top Tenth, 1917–2008

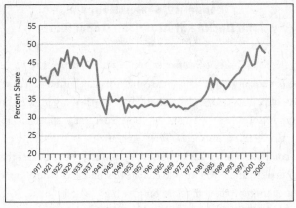

Facundo Alvaredo, Tony Atkinson, Thomas Piketty, and Emmanuel Saez, *World Top Incomes Database*, http://g-mond.parisschoolofeconomics.eu/topincomes/

Share Gains Within Top Tenth of Taxpayers, 1980–2008 (1980=100)

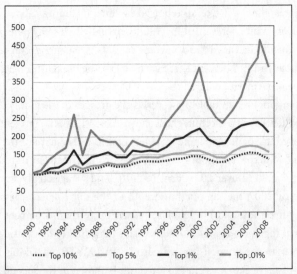

Facundo Alvaredo, Tony Atkinson, Thomas Piketty, and Emmanuel Saez, *World Top Incomes Database*, http://g-mond.parisschoolofeconomics.eu/topincomes/

Real Median Household Income, 1967–2009

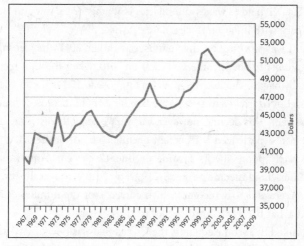

U.S. Census Bureau, http://www.census.gov/hhes/www/income/data/historical/household/index.html, Table H-3

Moreover, these changes occurred when most American households actually found their real incomes stagnant or declining. Median household income for the last four decades is shown in the chart above.

But this graph, disturbing as it is, conceals a far worse reality. The top 10 percent did much better than everyone else; if you remove them, the numbers change dramatically. Economic analysis has found that "only the top 10 percent of the income distribution had real compensation growth equal to or above…productivity growth."[14] In fact, most gains went to the top *1 percent*, while Americans in the bottom 90 percent either had declining household incomes or were able to increase their family incomes only by working longer hours. The productivity of working Americans continued to grow, particularly with the Internet revolution that began in the mid-1990s. But the benefits of productivity growth went almost entirely into the incomes of the top 1 percent and into corporate profits, both of which have grown to record highs as a fraction of GNP. In 2010 and 2011 corporate profits accounted for over 14 percent of total GNP, a historical record. In contrast, the share of U.S. GNP paid as wages and salaries is at a historical low and has not kept pace with inflation since 2006.[15]

As I was working on this manuscript in late 2011, the Census Bureau published the income statistics for 2010, when the U.S. recovery officially began. The national poverty rate rose to 15.1 percent, its highest level in nearly twenty years; median household income declined by 2.3 percent. This decline, however, was very unequally distributed. The top tenth experienced a 1 percent decline; the bottom tenth, already desperately poor, saw its income decline 12 percent. America's median household income peaked in 1999; by 2010 it had declined 7 percent. Average hourly income, which corrects for the number of hours worked, has barely changed in the last thirty years.

Ranked by income equality, the United States is now ninety-fifth in the world, just behind Nigeria, Iran, Cameroon, and the Ivory Coast.

This is not distinguished company. And it's not a statistical fluke. Americans don't like to face this, but America now has a true, increasingly permanent underclass living in near-subsistence conditions. There are now tens of millions of Americans whose condition is little better than many people in poor third-world nations. If you add up lifetime urban ghetto residents, illegal immigrants, migrant farmworkers, those whose criminal convictions sharply limit their ability to find work, those actually in prison, those with chronic drug-abuse problems, crippled veterans of America's recently botched wars, children in foster care, the homeless, the long-term unemployed, and other severely disadvantaged groups, you get to tens of millions of people trapped in very harsh, very unfair conditions, in what is supposedly the wealthiest, fairest society on earth.

At any given time, there are over two million people in U.S. prisons; over ten million Americans have felony records and have served prison time for non-traffic offenses. Many millions more now must work very long hours, and very hard, at minimum-wage jobs in agriculture, retailing, cleaning, and other low-wage service industries. Several million have been unemployed for years, exhausting their savings and morale. Twenty or thirty years ago, many of these people would have had—and some *did* have—high-wage jobs in manufacturing or construction. No more.

But in addition to growing inequalities in income and wealth, America exhibits growing inequality of *opportunity*, both economically and in all the determinants of a healthy, happy, secure life, ranging from health care to nutrition.

There are many facets to the decline in fairness and opportunity in American life. Perhaps the worst are the conditions now imposed upon young children born into the underclass and subjected to the recent evolution of American education. They are related, and they reinforce each other; their combined result is to condemn tens of millions of American children, particularly those born into America's new underclass, to a life of hardship and unfairness. For any young child whose parents don't have money, or who is the child of a migrant agricultural worker and/or an illegal immigrant, America's prenatal care, preschool, day care, after school, school nutrition, and foster-care systems are nothing short of appalling. And then comes school itself. Nowhere is America's rapidly growing denial of opportunity more severe or more devastating to the nation's economic future than in education.

The American dream, stated simply, is that no matter how poor or humble your origins—even if you never knew your parents—you have a shot at a decent life. America's promise is that anyone willing to work hard can do better over time, and have at least a reasonable life for themselves and their own children. You could expect to do better than your parents, and even be able to help them as they grew old.

More than ever before, the key to the American dream is education. The rise of information technology, and the opening of Asian economies, means that only a small portion of America's population can make a good living through unskilled or manual labor. But instead of elevating America's educational system and the opportunities it should provide, America has been going in exactly the wrong direction. As a result, America is developing not a class system, but, without exaggeration, a *caste* system—a society in which the circumstances of your birth determine your entire life.

As a result, the American dream is dying. Increasingly, the most important determinant of an American child's life prospects—future income, wealth, educational level, even health and life expectancy— is totally arbitrary and unfair. It's also very simple. American children's futures are increasingly determined by their parents' wealth, not by their own intelligence or energy. To be sure, there are a number of reasons for this. Income is correlated with many other things, and it's therefore difficult to isolate the impact of individual factors. Children in poor households are more likely to grow up in single-parent versus two-parent households, exposed to drugs and alcohol, with one or both parents in prison, with their immigration status questionable, and more likely to have problems with diet and obesity. Culture and race play a role: Asian children have far higher high school graduation rates, test scores, and grades than all other groups, including whites; Latinos, the lowest. So, yes, it's complicated.

But it's also simple, really. The largest single factor is the decline in educational opportunity and achievement, which are driven by money. If you don't have money, you lose—through the declining quality of public education in poor school districts, insufficient day care, inadequate preschool and after-school programs, financial and social pressure to quit school prematurely, and the soaring cost of college, both public and private. The historical accident that American public schools are funded through local property taxes plays a huge role here. As income inequality grows, so does the disparity between poor and wealthy school districts in the tax receipts available to fund schools.

So now, if your parents make enough money, they can live in a good public school district, and if they're really wealthy, they'll send you to private schools. The food will be good. You won't face pressure to drop out to take care of your younger sister; they can send her to day care or hire a babysitter. They'll buy you a computer, and piano lessons. Someone will be home, and you won't be left to fend for yourself on the streets. But if your parents don't have the money and they need to work two jobs, or if your parents have succumbed to alcohol or drugs, none of those nice things will happen, and you'll go to bad schools, and probably drop out of high school.

Increasingly, America has three parallel educational systems. There is an extremely high-quality, elitist, extremely expensive private system for the upper 5 percent or so. Second, there is a *reasonably good* system for comfortably middle-class professionals who can live in good public school districts and send their children to college. And then, there is a truly awful system for everyone else. The "everyone else" is now at least a quarter, and by some criteria may be nearly half, of the American population. That's a lot of people to waste.

America's high school graduation rate is difficult to estimate accurately, in part because government statistics at all levels—federal, state, local—often cover up the situation. But despite estimates that range surprisingly widely, the basic facts are clear. America's high school graduation rate is much lower than it should be, and it is *declining,* both absolutely and relative to the rest of the world. So is the quality of public education, even for those who do graduate. Anyone from Asia, or most of Europe, can tell you that most American high schools are a joke. And America's high school graduation rate is already inferior to that of most other developed nations, including those where graduating from high school means much more than it does in America. The best estimates place the current American high school graduation rate at 75–80 percent. Since graduation rates from exclusive private high schools are nearly 100 percent, America's *public* high school graduation rate is probably under 75 percent, and may be as low as 70 percent. In contrast many European and Asian nations have graduation rates of around 90 percent.

And, as with private planes and private elevators, so with private education; there has arisen an increasingly segregated system of private elementary and high schools for the wealthy. It's not very subtle. Where does John Paulson send his kids to school? His twin daughters attended preschool at the 92nd Street Y, which costs over $20,000 per student per year—yes, for preschool. Paulson is on their board. He also manages some of their investments, which he has guaranteed against losses. Many other board members have sent children to the school; four of them also manage money for the institution. This is not unusual. One of Mr. Paulson's daughters, having left nursery school behind, now attends Spence, another exclusive private school in Manhattan. Mr. Paulson is on their board too.[16]

Equally disturbing are trends in higher education. When I attended the University of California, Berkeley, in the mid-1970s, tuition for California residents was less than $700 per year. In 2011 undergraduate tuition for state residents was $14,260. Private universities have displayed similar changes. When I entered MIT as a first-year graduate student in 1978, annual tuition was $4,700. For the 2011–12 academic year, it was $40,460. In that same year, Harvard's tuition was $36,305. Harvard estimated its total annual costs (tuition, fees, room and board, supplies) at $52,652; so the total cost of sending your child to Harvard for four years, even assuming no further cost increases, was already over $210,000.

Harvard, and most other elite private schools, claim that their admissions are merit-based and need-blind, and that everyone who qualifies will receive enough financial aid to attend. This is bullshit, of course. If your parents went to Harvard (or Yale, Princeton, etc.) and have donated money, or if your father runs a huge global bank or is prime minister somewhere, your chances are surely somewhat improved. But forget about that—just look at the money and the students. In the 2011 academic year, Harvard's administration proudly announced that slightly over 60 percent of its undergraduates received some level of financial aid and also stated that no student whose family earned less than $180,000 per year would be required to pay more than 10 percent of their total costs.[17]

Think about that for a minute. If you're a Harvard student who receives no financial aid at all, you come from a family that makes *much* more than $180,000 per year. Let's say the eligibility cutoff for receiving any financial aid at all is $300,000 (Harvard doesn't reveal the number).

This means that nearly 40 percent of Harvard undergraduates came from families whose income is at the very upper end of the American income distribution. This means that Harvard's income distribution is probably even more skewed than America's: in the nation as a whole, in 2010 the top 1 percent of families received about 20 percent of all annual income.

At the same time as tuition is rising, there is a widening gulf in quality and resources between private universities and the public universities and community colleges that have traditionally provided the majority of educational opportunity for poor students. As income inequality has grown, donations to private universities have grown, as have their endowments, while government support for public education has stagnated or declined. As a result, between 1999 and 2009, spending per student at private universities grew from about $29,000 to nearly $36,000, while spending per student at community colleges remained nearly flat at about $10,000 per student. Since 2008, the situation has worsened; tuition at public universities and community colleges has increased sharply, while spending per student has declined, in some cases by more than 20 percent.[18] The University of California, the largest and best public university in the world, has seen its budget cut by over 20 percent since the financial crisis.

But there is yet another way in which America has become less fair, and it is even more disturbing than the growth in economic and educational inequality. It is this: increasingly, in America, you make more money by being crooked and destructive than you do by being productive and honest. Thankfully this isn't true everywhere—brains, work, and reputation still count in many places. (Once again, high technology stands out.) But in a sharply increasing, already frighteningly high percentage of American society, honesty is now a major professional and financial liability.

This pattern started, not surprisingly, in the same place as America's economic decline: the highly concentrated American industries that had become severely inefficient by the 1980s. The people who mismanaged America's automobile, steel, and telecommunications industries did not, in general, suffer for their incompetence. They stayed in their jobs and kept their perks, while their companies deteriorated. But now, with the financial sector and its friends free from any risk of prosecution, America has taken looting to a whole new level.

The Ultimate Insult:
The Financial Penalty for Being Decent

ANYONE WHO HAS ever lived or worked in a corrupt dictatorship knows what happens. When the system is rigged, when ordinary citizens are powerless, and when whistle-blowers are pariahs at best, three things happen. First, the worst people rise to the top. They behave appallingly, and they wreak havoc. Second, people who could make productive contributions to society are incented to become destructive, because corruption is far more lucrative than honest work. And third, everyone else pays, both economically and emotionally; people become cynical, selfish, and fatalistic. Often they go along with the system, but they hate themselves for it. They play the game to survive and feed their families, but both they and society suffer. In America, this issue is rarely mentioned in public or in the media, but in my personal experience it is increasingly discussed in private conversation.

Consider now the high-income, high-education sectors that are the principal subjects of this book: financial services, academia, politics, and policy making. Over the last several decades, the financial sector has sharply increased its share of GNP, total corporate profits, and employment. Its income per employee is now double the national average, and people at the top of the financial world today make phenomenal amounts of money. Over the same period, the industry's ethical standards deteriorated sharply.

Over the last decade executives, salespeople, and traders in the financial sector made truly obscene sums, by doing truly obscene things. With a few exceptions, the worst offenders made the most money. None of them have been prosecuted, and none of them have been forced to return the money. Most of them have kept their jobs. Even those who destroyed their own firms have remained both free and extremely wealthy. Jimmy Cayne saw his net worth decline from about $1.5 billion to a mere $600 million or so after Bear Stearns collapsed, but he can probably survive on that. Stan O'Neal received a severance of $161 million for being greedy and incompetent at Merrill Lynch. Henry Paulson made something like half a billion dollars turning Goldman Sachs into an organization that made money betting against its customers, and his successor Lloyd Blankfein hasn't done badly either. Angelo Mozilo still has his half a billion too. And so on.

Even worse, consider what it was like to be an honest person in one of those firms. We don't know if anyone ever knocked on Lloyd Blankfein's door and said, Listen, Lloyd, it isn't very nice to tell the world to buy this stuff when we know it's awful and we're making billions of dollars betting against it. And you shouldn't lie to Congress about it, either. Did anyone ever say that to Lloyd? Probably not. But if someone ever *did* tell him that, I rather doubt that he or she received an immediate promotion and a big bonus. And we do know what happened to a number of people, in various firms including Citigroup, Merrill Lynch, Countrywide, AIG, and others, who tried to call attention to the unethical and unsustainable behavior they saw. Almost without exception, they were severely penalized for it.

And yet, anyone graduating from business school, law school, or anyplace else anytime in the last two decades certainly noticed that finance was the quickest, surest way to get rich. This diverted a considerable number of America's smartest, most ambitious, best-educated people from productive work into quasi-criminal activities that have damaged, not improved, America's economic welfare. And while the financial bubble was the largest and worst of these activities, it was far from the only one.

Something similar now holds for economics and other academic disciplines relevant to politics and regulation (law, political science, and public policy). Which economists, finance professors, and industrial economists have made the most money, obtained the most senior positions, become the most famous, testified in Congress most frequently? Larry Summers, Glenn Hubbard, Laura Tyson, Frederic Mishkin, Martin Feldstein, Alan Greenspan, Hal Scott, Richard Schmalensee, Jerry Hausman...

Given this parade, put yourself in the shoes, once again, of someone young and honest, particularly someone who wants to do research on, say, the financial crisis. As we noted above, you would face a sobering tableau. Who would supervise your PhD thesis, judge your grant applications, consider whether to give you tenure, referee the articles you submit to journals? Answer: people who make millions of dollars defending the financial sector. In contrast, who is going to pay *you* hundreds of thousands of dollars per year to sit on their board of directors, testify in Congress on their behalf, advocate their interests in antitrust cases, appear for them before regulators? Nobody, is the answer.

As for politics, lobbying, and government policy—enough already said. At present, these are not professions that attract and reward the honest and selfless.

This is dangerous. A nation that allows predatory, value-destroying behavior to become systematically more profitable than honest, productive work risks a great deal. America, like all societies, depends heavily on idealism and trust, including the willingness of ordinary citizens to behave honestly and to make sacrifices. While many Americans do not yet realize how unfair their society has become, that condition will not last indefinitely. Unfortunately it will probably last long enough that the current generation of predators will die wealthy and comfortable. But most of us would not enjoy living in a society dominated by cynicism and dishonesty.

CHAPTER 10

WHAT SHOULD BE DONE?

WE ALL HAVE OUR own list of the reforms that America needs most. Here, very briefly, is mine. These are very easy things to write down, and very hard things to accomplish in America's current economic and political climate.

- Improving educational opportunity and quality is fundamental. The United States cannot compete economically, elect wise leaders, or call itself a fair society if it has a 25 percent high school dropout rate, if only the wealthy can attend good schools, and if only expensive private universities are adequately funded. Here, there is a fairness issue that not even a bank CEO can openly deny. If there is one thing that nearly everyone can agree on, amidst all of America's culture wars, it is that all children deserve a fair chance. If a child is born in a poor school district, or to drug-addicted parents, *it isn't the baby's fault.* And yet the ways America handles public school funding, after-school programs, child nutrition, foster care, and child poverty remain shameful, and if anything are becoming more so. Beyond this, a well-educated population yields a far happier, more prosperous society. As it stands, America is wasting a startlingly high fraction of its people, in ways that are painful and very expensive.

- Bring the financial sector under control. This, in turn, has many elements, most of which have been widely discussed. We need to reform, and tightly regulate, compensation structures at the individual, corporate, and industry levels; break up the largest banks; greatly strengthen the power and political independence of regulation and white-collar criminal law enforcement; tax financial transactions; tax financial sector income fairly; and close legal loopholes for activities such as "innovations" designed for tax avoidance or for betting against one's own securities. The natural result of proper re-regulation of the financial sector will be to reduce its size, concentration, and political power. This will have many benefits, ranging from increasing the supply of talented people for more productive activities to reducing pressures for political corruption.

- Control the impact of money on American politics. Easier said than done, but very important. Lobbying and political contributions should be heavily taxed; public sector and regulator salaries should be raised sharply, in return for strict prohibitions on revolving-door behavior; and some form of public campaign financing should be made mandatory.

- Reform the tax system, both individual and corporate, so as to raise revenues, increase fairness, and mitigate against the formation of hereditary and financial oligarchies. Extremely high estate taxes are one important element of this, as is the fair taxation of very high financial sector incomes.

- Greatly strengthen antitrust policy and the regulation of corporate governance. Antitrust policy and analysis have fallen victim to corruption in two ways: first, the corruption of federal policy through campaign finance, lobbying, and revolving-door hiring;

and second, the corruption of the economics discipline that supplies the economic analysis, and the personnel, behind antitrust decisions. In the areas of industrial organization, regulation, corporate governance, and antitrust theory, the economics discipline doesn't just need reform; it needs a five-organ transplant and a yearlong stay at a reeducation camp. More generally, America needs to figure out how to keep large, mature industries from going the way of General Motors, U.S. Steel, AT&T, Microsoft, or for that matter Citigroup and Merrill Lynch, either by deep reforms in corporate governance, by breaking up large and stagnant companies, or by creating other mechanisms for new entry in mature industries.

- Create a truly universally accessible, high-speed broadband Internet infrastructure, both wireline and wireless, for the United States. The United States should view broadband deployment in much the same terms that the Eisenhower administration viewed, and deployed, the nation's highway system beginning in the 1950s. If anything, broadband deployment is more important, both economically and as a way to enable the United States to deal with foreign energy dependence, homeland security problems, and global warming.

What the Future Holds

THERE IS A wide range of possible futures for the United States. One of them is simply more of the same, both economically and politically. In this case, America will be ruled by an ever more powerful oligarchy—roughly the top 1 percent—and will continue to function quite well for a sizable minority—roughly the top 10 percent—while becoming increasingly harsh for the majority of the population. Elite education will continue to supply people for high technology, financial services, and for the senior management of global companies whose markets and labor forces will be outside the United States. Most other

Americans will just survive, and America will have a very large, poor, angry underclass. One might call this a Brazilian outcome—although actually Brazil has been moving toward greater equality and opportunity, not less.

This outcome reflects not only America's current power arrangements but also, in part, the dark side of the Internet revolution. Although the Internet is overwhelmingly, and in so many ways, a force for good, for openness, and for the elimination of artificial barriers to knowledge and communication, it is also a powerful tool of managerial control. It is now possible to manage a gigantic global corporation from almost anywhere. As a result, the management of U.S.-headquartered firms may find it surprisingly easy to adapt to a world in which neither their employees nor their customers are primarily American.

In this case, American elites will remain extremely wealthy, and their political power could last a long time. But while such an outcome could last a couple of decades, there are several reasons to doubt that it will ultimately be sustainable. First, the financial sector will probably continue to produce bubbles and crises, and eventually their economic and political consequences will become impossible to ignore. Second, at some point the world will not allow the United States to continue borrowing unsustainably. Twenty years from now, China and India will have global currencies, and the world will start to treat the United States the way it is treating Europe now. And third, Americans are a rowdy lot, and they're not likely to put up with such a society forever.

However, the processes described above will not be reversed easily. And the general record of nations in decline suggests that internal reform occurs only under two conditions. The first is a very long period of growing frustration that finally boils over—as we saw in the Arab world. The second is a major crisis—as in the Great Depression. In 2008 many thought that the financial crisis might be enough, and that Barack Obama might seize his historical moment. Not so, as it turned out. Will it take another, even worse crisis?

Alas, as of this writing (early 2012), it appears possible that the European sovereign debt problem could eventually provide us with one.

Many of the same analysts who warned in vain about the mortgage bubble—Simon Johnson, Nouriel Roubini, and Charles Morris among them—are now warning that the unemployment and sovereign debt problems of Greece, Portugal, Ireland, Italy, and Spain are unsustainable and could trigger another crisis, one that would inevitably affect America.

Europe remains dangerously fragmented, both politically and economically, with the EU seemingly incapable of coherent action. Both the American and European economies remain weak, with high unemployment and low growth despite continued deficit spending. And the tools used to contain the crisis of 2008—zero interest rates, buckets of money for the financial system—are no longer as useful or available.

In this environment, instability may begin to enter politics and voter behavior as well as the economy. The question now is what will happen if popular frustration and desperation continue to grow, given that the American political duopoly does not allow for fundamental internal reform. Will America simply fester, will a movement arise to force real progress, or could America fall prey to extremist demagoguery? The answers to these questions are presently unknowable. There are both hopeful and alarming signals.

On the one hand, the fact that Michele Bachmann, Rick Perry, Ron Paul, Herman Cain, Newt Gingrich, and Sarah Palin could become major national figures, much less be taken seriously as candidates for president of the United States, is worrisome. So is the fact that major portions of American society seem not yet to understand the importance of education to their own, and the nation's, future prosperity. And for now, the influence of corporate money on both political parties seems completely intact. Those signs lead to pessimism.

On the other hand, the appearance of the Occupy Wall Street movement suggests that Americans are beginning to awaken. Other hopeful signs include Warren Buffett's public rebuke of his billionaire colleagues, and Starbucks CEO Howard Schultz's pledge to stop all campaign contributions until the federal government addresses America's fiscal problems. In several recent national elections, though not all, the

American people did the right thing. But America's current problems developed over several decades, and they won't be solved instantly.

In the meantime, Americans can do a number of things, both politically and personally. They can take to the streets; refuse to make political donations to the national party machines; support organizations such as Common Cause, Occupy Wall Street, and the Center for Responsive Politics; run for office themselves; and support candidates who do seem to care. At the personal level, we can save money; place our savings in local banks, credit unions, and mutual funds; invest prudently and ethically; and, above all, educate our children.

Since this book is being published in a presidential election year, I will close by saying that while President Obama has failed his country in major ways, he is the least of the available evils. So, yes, I recommend that you hold your nose and vote for him, as I will. But the very next day, I hope that you start thinking about how to replace him and the entire system that produced him.

How this can be accomplished is not yet clear. Earlier, I listed the three available avenues: an insurgency within one of the existing political parties; a third party; and a nonpartisan social movement. Any would face tough obstacles, and perhaps some combination of all three will be required. We might get lucky and one day find that America has elected a president who turns out to be deeply committed to fixing America's problems and willing to take a lot of heat. Time will tell. But America is a remarkable and beautiful country in so many ways. I hope that somewhere in the United States is a courageous young leader in the making, someone who can persuade the American people to rise up and throw the rascals out.

ACKNOWLEDGMENTS

There are so many people to thank. Many of them I can't name, for obvious reasons. And I'm sure I'm forgetting some—apologies in advance. First, Charlie Morris, for so much research and work and thinking and help and conversation. Everyone at Crown/Random House, especially Tina Constable, Mauro DiPreta, and Amanda Patten— you've been totally great, first and foremost for deciding to publish and support this book, which was a very gutsy thing to do. Thanks to everyone who talked to me, gave me information, corrected my misimpressions, guided me, and debated me, from Larry Diamond to Josh Cohen to Ralph Gomory and many others. And for sure, thanks to everyone who helped me make *Inside Job*—especially but not solely Audrey Marrs, Chad Beck, Adam Bolt, Alex Heffes, Kalyanee Mam, Will Cox, Matt Damon, my former assistant Anna Moot Levin, my current assistant Stacy Roy, Michael Barker, Tom Bernard, Diane Buck, Dylan Leiner, Christina Weiss Lurie, and John Sloss; everyone who appeared in the film; everyone who watched it; and the people at the Cannes, Telluride, Toronto, and New York film festivals who screened it. My book agent Max Brockman, my film agent Jeremy Barber, my film managers John Sloss and Dana O'Keefe, my wonderful lawyer Jackie Eckhouse, and bookkeeper Robin Cutter. Everyone in the film industry who has been so generous to me—which is to say, quite a few people.

Thanks to my lovely girlfriend, Audrey, and all my wonderful friends and family, who tolerated me and survived me and entertained me while I was In The Tunnel, and who keep showing up at my dinner parties even though the food is always the same. Athena Sofia, for being herself. My mother, for being a secret weapon of research. The

Mercer lobby staff, for the best office anyone could ever want. Craft and Giorgione, for all those very late dinners after a long day attacking the book. Everyone at Chez Panisse and Oliveto, too, for letting me show up really late but still feeding me so wonderfully when I was working in California.

I just wish that my thesis advisor, Carl Kaysen, could have lived to see the film and the book. The hard stuff about economists would have troubled him, but overall, I think he would have been pleased. Going to Carl's funeral was one of the toughest things I've ever done. I hope his widow, Ruth, and daughter, Zanny, will think that I've done him (or rather the education he gave me) justice by writing this.

Finally, my ridiculously patient and competent and effective assistant, Stacy Roy, who has endured my midnight phone calls, Sunday morning e-mails, crises, disorganization, overcommitment, and eccentricity—thank you, Stacy, for making everything possible. (And you—yes, YOU, whoever you are right now reading this, don't you dare hire her.)

Thank you all for making this possible. As grim as much of this book is, it was actually very enjoyable to write it, because I learned so much and had such good company all along the way.

NOTES

CHAPTER 1 Where We Are Now

1. Except as indicated, all U.S. economic data in this book are from the most recent official sources (i.e., as of 3Q 2011, if available).

2. William T. Vollman, "Homeless in Sacramento," *Harper's Magazine,* March 2011.

3. U.S. Census Bureau, "Income, Poverty, and Health Insurance Coverage in the United States: 2010," September 2011; Congressional Budget Office, "Trends in the Distribution of Household Income Between 1979 and 2007," October 2011, http://www.fns.usda.gov/pd/SNAPsummary.htm.

4. OECD StatExtracts: Labour Force Statistics, http://stats.oecd.org/index .aspx?queryid=251.

5. Emmanuel Saez and Thomas Piketty, "Income Inequality in the United States, 1913–1998," *Quarterly Journal of Economics,* 118(1) 2003, 1–39 (tables and figures updated to 2008 in Excel format, July 2010, http://elsa.berkeley .edu/~saez/); G. William Domboff, "Wealth Income and Power," Department of Sociology, UC Santa Cruz, November 2011, http://www2.ucsc.edu /whorulesamerica/power/wealth.html.

6. Julia B. Isaacs, "Intergenerational Comparisons of Economic Mobility," in Julia B. Isaacs et al., *Getting Ahead or Losing Ground: Economic Mobility in America,* 37–46, Brookings Economic Mobility Project, February 2008; Patrick M. Callan, "International Comparisons Highlight Educational Gaps Between Young and Older Americans," *Measuring Up 2006: The National Report Card on Higher Education,* http://measuringup.highereducation.org/commentary /introduction.cfm.

7. All company data are from annual reports and SEC filings.

1. Vincent Carossa, *Investment Banking in America: A History* (Cambridge, MA: Harvard University Press, 1970), 322–351.

2. Banking Act of 1933 (original version), Public Law 66, 73rd Congress, sec. 21(a)1.

3. Thomas Philippon and Ariel Resheff, "Wages and Human Capital in the U.S. Financial Industry: 1909–2006" (December 2008); draft available at http://pages.stern.nyu.edu/~tphilipp/papers/pr_rev15.pdf.

4. Lawrence J. White, *The S&L Debacle: Public Policy Lessons for Bank and Thrift Regulation* (New York: Oxford University Press, 1990); Martin Mayer, *The Greatest Ever Bank Robbery* (New York: Scribners, 1990). Mayer reprints the Greenspan letter on pp. 334–336.

5. The standard sources are James Stewart, *Den of Thieves* (New York: Touchstone, 1992); and Connie Bruck, *The Predators' Ball: The Inside Story of Drexel Burnham and the Rise of the Junk Bond Raiders* (New York: Penguin, 1989).

6. For a minute-by-minute account of the 1987 crash, see the Brady Commission Report, *Report of the Presidential Task Force on Market Mechanisms* (Washington, DC: USGPO, 1988).

7. Bethany McLean and Joe Nocera, *All the Devils Are Here: The Hidden History of the Financial Crisis* (New York: Penguin, 2010), chapter 2, "Ground Zero, Baby."

8. Yves Smith, *Econned: How Unenlightened Self Interest Undermined Democracy and Corrupted Capitalism* (New York: Palgrave Macmillan, 2010), 152.

9. Charles R. Morris, *Money, Greed, and Risk* (New York: Times Books, 1999), 168–171.

10. Alan Greenspan, "Testimony Before the House Committee on Banking and Financial Services," September 16, 1998.

11. Alan Greenspan, "Testimony Before the House Committee on Banking and Financial Services," October 1, 1998.

12. Alan Greenspan, "Remarks to the Chicago Conference on Bank Structure and Competition," May 8, 2003.

13. "Greenspan Admits 'Flaw' to Congress, Predicts More Economic Problems," *PBS NewsHour,* October 23, 2008, http://www.pbs.org/newshour/bb/business/july–dec08/crisishearing_10–23.html.

CHAPTER 3 The Bubble, Part One: Borrowing and Lending in the 2000s

1. Federal Reserve Board, "Selected Interest Rates," http://www.federal reserve.gov/releases/h15/data.htm.

2. Center for Responsible Lending, "Subprime Lending: A Net Drain on Home Ownership," *CRL Issue Paper* no. 14, March 27, 2007.

3. S&P/Case-Shiller U.S. National Home Price Index, http://www.standard andpoors.com/indices/sp-case-shiller-home-price-indices/en/us/. Between January 2000 and December 2005, the 10-City Index increased by 120 percent, the 20-City Index by 103 percent, and the National Index by 87 percent.

4. *The Financial Crisis Inquiry Report: Final Report of the National Commission on the Causes of the Financial and Economic Crisis in the United States* (New York: PublicAffairs, 2011), 89–90.

5. S&P/Case-Shiller index.

6. Rick Brooks and Constance Mitchell Forbes, "The United States of Subprime," *Wall Street Journal*, October 11, 2007. The article covers only "high-rate" loans, a category that excludes all the high-risk loans initiated with very low teaser rates, which may have been the majority of them.

7. *Financial Crisis Inquiry Report*, 89.

8. The primary source materials for WaMu are *Wall Street and the Financial Crisis: Anatomy of a Financial Collapse,* hearing before the U.S. Senate Permanent Subcommittee on Investigations (hereafter PSI), 111th Congress, 2nd sess., April 13, 2010, "Exhibits: The Role of High Risk Loans" (exhibits are not paginated); and *Federal Deposit Insurance Corporation v. Kerry K. Killinger et al.,* Complaint, U.S. District Court, Western District of Washington at Seattle, March 16, 2011.

9. PSI, *Wall Street and the Financial Crisis,* "Exhibits: The Role of High Risk Loans," Washington Mutual, "Higher Risk Lending Strategy," Finance Committee Discussion, January 2005, and Home Loans Discussion, Board of Directors Meeting, April 18, 2006.

10. Ibid. Washington Mutual, President's Club 2006—Kauai Business Meeting.

11. Ibid. Rotella to Killinger, April 27, 2006.

12. Ibid. Jill Simons to Timothy Bates, Risk Mit Loan Review Data "Confidential," e-mail, August 28, 2005.

13. *Cambridge Place Investment Management Inc. v. Morgan Stanley & Co.,*

Inc. et al., Superior Court of the Commonwealth of Massachusetts, Complaint and Jury Demand, July 9, 2010, 55–56; *The People of the State of New York v. First American Corporation et al.,* Supreme Court of New York, March 30, 2009.

14. *FDIC v. Killinger,* 23, 25.

15. PSI, *Wall Street and the Financial Crisis: Anatomy of a Financial Collapse,* Majority and Minority Staff Report, April 13, 2010, http://hsgac.senate.gov/public/_files/Financial_Crisis/FinancialCrisisReport.pdf.

16. http://www.nytimes.com/2011/12/14/business/ex-bank-executives-settle-fdic-suit.html.

17. *Financial Crisis Inquiry Report,* 89–90; "Final Report of Michael J. Missal, Bankruptcy Court Examiner" (hereafter Examiner's Report), *In re: New Century TRS Holdings, Inc. et al., Debtors,* U.S. Bankruptcy Court for the District of Delaware, 57.

18. Examiner's Report, 81–82.

19. Ibid., 2

20. Ibid., 127–128.

21. Ibid., 131.

22. Ibid. (Covers the accounting issues in detail; see esp. 177–212.)

23. Shawn Tulley, "Meet the 23,000% Stock," *Fortune,* September 15, 2003. The Countrywide account is based primarily on the e-mail trails and other documents assembled by the FCIC. The individual documents are available on a searchable website, http://fcic.law.stanford.edu/resource.

24. For one list, see http://en.wikipedia.org/wiki/Angelo_Mozilo#.22Friends_of_Angelo_.28FOA.29.22_VIP_program.

25. This account of Foster's experiences at Countrywide relies heavily on three sources. The first is the OSHA Finding letter describing her experiences after she filed a whistleblower lawsuit, which she won. The letter can be found online at http://www.documentcloud.org/documents/250789-cwd-ef-final-osha-order.html#document/p8. The second source is her interview with Steve Kroft, broadcast on *60 Minutes* in December 2011. This can be found online at http://www.cbsnews.com/8301-18560_162-57336042/prosecuting-wall-street/?pageNum=8&tag=contentMain;contentBody. The third source is Michael Hudson's articles based on his interview with her. Michael Hudson is a journalist working at the Center for Public Integrity. His articles can be found at http://www.iwatchnews.org

/2011/09/22/6687/countrywide-protected-fraudsters-silencing-whistleblowers
-say-former-employees.

26. See http://www.cbsnews.com/8301-18560_162-57336042/prosecuting
-wall-street/?pageNum=2&tag=contentMain;contentBody.

27. *Commonwealth of Massachusetts v. Fremont Invest & Loan et al.,* Final
Judgment by Consent, June 9, 2009. The final judgment included a $10 million
fine.

28. Cited in *Cambridge Place Investment v. Morgan Stanley,* 66.

29. Ibid., 69–74.

30. *Financial Crisis Inquiry Report,* 89, 12.

31. *Cambridge Place Investment v. Morgan Stanley,* 75–78.

32. *Washington Post,* June 10, 2008, see http://www.washingtonpost.com
/wp-dyn/content/article/2008/06/09/AR2008060902626.html.

33. Calculated from respective annual reports.

34. http://www.sec.gov/news/press/2011/2011-267.htm.

35. Alan Greenspan and James Kennedy, "Sources and Uses of Equity Extraction from Housing," Federal Reserve Board, 2007. Mr. Kennedy at the Fed
has kept the data up to date beyond the period in the study and furnishes them
upon request.

36. "A Home-Grown Problem," *Economist,* September 10, 2005.

CHAPTER 4 Wall Street Makes a Bubble and Gives It to the World

1. *Financial Crisis Inquiry Report,* 152–154.

2. http://www.finra.org/AboutFINRA/Leadership/.

3. *The Charles Schwab Corporation v. BNP Paribas Securities, Inc., et al.,*
Amended Complaint, Superior Court of the State of California, August 2, 2010.

4. *Financial Crisis Inquiry Report,* 166.

5. *Ambac Assurance Corporation et al. v. EMC Mortgage Corporation et al.,*
Complaint, Supreme Court of the State of New York, February 2, 2011.

6. Consolidated Amended Class Action Complaint, *American Home Mortgage Securities Litigation,* U.S. District Court, Eastern District of New York,
June 3, 2008.

7. *Ambac v. EMC,* 70.

8. Ibid., 71n181.

9. Ibid., 71.

10. Ibid., 72, 72n185.

11. Ibid., 74–76.

12. Ibid., 81–83.

13. Ibid., 78, 86–87.

14. Ibid., 93, 93n255.

15. Ibid., 65, 66n161, 69.

16. Ibid., 99–100.

17. Ibid., 97.

18. Ibid., 103.

19. Ibid., 104.

20. Allan Sloan, "House of Junk," http://money.cnn.com/2007/10/15/markets/junk_mortgages.fortune/index.htm.

21. *Employees' Retirement System of the Government of the Virgin Islands et al. v. Morgan Stanley & Co., Incorporated, et al.,* Class Action Complaint, U.S. District Court, Southern District of New York, December 24, 2009.

22. Ibid., 13.

23. Ibid., 15.

24. *In re: Morgan Stanley & Co., Incorporated,* Assurance of Discontinuance, Superior Court of the Commonwealth of Massachusetts, June 24, 2010.

25. *Virgin Islands v. Morgan Stanley,* 11.

26. For an interesting and extended dissection of this episode, including Hubler's relationship to his boss Zoe Cruz and the possible role of sexism in allowing Hubler's losses, see http://nymag.com/news/business/46476/.

27. *Financial Crisis Inquiry Report,* "Testimony of Richard M. Bowen," III, 1–2.

28. See the SEC complaint in the most publicized case, available at http://dealbook.nytimes.com/2011/10/26/in-fight-against-securities-fraud-s-e-c-sends-wrong-signal/.

29. *HSH Nordbank AG v. UBS AG and UBS Securities, LLC,* Summons and Complaint, Supreme Court of the State of New York, February 25, 2008.

30. The discussion here is drawn from PSI, *Wall Street and the Financial Crisis,* 243–317.

31. *Financial Crisis Inquiry Report,* "Interview of Robert Rubin," March 11, 2010.

CHAPTER 5 All Fall Down: Warnings, Predators, Crises, Responses

1. Raghuram G. Rajan, "Has Financial Development Made the World Riskier?" proceedings, Federal Reserve Bank of Kansas City, August 2005, 313–69, www.kc.frb.org/publicat/sympos/2005/pdf/rajan2005.pdf.

2. Wyatt, Edward, "Judge Blocks Citigroup Settlement with SEC," *New York Times,* November 28, 2011, http://www.nytimes.com/2011/11/29/business/judge-rejects-sec-accord-with-citi.html?_r=1.

3. PSI, *Wall Street and the Financial Crisis,* "Exhibits: Role of Investment Banks," David Viniar to Tom Montag, e-mail, December 15, 2006, and trail; Fabrice Tourre to Geoffrey Williams et al., e-mail, December 18, 2006.

4. Ibid. "The Subprime Meltdown: Timeline of Recent Events," presentation to Goldman Sachs board of directors, subprime mortgage business, March 26, 2007; Daniel Sparks to Gary Cohn et al., e-mail and trail, February 8, 2007.

5. Ibid. Sparks to Montag et al., e-mail, February 14, 2007.

6. Ibid. Sparks to Josh Birnbaum et al., e-mail, February 22, 2007.

7. Ibid. Sparks to Jon Winkelried, e-mail, February 21, 2007.

8. Ibid. Viniar to Gary Cohn, e-mail, July 25, 2007.

9. Ibid. Birnbaum to [redacted], e-mail, July 12, 2007.

10. Ibid. *Code of Business Conduct and Ethics,* May 2009.

11. Ibid. Fabrice Tourre to Jonathan Egol, e-mail, December 28, 2006.

12. Ibid. Jonathan Egol to Geoffrey Williams, e-mail, October 24, 2006, and trail.

13. Ibid. E-mails: Aliredha Yusuf to Sparks, March 9, 2007; Peter Ostrem to Sparks, March 9, 2007; Robert Black to ficc spcdo et al., March 21, 2007; Omar Chaudary to David Lehman, June 7, 2007; exchange of e-mails between Sparks and Bohra Bunty, April 19, 2007.

14. Ibid. Darryl Herrick to Mahesh Ganapathy, e-mail, October 12, 2006; sales book, Hudson Mezzanine Funding 2006-1, Ltd., October 2006.

15. Ibid. Sales book, Hudson.

16. Ibid. Ostrem to team, e-mail, October 30, 2006; Sparks to Montag, e-mail, January 27, 2007.

17. PSI, *Wall Street and the Financial Crisis,* Majority and Minority Staff Report, 585.

18. PSI, *Wall Street and the Financial Crisis,* "Exhibits: Role of Investment Banks," Salem Deeb to Michael Swenson, e-mail, December 15, 2006, and trail.

19. Ibid. GS Syndicate to T–Mail Subscribers, e-mail, March 28, 2007.

20. Ibid. Montag to Sparks, e-mail, June 22, 2007.

21. Ibid. Matthew Bieber to Christopher Creed, e-mail, September 17, 2007 and trail.

22. Gregory Zuckerman, "Profiting from the Crash," *Wall Street Journal,* October 31, 2009; http://online.wsj.com/article/SB10001424052748703574604574499740849179448.html.

23. Tourre to Egol, e-mail, December 18, 2006, "Wall Street and the Financial Crisis," hearing exhibits.

24. *Securities and Exchange Commission v. Goldman Sachs & Co. and Fabrice Tourre,* Complaint, U.S. District Court, Southern District of New York, April 16, 2010, 10.

25. PSI, *Wall Street and the Financial Crisis,* "Exhibits: Role of Investment Banks," sales book, ABACUS 2007-AC1, March 23, 2007.

26. http://www.nytimes.com/2010/04/21/business/21deals.html.

27. The financial details are those stated in *SEC v. Goldman,* which were the basis for the settlement.

28. *SEC v. Goldman,* Consent of Defendant Goldman Sachs & Co., July 16, 2010.

29. See the series by Jake Bernstein and Jesse Eisinger, commencing with "The Magnetar Trade: How One Hedge Fund Helped Keep the Bubble Going," *ProPublica,* April 9, 2010; Smith, *Econned,* 257–263.

30. Smith, *Econned,* 260.

31. http://www.bloomberg.com/apps/news?pid=newsarchive&sid=ax3yON_uNe7I.

32. *Financial Crisis Inquiry Report,* 243–44, 265–75.

CHAPTER 6 Crime and Punishment:

Banking and the Bubble as Criminal Enterprises

1. http://www.nytimes.com/interactive/2011/11/08/business/Wall–Streets–Repeat–Violations–Despite–PromisesStsssss.html?ref=business.

2. The standard account is Kurt Eichenwald's *Conspiracy of Fools: A True Story* (New York: Broadway Books, 2005).

3. For the Citi and Chase transactions, see *In re Enron Corporation Securities Litigation,* First Amended Consolidated Complaint, U.S. District Court, Southern District of Texas, May 14, 2003, 35–39 (this is the primary class-action suit filed by Enron shareholders); *SEC v. JPMorgan Chase,* Complaint, U.S. District Court, Southern District of Texas, July 28, 2003; Securities and Exchange Commission, Accounting and Auditing Enforcement Release no. 1821, in the matter of Citigroup, Inc., respondent, July 28, 2003.

4. *In re Enron Corporation,* 500–501; *SEC v. Merrill Lynch, & Co., Inc., et al.,* Complaint, March 17, 2003, U.S. District Court, Southern District of Texas at Houston.

5. Harold Meyerson, "The Enron Enablers," *American Prospect,* May 10, 2007.

6. Charles R. Morris, "The Hole in the Economy," *Boston Globe,* July 7, 2002.

7. Geoff Lewis, "The Bloody Mess After the Internet Bubble," *Registered Rep,* May 1, 2005.

8. Ibid.

9. William H. Donaldson, "Testimony Concerning Global Research Analyst Settlement," Senate Committee on Banking, Housing and Urban Affairs, May 7, 2003; Securities and Exchange Commission, Litigation Release, "Federal Court Approves Global Research Analyst Settlement," October 31, 2003; Securities and Exchange Commission, Administrative Proceeding, *In the Matter of Jack Benjamin Grubman,* October 31, 2003; Securities and Exchange Commission, Administrative Proceeding, *In the Matter of Henry M. Blodget,* October 31, 2003.

10. The account of this episode is drawn from *SEC v. Charles E. LeCroy and Douglas W. MacFaddin,* Complaint, U.S. District Court, Northern District of Alabama, November 4, 2009; SEC, Administrative Proceeding, *In the Matter of JPMorgan Securities, Inc.,* Order Instituting Administrative and Cease-And-Desist Proceedings, November 4, 2009; and William Selway and Martin Z. Braun, "JPMorgan Swap Deals Spur Probe as Default Stalks Alabama County," Bloomberg, May 22, 2008.

11. The narrative is from Martin Z. Braun, "Auction Bond Failures Roil Munis, Pushing Rates Up," Bloomberg, February, 10, 2008; Liz Rappaport and Randall Smith, "Credit Woes Hit Funding for Loans to Students," *Wall Street Journal,* February 13, 2008; Floyd Norris, "Auction Market Chaos for Bonds," *New York Times,* February 20, 2008.

12. *SEC v. Banc of America Securities LLC et al.,* Complaint, U.S. District

Court, Southern District of New York, June 9, 2009, 7. This and other complaints provide a complete description of the process.

13. Expected settlement costs from SEC press releases on each case.

14. SEC litigation releases.

15. http://dealbook.nytimes.com/2011/02/15/del-monte-ruling-challenges-cozy-buyout-bids/.

16. The account here is distilled from U.S. Department of Justice Press Release, "Justice Department & IRS Announce Results of UBS Settlement & Unprecedented Response to Voluntary Tax Disclosure Program," November 17, 2009; Carolyn B. Lovejoy, "UBS Strikes a Deal: The Recent Impact of Weakened Bank Secrecy on Swiss Banking," *North Carolina Banking Institute Journal* 14 (February 10, 2010): 435–466; Joann M. Weiner, "Brad Birkenfeld: Tax Cheat and UBS Informant Doesn't Deserve Pardon," *Politics Daily,* June 2010; Carlyn Kolker and David Voreacos, "UBS Tax Net Snares Credit Suisse, Julius Baer Clients," Bloomberg, September 18, 2009; and Cyrus Sanati, "Phil Gramm and the UBS Tax Case," *New York Times,* August 20, 2009.

17. William Wechsler, "Follow the Money," *Foreign Affairs,* July/August 2001.

18. *United States of America v. Credit Suisse, AG,* Deferred Prosecution Agreement, U.S. District Court for the District of Columbia, December 16, 2008. Details from Exhibit A, Factual Statement.

19. Press Release, New York County District Attorney's Office, "Barclays Bank PLC Agrees to Forfeit $298 Million in Connection with Violations of the International Emergency Economic Powers Act and the Trading with the Enemy Act," August 18, 2010; and Press Releases, U.S. Department of Justice, "Credit Suisse Agrees to Forfeit $536 Million in Connection with Violations of the International Emergency Economic Powers Act and New York State Law," December 2, 2009, and "Lloyds TSB Bank Plc Agrees to Forfeit $350 Million in Connection with Violations of the International Emergency Economic Powers Act," January 9, 2009.

20. See http://www.nytimes.com/2010/06/05/nyregion/05hawala.html.

21. Kevin Roose, "JPMorgan to Pay $88.3 Million for Sanctions Violations," *New York Times,* August 35, 2011.

22. Robert H. Hast, "Private Banking: Raul Salinas, Citibank, and Alleged Money Laundering," testimony before the Permanent Subcommittee on Inves-

tigations, Committee on Governmental Affairs, U.S. Senate, November 9, 1999 (Washington, DC: U.S. GAO, 1998).

23. U.S. Senate, Permanent Subcommittee on Investigations, "Money Laundering and Foreign Corruption: Case Study Involving Riggs Bank," July 15, 2004.

24. Ed Vulliamy, "How a Big US Bank Laundered Billions from Mexico's Murderous Drug Gangs," *Guardian,* April 2, 2011, http://www.guardian.co.uk /world/2011/apr/03/us-bank-mexico-drug-gangs; Andrew Nill Sanchez, "Big Bank Ignored Warnings That It Was Being Used to Launder Money by Mexican Drug Cartels," *ThinkProgress,* April 20, 2011, http://thinkprogress.org /economy/2011/04/20/159951/wachovia-banks-drug-cartels/.

25. http://thinkprogress.org/economy/2011/04/20/159951/wachovia-banks -drug-cartels/.

26. David Voreceos et al., "Banks Financing Mexico Drug Gangs Admitted in Wells Fargo Deal," Bloomberg, June 28, 2010; *United States of America v. American Express Bank International,* Deferred Prosecution Agreement, U.S. District Court, Southern District of Florida, August 6, 2007.

27. For settlement and other statistical data, see *Securities Investor Protection Corporation v. Bernard Madoff Investment Securities, LLC,* U.S. Bankruptcy Court, Southern District of New York, Trustee's Fifth Interim Report for the Period Ending March 31, 2011.

28. Andrew Cave, "Bernard Madoff Fraud: Increased Scrutiny in Hedge Fund Industry," *Daily Telegraph,* December 20, 2008.

29. *Irving H. Picard Trustee v. Citibank NA et al.,* Complaint, U.S. Bankruptcy Court, December 8, 2010; *Picard v. Merrill Lynch International,* Complaint, U.S. Bankruptcy Court, December 8, 2010; *Picard v. ABN Amro,* Complaint, U.S. Bankruptcy Court, December 8, 2010.

30. http://www.forbes.com/sites/robertlenzner/2010/11/28/suit-says-ubs -feeder-funds-knew-madoff-was-fishy-back-in-2006/.

31. http://www.ft.com/cms/s/0/e544bb08-0954-11e0-ada6-00144feabdc0 .html#axzz1fKjlttnW.

32. *Picard v. UBS AG et al.,* Complaint, U.S. Bankruptcy Court, December 7, 2010, 24.

33. *Picard v. JPMorgan Chase & Co., et al.,* Complaint, U.S. Bankruptcy Court, December 2, 2010, 44.

34. Ibid., 1; Diana R. Henriques, "Bankers Named Who Doubted Madoff," *New York Times,* April 14, 2011, http://www.nytimes.com/2011/04/15/business /15madoff.html.

35. http://www.whitehouse.gov/the–press–office/2011/10/06/news –conference–president.

36. The relevant FCIC transcript can be found here, as well as on the FCIC website: http://cybercemetery.unt.edu/archive/fcic/20110310173928/ and http:// www.fcic.gov/hearings/testimony/subprime-lending-and-securitization-and-enterprises.

37. The letter is available online at http://dealbook.nytimes.com/2010/03/19 /the-letter-by-lehman-whistle-blower-matthew-lee/.

38. See http://dealbook.nytimes.com/2010/03/15/auditor-could-face-liability -over-lehman/.

39. For one discussion of the cartelistic nature of the industry as reflected in these fee structures, see http://www.bloomberg.com/news/2012-01-09/cohan -how-wall-street-turned-a-crisis-into-a-cartel.html.

40. http://www.consumeraffairs.com/news04/2005/credit_card_fee_suit .html; see also http://finance.yahoo.com/news/bank-america-big-banks-face -113000788.html.

41. http://www.bloomberg.com/news/2011–11–28/secret–fed–loans –undisclosed–to–congress–gave–banks–13–billion–in–income.html.

42. http://www.nytimes.com/2011/12/04/business/secrets-of-the-bailout -now-revealed.html?_r=1&scp=1&sq=federal%20reserve%20sec%20disclosure %20lynn&st=cse.

CHAPTER 7 Agents of Pain: Unregulated Finance as a Subtractive Industry

1. Federal Reserve, Flow of Funds reports for respective years.

2. William J. Holstein, "Personal Business; The Home Equity Highway: Busy and Hazardous," *New York Times,* December 23, 2001; Alan Greenspan and James Kennedy, "Sources and Uses of Equity Extraction from Housing," (Washington, DC: Federal Reserve Board, 2007; data updated through 2008 by Mr. Hamilton); Bureau of Economic Analysis, "U.S. International Trade in Goods and Services," Federal Reserve, Flow of Funds.

3. "Global House Priers: A Home-Grown Problem," *The Economist,* Septem-

ber 8, 2005, at http://www.economist.com/node/4385293. Christopher B. Leinberger, "The Next Slum," *Atlantic Monthly*, March 2008.

4. For a detailed examination of this and other questions related to the federal deficit and U.S. national debt, see Simon Johnson and James Kwak, *White House Burning: The Founding Fathers, Our National Debt, and Why It Matters to You* (2012).

5. The most detailed account is Andrew Ross Sorkin, *Too Big to Fail* (New York: Viking, 2009).

6. Audio recording of the entire SEC meeting available at http://graphics8 .nytimes.com/packages/audio/national/20081003_SEC_AUDIO/SEC_Open _Meeting_04282004.mp3.

7. All company financial information is drawn from annual 10K filings.

8. I am indebted to Charles Morris for this observation, and for the phrase.

9. For the "repo run," see Gary Gorton and Andrew Metrick, "Securitized Banking and the Run on the Repo," National Bureau of Economic Research Working Paper no. 15223, November 10, 2010.

10. http://www.huffingtonpost.com/2011/10/14/goldman-sachs-for-profit -college_n_997409.html?page=1.

11. http://chronicle.com/article/Education-Management-Corp/128560/.

12. http://www.nytimes.com/2009/10/05/business/economy/05simmons .html?pagewanted=2&dbk.

13. http://www.bloomberg.com/news/2012-02-11/sec-looking-into-private -equity-firms-valuation-of-assets.html.

14. Adair Turner, "Reforming Finance: Are We Being Radical Enough?" 2011 Clare Distinguished Lecture on Economics and Public Policy, February 18, 2011.

15. Vito Racanelli, *Barron's*, January 27, 2011.

CHAPTER 8 The Ivory Tower

1. Justin Bekelman, "Scope and Impact of Financial Conflicts of Interest in Biomedical Research," *Journal of the American Medical Society* 289 (2003): 454–486; George Khusuf et al., "Understanding, Assessing, and Managing Conflicts of Interest," in Lawrence B. McCollough et al., *Surgical Ethics* (New York: Oxford University Press, 2006), 343–366, quote on 351; U.S. Senate, Committee

on Finance, "Staff Report on Sanofi's Strategic Use of Third Parties to Influence the FDA" (May 2011); for the three settlements see Justice Department press releases on TAP (an Abbott-Takeda joint venture), October 3, 2001; Astra-Zeneca, June 20, 2003; and Warner-Lambert (now part of Pfizer), May 13, 2004; "Stanford Won't Let Doctors Accept Gifts," Associated Press, September 12, 2006, MSNBC.

2. www.brg-experts.com.

3. Ibid.

4. www.theanalysisgroup.com.

5. www.compasslexecon.com.

6. Company website at www.crai.com; for revenues and employment practices, see Charles River Associates, Inc., 10K filing for 2010.

7. R. Glenn Hubbard, "How Capital Markets Enhance Economic Performance and Facilitate Job Creation" (with William C. Dudley) (New York: Goldman Sachs Global Markets Institute, 2004).

8. 2011 company proxy statements.

9. This was true as of late February 2012. See his Columbia CV at http://www0.gsb.columbia.edu/faculty/ghubbard/cv.html.

10. The testimonials page is http://www.harrywalker.com/speaker/R-Glenn-Hubbard-ovations.cfm?Spea_ID=646.

11. Steven Gjerstad and Vernon L. Smith, "Monetary Policy, Credit Extension, and Housing Bubbles: 2008 and 1929," *Critical Review* 21, nos. 2–3 (2009): 269–300, quote on 286.

12. David Goldman, "What Did Larry Summers Do at DE Shaw?" *Asia Time: Inner Workings,* April 6, 2009, http://blog.atimes.net/?p=867.

13. You can see the full interview, together with Felix Salmon's commentary on it, on Salmon's blog: http://blogs.reuters.com/felix-salmon/2012/01/27/summers-inside-job-had-essentially-all-its-facts-wrong/.

14. See, for example, http://www.rkmc.com/Credit-Default-Swaps-From-Protection-To-Speculation.htm.

15. The article can be found at http://www.nytimes.com/2009/04/06/business/06summers.html.

16. Summers has two web pages on the Harvard website. One is at http://www.hks.harvard.edu/about/faculty-staff-directory/lawrence-summers. The other is http://www.hks.harvard.edu/fs/lsummer/index.htm.

17. The web page is http://www.harrywalker.com/speaker/Lawrence-Summers-ovations.cfm?Spea_ID=450.

18. Heather Timmons, "Iceland's Fizzy Economy Faces a Test," *New York Times,* April 18, 2006.

19. Frederic S. Mishkin and Tryggvi Thor Herbertson, "Financial Stability in Iceland," Iceland Chamber of Commerce (May 2006), 49, 42.

20. Frederic S. Mishkin, "Policy Remedies for Conflicts of Interest in the Financial System," conference paper, *Macroeconomics, Monetary Policy and Financial Stability: A Festschrift for Charles Freedman* (July 2003), 10–11.

21. "Fed Governors' Financial Disclosures: 2006," Financial Markets Center (October 11, 2007).

22. http://www.leighbureau.com/speaker.asp?id=501

23. Company proxy filings.

24. The page is http://www.harrywalker.com/speaker/Laura-Tyson-ovations .cfm?Spea_ID=43.

25. His speaker's bureau biography is at http://www.washingtonspeakers .com/speakers/biography.cfm?SpeakerID=1760.

26. http://www.prnewswire.com/news-releases/media-advisory-hal -scott-urges-narrow-application-of-volcker-rule-to-allow-bank-market -making-hedging-other-dodd-frank-permitted-activities-124002944 .html.

27. See http://www.law.harvard.edu/programs/corp_gov/media.shtml.

28. http://www.compasslexecon.com/Pages/default.aspx.

29. Anthony Giddens, "My Chat with the Colonel," *Guardian,* March 9, 2007.

30. Benjamin R. Barber, "Gaddafi's Libya: An Ally for America?" *Washington Post,* August 15, 2007.

31. Joseph S. Nye, Jr., "Tripoli Diarist," *New Republic,* December 10, 2007.

32. David Corn and Siddhartha Mahanta, "From Libya with Love: How a US Consulting Firm Used American Academics to Rehab Muammar Qaddafi's Image," *Mother Jones,* March 3, 2011.

33. 22 U.S.C. Sec. 611 (c)(1)(ii), http://www.fara.gov/.

34. Reported in http://mobile.bloomberg.com/news/2012-01-07/on-the -capture-of-economists-the-ticker.

35. See http://www.bloomberg.com/news/2012-01-17/economists-inside-job -conflicts-beg-for-more-than-pay-disclosure-view.html.

1. See, for example, my articles at http://www.huffingtonpost.com/charles-ferguson/the-financial-crisis-and-_1_b_782927.html and also http://www.salon.com/2010/10/27/barack_obama_wall_street/.

2. See James Womack, Daniel T. Jones, and Daniel Roos, *The Machine That Changed the World* (Cambridge, MA: MIT Press, 1991; rev. 2007), or Kim B. Clark and Takahiro Fujimoto, *Product Development Performance* (Cambridge, MA: Harvard Business School Press, 1991).

3. See Ramchandran Jaikumar, "Postindustrial Manufacturing," *Harvard Business Review* (November/December 1986).

4. http://www.digitimes.com/news/a20120131PD200.html.

5. http://mediadecoder.blogs.nytimes.com/2011/12/02/with-verizons-3-6-billion-spectrum-deal-cable-and-wireless-inch-closer/?scp=1&sq=verizon%20cable%20spectrum%20deal&st=cse.

6. See, for example, http://www.offthechartsblog.org/what-should-corporate-tax-reform-look-like/ and http://www.nytimes.com/2011/08/06/business/workers-wages-chasing-corporate-profits-off-the-charts.html.

7. For the Senate, see http://www.cfinst.org/pdf/vital/VitalStats_t5.pdf. For the House, see http://www.cfinst.org/pdf/vital/VitalStats_t2.pdf.

8. http://sunlightfoundation.com/blog/2011/12/13/the-political-one-percent-of-the-one-percent/?utm_source=The+Balance+Sheet&utm_campaign=36e95872b7-Balance_Sheet_12_02_1112_2_2011&utm_medium=email.

9. http://www.opm.gov (U.S. Government Office of Personnel Management).

10. PSI, *Wall Street and the Financial Collapse*, "Majority and Minority Staff Report," 349.

11. See http://www.reuters.com/article/2012/01/20/us-usa-holder-mortgage-idUSTRE80J0PH20120120.

12. See for example the firm's own website: http://www.cov.com/practice/white_collar_and_investigations/.

13. http://www.economicpolicyjournal.com/2011/01/blankfein-dimon-attending-white-house.html.

14. Ian Dew-Becker and Robert J. Gordon, "The Rise in American Inequality," *Vox* (June 19, 2008), www.voxeu.org/index.php?q=node/1245.

15. http://www.nytimes.com/2011/08/06/business/workers-wages

-chasing-corporate-profits-off-the-charts.html?scp=1&sq=floyd%20
norris%20u.s.%20corporate%20profits%20record%20gnp%20share&st=Search.

16. http://dealbook.nytimes.com/2011/11/29/at-the-92nd-st-y-a
-cushion-against-wall-st-worries/?hp.

17. http://www.thecrimson.com/article/2011/2/25/aid-financial
-percent-year/.

18. http://www.nytimes.com/2011/09/14/education/14delta.html?_r=1&sq
=private%20universities%20public&st=cse&adxnnl=1&scp=1&adxnnlx
=1323636060-50gcU9ysLdyDB7PikH05yg.

GLOSSARY

ADJUSTABLE RATE MORTGAGE (ARM) A mortgage with an interest rate that varies over time, usually with reference to some external rate.

ALT-A MORTGAGE Originally, a mortgage offered to a borrower with a good credit rating but without full documentation (an alien, for example). During the bubble, Alt-A mortgages were used to mask the borrower's financial incapacity, becoming known in the trade as "liar loans."

BANK HOLDING COMPANY A corporation that owns a regulated deposit-taking bank, usually along with other financial services entities that may or may not be regulated.

BROKER-DEALER A firm that is in the business of buying and selling securities for its customers. Broker-dealers are often subsidiaries of investment banks.

COLLATERALIZED DEBT OBLIGATION (CDO) A security that is backed by a range of other securities, often of multiple types, including mortgages, bank loans, bonds, and so forth. A CDO is almost always *structured;* that is, it will offer a hierarchy of bonds ranked by their payment priority. The cash flows from the securities supporting the CDO are directed first to the top-ranked bonds, then to the second-ranked, and so on down the "subordination" ladder. The bottom-ranked CDO bonds therefore absorb the first losses. CDOs played an important role in the financial crash, because their structure was inherently opaque and

CDO creators loaded them up with very risky instruments, like subprime, often fraudulent, mortgages. A CDO SQUARED (CDO²) is a CDO constructed from risky pieces of other CDOs.

COMMODITY FUTURES TRADING COMMISSION (CFTC) An independent federal agency that regulates trading in futures and options.

COMMUNITY REINVESTMENT ACT (CRA) A 1977 federal law that required regulated lenders to make loans and provide services to their local communities.

CREDIT DEFAULT SWAP (CDS) A form of derivative that transfers the default risk of a debt security, like a bond or a loan. The *protection buyer* pays a stream of interest-like payments to the *protection seller,* who agrees to make the protection buyer whole if the instrument defaults. Neither the protection buyer nor the protection seller needs to own the underlying instrument. CDSs grew at an extraordinary rate during the bubble because they were a convenient way for traders to simulate bond portfolios with minimal cash outlays.

CREDIT RATING AGENCIES Private companies that evaluate the risk and credit quality of securities and provide ratings based on their analysis. The largest credit raters are Fitch Ratings, Moody's Investor Services, and Standard & Poor's.

DEPOSITARY INSTITUTION A financial institution, which may be a bank, a thrift (savings and loan), or a credit union, that accepts deposits.

DERIVATIVE A financial contract with a value that is determined by the value of some other underlying asset, rate, or event.

FANNIE MAE Short for the Federal National Mortgage Association (FNMA), a government-sponsored enterprise that provides financing for the home mortgage market.

FEDERAL DEPOSIT INSURANCE CORPORATION (FDIC) An independent federal agency that insures the deposits of federally chartered banks and savings banks, as well as state-chartered institutions that elect to join the Federal Reserve System. It is financed entirely by the insured institutions. To prevent insurance losses it examines the books and safety of insured institutions; if an institution does fail it has the power to take over, reorganize, sell, or otherwise dispose of such institutions in order to recover its insurance payouts.

FORECLOSURE The legal process by which a mortgage lender takes ownership of a property securing a defaulted mortgage.

FREDDIE MAC Short for the Federal Home Loan Mortgage Corporation (FHLMC), a government-sponsored enterprise that provides financing for the home mortgage market.

GLASS-STEAGALL ACT The Banking Act of 1933 that, among other things, prohibited commercial banks from underwriting or dealing in most types of securities, and prohibited banks from affiliating with securities firms. In 1999 the Gramm-Leach-Bliley Act repealed the provisions of Glass-Steagall that prohibited affiliations between commercial banks and securities firms.

GRAMM-LEACH-BLILEY ACT The 1999 law repealing provisions of the Glass-Steagall Act prohibiting affiliations between banks and securities firms.

HEDGE FUND A privately owned investment vehicle exempted from most regulation and oversight; generally open only to high-net-worth investors. Hedge funds follow a great variety of investment strategies that may or may not involving hedging.

LEVERAGE A measure of the extent to which an asset is financed with borrowed money. A $100,000 home that is purchased with $10,000 cash and a $90,000 mortgage is leveraged at ten to one (the home value divided by the homeowner's equity). The danger of leverage becomes clear when asset prices fall. If the value of the home dropped to $80,000, the homeowner would have lost his or her entire cash investment, and could not cover the mortgage even by selling the home. Investment banks like Lehman Brothers were typically leveraged at thirty to one before the crash ($3 billion in assets would be financed with $100 million of equity and $2.9 billion of borrowings). To make matters worse, the borrowing was often short-term, so it had to be paid back in full and refinanced several times throughout the year. When financial assets plummeted during the crash, many Wall Street firms were immediately insolvent.

LIQUIDITY The state of availability of cash or financial instruments that can be quickly converted to cash.

LIQUIDITY PUT A financial contract that requires one party to refinance or purchase an asset held by the other party under certain conditions.

LOAN-TO-VALUE RATIO (LTV) The ratio between the principal amount of a mortgage or mortgages and the market value of real property securing the mortgage(s), usually expressed as a percentage.

MARK-TO-MARKET An accounting convention by which the carrying values of securities are regularly adjusted to reflect their current market values.

MORTGAGE-BACKED SECURITY (MBS) A credit instrument supported by residential or commercial mortgages. An MBS may or may not be structured. (See entry for collateralized debt obligation.)

OFFICE OF THE COMPTROLLER OF THE CURRENCY An arm of the Treasury Department that charters, regulates, and supervises all national banks and certain branches and agencies of foreign banks in the United States.

OPTION-ARM An adjustable rate mortgage, usually with a "teaser," or below-market initial interest rate, that allows borrowers, at their option, to make lower than scheduled payments during the early years of the loan. When the rate is reset to a market rate, the accumulated payment shortfalls are added to the loan principal.

PRIVATE-LABEL SECURITIES Mortgage-backed securities constructed and distributed by private investment banks and securities dealers (as opposed to MBSs distributed by Fannie Mae, Freddie Mac, or other federal mortgage agencies).

SECURITIES AND EXCHANGE COMMISSION (SEC) Independent federal agency responsible for protecting investors by enforcing federal securities laws, including regulating security and security options exchanges, broker-dealers, investment companies, and other securities professionals, and the issuance and sale of securities.

SECURITIZATION The process of pooling mortgages, credit card receivables, or other instruments in a separate legal entity to secure the issuance of new financial instruments to investors.

SHADOW BANKING SYSTEM Nonbank financial institutions, like hedge funds, private equity funds, mutual funds, and other investment vehicles, that often provide credit and perform other activities that parallel the formal banking system. The ballooning of the shadow banking system in the 2000s made it difficult for regulatory officials to track the volume of credit in the financial system.

SYNTHETIC CDO A collateralized debt obligation that is constructed of credit default swaps rather than of real securities. By using synthetic CDOs to reference very high-risk real CDOs, Wall Street greatly increased the volume of very risky assets in the market.

TRANCHE The French word for "slice," used to refer to the various layers of securities making up a structured financial instrument.

UNDERWRITING The process of determining the risk and value of a security. Investment banks underwrite securities when they evaluate the creditworthiness of issuers and establish a price for distributing the securities to investors; mortgage lenders underwrite mortgages by evaluating the creditworthiness of the borrower and the market value of the underlying property.

WRITE-DOWN An accounting process by which the value of an asset is reduced from a previous accounting value. Frequently, when a company writes down an asset, the amount of the write-down must be deducted from reported profits.

INDEX